SERGEJ ESENIN

A BIOGRAPHICAL SKETCH

8

SLAVISTIC PRINTINGS AND REPRINTINGS

55

edited by

C. H. VAN SCHOONEVELD

Stanford University

LV

1966

MOUTON & CO.

LONDON · THE HAGUE · PARIS

SERGEJ ESENIN:

A Biographical Sketch

by

FRANCES DE GRAAFF

*Bryn Mawr College
and Haverford College*

1966
MOUTON & CO.
LONDON · THE HAGUE · PARIS

PRINTED IN THE NETHERLANDS BY MOUTON & CO., PRINTERS, THE HAGUE

TABLE OF CONTENTS

Note   6

   I.   Early Years: 1895–1912   7

   II.   Moscow and Petrograd: 1912–1916 15

  III.   Early Poems and Prose. 27

  IV.   The Russian Revolution 40

   V.   Imagism: 1919–1921 60

  VI.   Marriage and Travel Abroad: 1921–1923 94

 VII.   Poet of the New Russia: 1923–1925 116

VIII.   The Last Year: 1925 146

Bibliography 161

NOTE

Esenin's poetry will be quoted from the new edition of his collected works in five volumes, *Sobranie Sočinenij* (Moscow, 1961). This edition will be indicated in the notes by *Sobr. Soč.*

Some works will be quoted from the first edition, *Sobranie Stixotvorenij* (Moscow, 1926) in four volumes, indicated in the notes by *Sobr. Stix.*

I

EARLY YEARS: 1895–1912

Sergej Aleksandrovič Esenin was born in the province of Ryazan, one of the most fertile parts of the Russian "black earth", a region of rich fields, of hills and forests, rivers and marshes and many little lakes. On the fourth of October 1895, in the village of Konstantinovo, he began a life that thirty years later would end in tragedy and suicide.

His parents were poor farmers who could hardly provide enough food and money to support themselves and their two little daughters with the products of the few acres of land they possessed. Before Sergej was born his father had left the village to try to earn money in Moscow. He found work in a butcher's store and for about two years he was able to send home some money regularly. His family remained in Konstantinovo where his wife worked the land and took care of the children. She had married against the wishes of her father, the miller of the village, a rich man compared to most of the farmers. Since she had not obeyed him he at first refused to help her. When her husband stopped sending money and it was impossible to support herself and the children, she decided to move to Ryazan to find work as a servant. Then at last her parents took pity on her and offered to take young Sergej to live with them, an offer that was gratefully accepted. And so, from his second year on,[1] Sergej spent his childhood and early youth with his grandparents, the Titovs.

His grandfather, Sergej Andreevič Titov, was a remarkable man who left a great impression on his grandson. He belonged to the religious sect of the Old Believers and was an assiduous Bible-reader. He knew many folk-songs and religious poems by heart and liked to recite them before

---

[1] This is the age Esenin mentions in his autobiographies. V. Xodasevič, in his otherwise well-documented article "Esenin", in *Sovremennye Zapiski*, XXVII (1926), says that Sergej was four years old when his mother had another child. Then her husband stopped sending money home and Sergej went to live with his grandparents. We have found no confirmation of this information and have, therefore, kept the dates furnished by Esenin. On the poet's early years see also: Ekaterina Esenina, "V Konstantinove", *Al'manax Literaturnaja Rjazan'*, II (1957), pp. 305–317.

his grandson. He was vigorous and <u>liked to drink</u>, but never to excess. Esenin's sister, Aleksandra, wrote in an article about Sergej's youth:

> Grandfather was a man who did things in a large way, he loved to have a good time and make merry. When he came back from a trip to Petersburg he used to give parties which lasted several days. Wine was served in buckets... And nearly the whole village drank and feasted... Accordeon music, songs, dances and laughter sometimes went on for a week. But afterwards, when the fun was over, grandfather began to count every cent and, according to my mother, he used to grumble that "too much salt had been used, too many matches had been burnt".[2]

Grandfather wanted Sergej to become as strong and independent as he was and nothing pleased him more than seeing his grandson coming home covered with blood and dirt after a fight with the village boys. When his wife tried to console or gently scold the little boy, he became angry and shouted: "Leave him alone, he'll get stronger when he fights!"

His wife, a deeply religious woman, adored her grandson. She took him with her when she went to visit the monasteries in the neighborhood. Sergej never tired of listening to the folk-tales she told him. Her house was always open to the many itinerant monks and beggars who passed through the village. She used to invite them to share their meals and afterwards they sat around and talked or sang. Sergej loved to listen when they spoke of their travels, of the monasteries they had visited and the strange and interesting things they had seen.

The Titovs had three grown-up sons, living at home. They seem to have been rather crude and quarrelsome young men who loved to tease their little nephew. When Sergej was only three years old, they put him on an unsaddled horse and sent it galloping away. Screaming, Sergej clung to the horse's mane, but he did not fall off and soon became an excellent rider. They also taught him to swim by throwing him into the water. Later he often served them as a hunting dog, swimming after the ducks they had shot over the lake.

In one of the four autobiographies[3] where these details about Esenin's

---

[2] Aleksandra Esenina, "Èto vse mne rodnoe i blizkoe. O S. Esenine", *Molodaja Gvardija*, 1960, no. 7, pp. 207–220; no. 8, pp. 206–221.

[3] Esenin wrote his first autobiography in Berlin in 1922. There it was published in *Novaja Russkaja Kniga* (1922), no. 5. After his return from Europe he wrote the second, published in an article by S. Borisov, "K biografii S. Esenina", *Krasnaja Niva* (1926), no. 2. A third one, written in June 1924, can be found in the Esenin Archives in the Central State Archives of Literature and Art of the U.S.S.R. (Moscow), fund 190. The fourth, "O sebe", was first published in *Pamjatka o Sergee Esenine* (Moscow, 1926) and reprinted in the first volume of the four-volume collected works of Esenin, *Sobranie Stixotvorenij* (Moscow, 1926), pp. XXXVII–XL. All four autobiographies are reprinted in volume V of *Sobranie Sočinenij*, p. 7–22.

early youth are recounted, he also mentions another uncle who suffered from epileptic attacks. This uncle was very kind to him and often took him on long walks through the countryside.

Life with the Titovs was pleasant and carefree for Sergej. Even though his uncles sometimes made him suffer, there was always his grandmother to love and protect him. He was the only child among grownups and he felt secure and important. Visitors were always charmed by the young boy, for he was a beautiful child, with lovely golden curls and clear blue eyes, not very tall for his age, rather delicately built, but well-proportioned. His grandparents were not strict with him and he was free to roam in the country and play as much as he liked. He loved to walk through the fields, to climb trees and to play and fight with the village boys. In their games he was always the leader. Intelligent and quick of mind and body, he felt superior to the other boys, who were poorer and more shabbily dressed. This feeling of superiority was strengthened by his successes in the village school. Learning came easily to Sergej. Without effort he was always first in his class.

In May 1909 Sergej had finished the village school. His father wanted him to come to Moscow to learn the butcher's trade, but his grandfather had other plans. He decided that Sergej should continue his education to become a schoolteacher. Since there was no secondary school in the neighborhood, he had to go to another town, Spas-Klepiki, about forty miles away, where he could enter a boarding-school for the preparation of teachers of church-supported elementary schools.

At first Sergej had been excited about the idea of further study, but when he arrived at the school, he felt scared and terribly alone. His schoolmates were different from the ragged village boys with whom he used to play and who regarded him as their leader. Here nobody knew him, nobody loved, admired or pampered him. The somber buildings, the many rules and regulations scared and repelled him. He longed for his grandmother and the carefree life at Konstantinovo. After a few days at school, Sergej decided that he definitely did not like it. He ran away, walked the forty miles back home and arrived dirty and exhausted at his grandfather's house. This time, however, he found little sympathy and tenderness. He was severely scolded and sent back to school the next day. But now his position at school was greatly changed. He was no longer just one of the unimportant "new boys". He was now "the boy who had dared to run away", "the boy who had walked forty miles all by himself". Even the teachers paid more attention to him and Sergej gradually became reconciled to his fate.

Among the manuscripts in the Esenin Collection[4] are the notes of one of Sergej's teachers who, when Esenin had become famous, wrote down what he remembered about him. He tells us that at this time Sergej was not very different from the other boys. Though noisy in class, he was on good terms with his teachers and friendly and sensible when one talked kindly to him. He was rough when he played with the other pupils, and after a fight often came back to school dirty and with torn clothes. But generally he was clean and took good care of his appearance. His blond, curly hair was his pride; he brushed it carefully before going to church or town. Every time the boy's heads were shorn – a customary practice in Russian schools – he suffered agonies and felt humiliated and ugly without his curls.

Going to church in town was the only event which broke the monotony of school life. Sergej went to all the services and took an active part in the religious life of the school, but it is doubtful whether this was the result of strong religious feelings. Going to church meant also that you could put on your best clothes and could see the girls and perhaps even exchange a few words with them. The only other occasion when the boys could meet the opposite sex was in winter on the ice. During his last year at school Sergej was an enthusiastic skater and one can easily imagine how popular the handsome blond boy was with the girls.

There were other qualities which made him stand out among the pupils. It soon became known that he wrote poetry – not unusual, for many of his friends did the same – but Sergej wrote with such ease and fluency that he became the foremost poet of the school. He began to write while still in Konstantinovo, when he noted down the stories his grandmother told him. Often he changed the endings when they were too sad for his taste. Now he turned to poetry and began to take his writing more seriously. He read a great deal during his school years, especially the great Russian poets – Puškin, Lermontov and Nekrasov. As with most young poets, his work was still too much in the style of the writers he admired. It lacked depth and was too hastily written, but he already showed an easy mastery of the language and an amazing smoothness of style. His poems gave him what he desired most, the admiration and praise of his teachers and fellow students. He was proud and happy to be considered the first among the school poets, and this bolstered his self-confidence. It is quite understandable that his boastful attitude often made him rather unpopular with the others.

[4] Esenin's works and books and articles about him can be found in the Central State Archives of Literature and Art of the U.S.S.R. (Moscow).

Although Sergej was a bright student, he never spent much time on his lessons. He did not care whether he received good grades and usually a hasty glance into his books between the courses was sufficient to obtain a passing grade. He detested the boys who studied hard for good grades and they, of course, hated him. Continuous fights and quarrels were the result.

In his autobiographies Esenin says very little about his school years. In one of them he mentions that he ran away and, in the third one, he says that the only thing he learned at school was a good knowledge of the Church-Slavonic language. For the rest, he says, he studied mostly outside the classroom, under the guidance of one teacher who made him read modern Russian literature and advised him against imitating the old writers. He never mentioned his school friend, Panfilov, a great admirer of Dobroljubov and other 19th century revolutionaries. After leaving school he continued to correspond with him until 1913 and through him undoubtedly became acquainted with many ideas not included in the school program.[5]

After his graduation in 1912 Sergej was expected to continue his studies at a Teachers' Institute in Moscow. In 1922 he wrote in his autobiography: "Luckily that did not happen. The courses in teaching methods and education irritated me so much that I did not even want to listen to the teachers".

And so, at the age of sixteen, Sergej returned to his grandparents in Konstantinovo, having decided to become a poet. He was convinced that he would soon be famous throughout the country. Happy to have him back with them, his grandparents were not opposed to his plans. "Let him try what he can do", they decided, "time will tell."

Sergej was happy to be free again. He spent his days reading and writing. He roamed through the fields and the forests. Nobody made him do anything he didn't want to do. He could lie in the grass, dream and think at his leisure. He saw the life of the peasants around him, but he did not realize what it meant to be poor, to go hungry, to work from morning till night. When he felt like it, he took part in the work for a few hours. He knew how to handle a scythe, to bring in the hay. He especially liked to join the men when they camped near the river to harvest the distant fields, or to go to the hills with the boys to guard the horses and sleep around the camp fire. In the evening he often promenaded with the other young people through the village street and sang and danced to the music of an accordion.

He loved to walk alone at night through the fields when the farmers had

[5]   See K. Zelinskij, "O Esenine", *Oktjabr'* (1955), no. 10, pp. 176–86.

gone home. The sweet melancholy of the night sharpened his senses. Then inspiration came and the lines started to flow in his head. He thought about himself, about his life and he gradually began to feel restless and sad. All around him everyone was working or resting after a tiring day. Everybody knew what they had to do the next day and for years to come. His school friends had chosen their professions. They had an aim in life. Only he was still searching, hesitating, doing little. Certainly, he wanted to be a poet, the best poet of his country, but fame seemed far away. It was not enough to have been the first poet of his school. The world, even his own country, still ignored his existence.

The poems Sergej wrote during these years reflect his thoughts and moods. Often they are only short descriptions of a landscape, a sunset, or an early summer morning, such as the following four lines which he wrote at the age of fifteen:

> Там, где капустные грядки
> Красной водой поливает восход,
> Клененочек маленький матке
> Зеленое вымя сосет.

> There, where the sunrise throws
> Red water over the cabbage fields,
> A little maple tree sucks
> The green udder of its mother.[6]

Here we have one of the earliest examples of his use of imagery, which later was to be one of the characteristic traits of his poetry. Another theme, his sympathy and love of animals, is also already evident, as in the poem about the pitiful fate of birds in winter.[7]

The mood of many of these poems is still gay and happy. When he was fifteen years old, Esenin seems to have had a happy love affair and speaks of it in joyful lines.[8] It did not last, perhaps because his girl preferred another and the first notes of real melancholy and despair are heard in the lines:

> Догадался и понял я жизни обман,
> Не ропщу на свою незавидную долю.
> Не страдает душа от тоски и от ран,
> Не поможет никто ни страданьям, ни горю.

> I have guessed and understood the betrayal of life,
> I do not protest against my miserable fate,
> My soul does not suffer from anguish and wounds,
> Nobody can alleviate suffering and sadness.[9]

[6] *Sobr. Soč.*, I, p. 56.
[7] *Ibid.*, p. 57–58.
[8] *Ibid.*, p. 60.
[9] *Ibid.*, p. 74.

And the following poem ends with the words: "What has been, one can never bring back."

The subject matter and vocabulary of these early poems are clearly those of a boy reared among peasants. The life of the farmers, however, with its joys and sorrows, is never mentioned. Even at this time Esenin is already an outsider who observes the work around him, but does not take part in it. He is a poet of the village, but not a peasant-poet, as he often has been called.

Much has been written about the religious content of Esenin's early poems. It is true, of course, that the vocabulary and subject matter of many early poems show his close contact with the Christian faith, but whether the poet had strong convictions in this field seems doubtful. In a conversation with his friend, Rozanov, Esenin once said: "Early in my life I was torn by religious doubts. In my childhood I went from one extreme to the other. Periods of prayer were followed by periods when I was extremely insolent. I went even so far that I wanted to make fun of holy things and to blaspheme".[10]

The influence of the patriarchal way of life of his grandparents was very strong on Esenin. Through his grandfather he knew the religious traditions of the Old Believers. The symbolism of this faith, the old customs, attracted him. He was also influenced by the many religious sects who sought a new religious form. Their religion was nearer to the earth and they even dared to criticize the Bible. But he did not adhere to any specific creed and his faith remained vague. He believed in God like all the people around him. He imagined God as an old bearded man who sits in heaven in a village where there is no misery and poverty. The Virgin Mary sits at her open window and throws grain to the pigeons.[11] When God visits the earth, he comes in the form of an itinerant beggar pleasantly surprised when a miserable old peasant, who is eating his last crust of bread, offers him a piece with the words: "Here, eat it … it will make you a little stronger."[12] God and and his family are real people, like the villagers, only better and of a great simplicity. Esenin never questioned his faith intellectually and it remained vague and rather superficial. As soon as he left the village and was among people who were not religious, he lost his primitive beliefs. Only the memories of his grandparents, of the itinerant monks who came to their house and sang their religious songs, of

---

[10] I. Rozanov, *Esenin o sebe i drugix* (Moscow, 1926), p. 18.
[11] *Sobr. Soč.*, I, p. 92–93.
[12] *Ibid.*, p. 122.

the monasteries he visited with his grandmother, would always leave their imprint on his mind.

A Soviet critic, A. Voronskij, who wrote the introduction to the 1926 edition of the Complete Works of Esenin, maintains that the real village was hidden from Esenin because of his religious feelings. This explanation is too simple and ignores the fact that Esenin never was a peasant-poet, although he later liked to pose as one. When at the age of sixteen, after his school years, he returned to the village, he felt that he was an outsider, that he did not share the life of the people around him. Already he felt alone, different from the others, isolated and without roots. He wanted to share only in what was beautiful in country life, to admire the plants, trees and animals, the beautiful sunsets and the pleasures of life. His religious feelings helped him to flee or to ignore the ugliness of daily life.

II

MOSCOW AND PETROGRAD: 1912–1916

Although life in the country without obligations was pleasant, Esenin soon realized that it could not last forever. It was difficult to become known as a poet and his poetry could not support him. When in 1912 his father again urged him to come to Moscow where he had found him a job in a merchant's office, Sergej decided to move to the city. He expected soon to be famous and considered the job a temporary necessity. And, indeed, he worked only a week in the office. He disliked the owner, the monotonous work bored him and he hated to obey orders. Since his pen could not support him, he found work as a clerk in a bookstore. Here he worked with more enthusiasm. He loved to be among books, to read whenever he had time. Soon he became acquainted with other young writers and poets. They were members of the Surikovskij Club for writers and Esenin joined them. In 1912 the club was a rather large organization of proletarian and peasant writers. According to its statutes its aim was to unite writers who had come from the working class or peasants and to help them in their literary work. Only those who had not lost their spiritual link with the working people could be active members.[1] An article about the club stated that it strove "to throw a ray of light into the soul of every farmer, factory worker, office worker etc., so that they might acquire a deeper consciousness of their human self".[2] Many of the members were politically active and were Social-Revolutionaries or Social-Democrats. At their meetings they discussed politics, as well as literature, and many took part in illegal political work. What attracted Esenin most was the fact that at last he was among people who attached the same importance to literature and poetry that he did, who appreciated him as a poet and gave him the encouragement and admiration he craved.

Then, just when he felt happy and at ease with his new literary friends, the bookstore where he had worked for six months was closed. Unable

[1] See *Drug Naroda* (1918), no. 1, p. 4.
[2] *Ežemesjačnyj Žurnal* (1915), no. 6, p. 155.

to find another job, Sergej was forced to return to Konstantinovo. It was disappointing and dull to live in the village after the six exciting months in Moscow. He wrote desperate letters to his friends, urging them to find some work for him which would enable him to earn a living. At last, in May 1913, they found him a job as proof reader in a printing shop and Esenin returned immediately to Moscow.

His job brought him into direct contact with the workers of the printing plant and strengthened his interest in politics and the workers' movement.[3]

He stayed at his job for more than a year and during this time became more and more involved in the work of his friends who belonged to the Social Revolutionary party. He became one of the most active members of the Surikovskij Club and was appointed its secretary. He distributed illegal literature, spoke at workers' meetings and faithfully fulfilled his political duties, often risking imprisonment and exile. But he never became a socialist, he never completely accepted the ideology of the party. He was still searching for ideals and something in which he could believe. At first he had been strongly influenced by Tolstoj's teachings. In a letter to his former schoolfriend Panfilov he had written:

And so I have given up eating meat, nor do I eat fish; I don't use sugar, I want to discard anything made of leather, but I don't want to be called a "vegetarian".[4]

Also, early in 1913 he wrote again:

The question whether I have changed in some ways made me think and analyse myself. Yes, I have changed. I have changed in my opinions, but my convictions are the same and have settled even deeper in my soul. Because of personal convictions I have given up eating meat and fish and fancy things such as chocolate and cocoa, I don't drink coffee and I don't smoke. Soon it will be four months since I started. I also have begun to have different opinions about people. A genius for me is a man of words and deeds, like Christ. All the others, except Buddha, are nothing but lechers who have fallen into the abyss of depravity. Of course, I feel sympathetic towards people like Belinskij, Nadson, Garšin, Zlatovratskij and others... Recently I have begun to make propaganda among the workers through letters. I have spread among them the monthly magazine "Ogni" which has a democratic trend. It is very good.[5]

---

[3]   D. Zolotnickij, "Iz rannix stixov Sergeja Esenina", *Neva* (1955), no. 3, pp. 169–170, says that Esenin came to Moscow in the winter of 1913 and that he worked in a cartridge factory. We have found no proof of this information.
[4]   *Sobr. Soč.*, V, p. 99.
[5]   *Ibid.*, pp. 92, 93. *Ogni* mentioned here by Esenin published in 1913 popular articles, f.i. about Marx's *Kapital*, about the position of women and similar ones. In literature it rejected art for art's sake and stressed the importance of the social task of literature.

G. Deev-Xomjakovskij, who knew Esenin at this time, wrote in his article "The Truth about Esenin",[6] that at one moment he became so interested in his political work that he wanted to devote all his free time to it and give up his literary work. His friends were appalled at the idea and urged him to continue his poetry. And, in fact, he did write many lyrical poems during his stay in Moscow. It is striking, however, that he very rarely mentions his life in the city or his contact with the workers' movement. Only one poem, "The Blacksmith", reflects his political convictions. In it he describes a blacksmith at work. He then adresses him:

> Куй, кузнец, рази ударом,
> Пусть с лица струится пот.
> Зажигай сердца пожаром,
> Прочь от горя и невзгод!
> Закали свои порывы,
> Преврати порывы в сталь
> И лети мечтой игривой
> Ты в заоблачную даль.
> Там вдали, за черной тучей,
> За порогом хмурых дней,
> Реет солнца блеск могучий
> Над равнинами полей.
> Тонут пастбища и нивы
> В голубом сиянье дня,
> И над пашнею счастливо
> Созревают зеленя.
> Взвейся к солнцу с новой силой,
> Загорись в его лучах.
> Прочь от робости постылой,
> Сбрось скорей постыдный страх.

> Hammer, blacksmith, strike your blow,
> Let the sweat run from your brow.
> Light the hearts with fire,
> Away from misery and adversity!
> Temper your impulses,
> Turn them into steel
> And fly like a playful dream
> Far away above the clouds.
> There afar, behind the black cloud,
> Beyond the threshold of gloomy days,
> Hovers the mighty brilliance of the sun
> Over the plains and fields.
> The pastures and cornfields are drowned
> In the blue radiance of the day,
> And over the fields, happily,
> The green is ripening.
> Soar up toward the sun with new force,

[6]   G. Deev-Xomjakovskij, "Pravda o Esenine", *Na Literaturnom Postu* (1926), no. 4, p. 33.

> Catch fire in its rays.
> Away from hateful timidity,
> Quickly throw off the shameful fear.[7]

But his other poems were about the village, nature, plants and animals. Although he speaks about his feelings and emotions, he does not mention his love for one of the girls who worked in the printing plant, A. R. Iz-rjadnovaja, with whom he lived and who bore him a son. This, as well as the fact that within a year he could abandon his family and politics so easily, seems to prove that they had not touched his inner life very deeply. What had attracted him first of all towards the group of politically conscious writers was that they recognized his talent as a poet, and in addition he felt close to several members of the group who called themselves peasant-poets and who had the same background as he had. Although he was never much interested in political theory, he felt attracted toward the Social-Revolutionaries because they were convinced that the peasants would play the most important role in the society of the future. And finally the adventurous life of a revolutionary attracted him. He was clever at dodging the police and enjoyed his illegal activities. He liked to break laws, to live dangerously, to see himself as an outcast of the society of law-abiding, respectable citizens. He wrote at that time to Panfilov:

Your carelessness nearly got me into prison. Didn't I tell you to change your envelopes and handwriting? I am being followed and quite recently they have searched my rooms. I am not going to explain it all in my letter, for one can't even hide a pin from these pasha's with their all-seeing eye. I must keep silent. Somebody reads my letters, but very carefully, not tearing the envelope. Once more I beg you, please cut out any sharp tone in your letters, otherwise it will end badly, for me as well as for you. I'll explain the reasons for all this later, when – I don't know. Anyhow, when this threatening thunderstorm has passed.[8]

And in another letter:

I can't write in detail. Eight comrades have been arrested for their past solidarity-action for the streetcar-workers. There is a lot of trouble and I am very busy...[9]

But even though it is evident from these letters that Esenin was actively involved in illegal political work, his deepest desire remained, as before, to become a great poet. Gradually, when he came to know more intellectuals, he began to realize that he needed to know more, especially in the field of history and world literature, in order to become a real writer. Therefore, in 1913 he enrolled in evening courses of the Šanjavskij Peo-

---

[7]   *Sobr. Soč.*, I, p. 97–98. This poem was published in 1914 in *Put' Pravdy* which was then a newspaper of the bolshevists.
[8]   *Ibid.*, V, p. 104.
[9]   *Ibid.*, p. 103.

ples' University in Moscow, and for a year and a half he studied diligently.

Esenin's work as secretary of the Surikovskij Club became more and more difficult. There was never enough money to do what the club had planned. They had, for instance, decided to start the publication of works of their members, a project which seemed of the utmost importance to Esenin, whose poems would form one of the first books. Funds were lacking and the publication had to be postponed indefinitely. He became more and more discouraged. His job as a proof reader began to bore him. He lacked the will power and the mental strength to persevere when the odds were against him. In May 1914 when the snows melted and the first sunny days warmed the city, he suddenly abandoned his job and his work for the club and took a train to the South. A month later he had to beg his father to send him money for the return trip to Moscow.

When he came back he had, of course, lost his job. The small sum of money he had been able to save had been spent. Unable to find other work, he returned to Konstantinovo to live with his grandparents. He was there in August 1914 when war was declared. Esenin hated the idea of war and was terribly afraid of being drafted. Luckily he was exempted from service for a year. He frequently visited his friends in Moscow and continued to participate in their work. When in August 1914 a group of Social Democrats wanted to issue an appeal against the war, Esenin collaborated with a poem, "The Crows", in which he described Russian soldiers fleeing in Prussia and wives and mothers weeping over their lost ones.[10] The group decided to publish a new periodical, "The Friend of the People", and Esenin became secretary to the editors. Each member paid a few rubles to cover the cost of publication. With this journal they hoped to attract all those who were opposed to war. This was not an easy task, since of course, any public protest was forbidden. Esenin's poem, "The Crows", which was to be published in the first issue, was confiscated by the censor. He then contributed another, less outspoken poem, "Uzory" (Pattern),[11] about a girl who embroiders a picture of her fallen lover. The first and only issue of the journal finally appeared. From Petrograd Esenin received several letters with high praise of his poetry.

At the end of December 1914 Sergej met several writers from Petrograd. He saw more and more clearly that he could only become known outside his little group if he moved to Petrograd where the greatest writers and poets lived. In March 1915 he left his friends, his political work,

[10]   This poem has not been preserved.
[11]   *Sobr. Soč.*, I, p. 112.

his wife and child, to try his fortune in Petrograd. He wanted to meet great poets like Aleksandr Blok, Zinaida Gippius, Gorodeckij, Sologub and Vjačeslav Ivanov and the novelists Merežkovskij, Bunin and Kuprin. But how to approach them? He realized that they were different from his leftist friends in Moscow, that they were not particularly interested in politics or the workers' movement. He felt that he would not impress them as a student of the Šanjavskij University or the secretary of the Surikovskij Club. He knew that it was the fashion among certain intellectuals in Petrograd to adore "the Russian peasant", the "people" in general. Since he did not mind acting a little, if this could open the doors for him, he decided to pose as the naive peasant, primitive and hardly literate, who had written his poems in the woods and was unconscious of their value.

Anatolij Mariengof, who later became one of Esenin's intimate friends, has written about Esenin in his "Novel Without Lies".[12] This book often gives a somewhat distorted picture of the poet, and when we quote the page where he gives Esenin's account of his introduction into the literary world of Petrograd, one should keep in mind that Mariengof is often not quite reliable. That at least some of it is true is proved by the account of several other writers who knew Esenin after his arrival in Petrograd. Zinaida Gippius, the well-known poetess and wife of Merežkovskij, wrote in an article in the *Poslednie Novosti* in 1926 her recollection of Esenin's visit. He was dressed in a peasant costume, wearing high boots.[13] Gorodeckij mentions that when Blok had sent Esenin to him, he arrived with his poems knotted in a peasant handkerchief.[14] Mariengof quotes Esenin as follows:

Do you know how I arrived on Parnassus? Well, brother, you have to be clever. I told myself that I would let everybody believe that it was thanks to him that I came into Russian literature. That is pleasant for them and I don't give a damn. Did Gorodeckij introduce me? – Fine. Did Kljuev do it? – Good. Did Sologub and Čebotarevskaja introduce me? – Good. In one word: Merežkovskij as well as Gippius, and Blok, and Rjurik Ivnev... I remember how he stared at me through his glasses, and I had hardly read twelve lines when he said in a very thin voice: "Oh, but that is remarkable, the work of a genius, really...," and taking me by the arm he dragged me from one celebrity to the other. As for me, I couldn't be more modest. I blushed like a girl at every word of praise and I was so shy that I couldn't look anybody in the face. What fun it was! And you know, never in my life had I worn such shabby boots or such a torn shirt as I was wearing at that time. I told them that I was on my way to Riga to load barrels. That I had nothing to eat. That I was for a few days in Petrograd waiting for my gang of dockworkers. And about what barrels was I talking?

[12]   A. Mariengof, *Roman bez vran'ja* (Berlin, 1929).
[13]   Zinaida Gippius, "Sud'ba Eseninyx", *Poslednija Novosti* (28 January, 1926).
[14]   S. Gorodeckij, "O S. Esenine, Vospominanija", *Novyj Mir* (1926), no. 2, p. 138.

I had come to Petrograd for world fame, for a monument in bronze... Well, for three weeks they dragged me from one drawing-room to the other to sing dirty songs. First, for appearance's sake they asked for poems. I read two or three and they yawned behind their hands and then for the rest of the night they wanted dirty songs... O, how I hate all those Sologubs and Gippius'![15]

In his autobiography Esenin says that he first went to see Aleksandr Blok when he arrived in Petrograd: "When I saw Blok", he writes, "my face dripped with perspiration, for the first time I saw a poet". It seems that Blok gave him an introduction for Gorodeckij and Esenin lived for some time at Gorodeckij's apartment. The latter was a young writer who was very interested in folk-songs and he was glad to meet the peasant-poet. He brought Sergej into contact with other writers and soon Esenin enjoyed great popularity. It is probably true that on several occasions late in the evening, when the more sedate guests had left and ample drinks had been consumed, Esenin had more success with his bawdy songs than with his serious poetry. But nevertheless his talent as a poet was generally recognized. His descriptions of nature and of the simple life in the country appealed immensely to the literary intellectuals in Petrograd.

A writer who had been introduced to Esenin at a poetry evening in one of the large halls of Petrograd in March 1915, describes the impression Esenin made on him:

A group of people who surrounded him listened with growing enthusiasm to what he was saying. He talked somewhat shyly, it seemed, but with a certain pride and with a strong provincial accent, of his life in the village; he felt, and certainly not for the first time, how interested we were in this life; he told how he had started to write poems – "you go fishing and then you don't return home for two months! You have just enough money to buy paper." The people around him were rapt with admiration. From the first moment, even not knowing his poetry, these "intellectuals" felt his wonderful freshness, his unspoilt health, without crudeness, his half-shy and half-insolent youth, they smelt the odor of the far-away village which seemed so wholesome to them.[16]

Although Esenin may not have felt a great sympathy for his admirers he was, nevertheless, very happy during his first months in Petrograd. At last he was fully recognized as a poet, at last he was famous. And though he continued acting the naive peasant boy in the drawing-rooms and among the more fashionable writers, he also became acquainted with some proletarian writers and leftist critics, among whom he could show his real self. One of these critics, Klejnbort, arranged for Esenin to become an editor of the political and literary journal *Severnye Zapiski* (Northern

[15]   Mariengof, *Roman bez vran'ja*, p. 16, 17.
[16]   Vl. Č-sky, "Pervye šagi", *Zvezda* (1926), no. 4, p. 214.

Notes). Esenin remained in correspondence with his friends in Moscow and occasionally went to see them. Deev-Xomjakovskij tells us how you could see from Sergej's letters that he was torn between his political friends and his other admirers. In Moscow he told his friends how boring life in Petrograd was for him and how he wanted to commit suicide. But his visits to Moscow always refreshed him and gave him new courage. His friends were convinced that he would again devote his energy to political activities.

Whatever intentions he may have had, his visits to Moscow became less and less frequent and soon Esenin turned away from politics. He gave up his editorship of the *Severnye Zapiski* and sought the company of other poets who wrote about the village and called themselves peasant-poets. One of these, Nikolaj Kljuev, became a very close friend and had considerable influence on Esenin.

Kljuev was eight years older than Esenin. According to Mariengof, he had introduced himself in Petrograd very much as Esenin had done. He had played the part of a simple house-painter and had worked in Gorodeckij's apartment. There he "forgot" his poems on the kitchen table. Gorodeckij read them and was deeply impressed and excited by his discovery of a new talent. This story may be apocryphal, but there is no doubt that Kljuev, like Esenin, pretended to have come straight from the village. He was very proud of his background and stressed it by always wearing a peasant shirt and heavy high boots. In this outfit he went into the most elegant restaurants and soon became a well-known figure in the streets of Petrograd. Kljuev had elaborated a whole theory about the future of Russia in which the peasant would play the most important part. His ideas can be summarized as follows:

Russia is a peasant country. The peasant is the bearer of the only true religious and social ideas. At the moment the peasant is oppressed and exploited by people who belong to other social classes. Those classes must disappear. Then the peasant will create a new Russia with a new conception of truth and with new laws, for he himself is the source of truth and law. The present laws have been invented by people who work in offices in Petrograd. The peasant will reintroduce natural laws and he will also change religion. Instead of the existing church he will erect a green forest-church, a church of the soil. Then Ivan the Stupid will become Ivan Tsarevich.[17] But this will happen in the future. At present the enemy is still too strong. The peasant must wait till the enemy has been weakened by internal quarrels. Then the moment will come. The peasant will then

[17] Allusion to a folk-tale.

join forces with any group which will first light the fire to burn up the existing order. It does not matter whether it comes from the right or the left, from above or below, so long as it starts burning.[18]

These theories held immense appeal for Esenin. The peasant who would play such an important role in the future was not just any farmer, but only he who knew the old traditions, the old legends, who knew the Bible and the symbols of Russian peasant life. They were the people like his grandfather, and he believed himself to be one of them. He felt himself glorified in Kljuev's theories. If Kljuev was right, it meant that he had a great part to play in the coming events, that the future belonged to him.

Esenin's admiration for Kljuev was quite sincere. He learned a great deal from him and he certainly felt much happier in his new role of the peasant-prophet than in that of the naive village boy. It was now no longer necessary to amuse an audience who regarded him as a curious, interesting phenomenon. He could feel far superior to them and despise them as city-dwellers to whom the future did not belong.

The other writers and poets in Petrograd whom Esenin admired and who appreciated his talent were mostly more cultured and better educated. He hated to feel inferior to others. Kljuev's theories stressed the importance of the one field where his knowledge was indeed greater than that of the most famous writers. Perhaps this alone was enough to make him a fervent follower of Kljuev's theories.

Whether Esenin was really convinced of the truth of these theories, or whether he wanted to believe them because they flattered his ego, is difficult to ascertain. His occasional spells of melancholy, his moments of despair when he even contemplated suicide, seem to indicate that his faith in the great future of the peasant was not too deeply founded. In his moments of complete sincerity he must have realized that again he was acting a part. He already knew how easy it was to fool people, to be admired and applauded for what he pretended to be. But these moments of sincerity were still rare and in general he seems to have enjoyed his new importance as the peasant-prophet.

After two months in Petrograd, Esenin returned at the end of April 1915 to Konstantinovo to spend the summer in the country. He was again exempted from military service. He spent his days reading and writing and enjoyed the talks with his grandparents and the other farmers of the older generation. When he returned to Petrograd in October, he stressed his peasant background more than ever before. With other peas-

[18]   See V. Xodasevič, "Esenin", *Sovremennye Zapiski*, XXVII (1926), p. 298.

ant-poets – Kljuev, Gorodeckij, Klyčkov and others – he founded the Krasa Group. They organized poetry evenings where the members of the group read their poems. Again Sergej began to walk around dressed like a peasant, but no longer in the shabby clothes he had worn when he came to Petrograd. He now imitated Kljuev and wore magnificent boots of shiny black leather, a blue silk peasant shirt girded with a golden belt to which a little comb was attached. He had let his hair grow and it hung in long golden curls on his shoulders.

The Krasa Group was not active for long. Differences of opinion developed and the members soon drifted apart. Kljuev gradually drew Esenin away from Gorodeckij. Although Sergej still admired Kljuev and was influenced by him, he began more and more to resent his leadership. He was especially irritated by the fact that when the critics wrote about the peasant-poets, they always linked Esenin's name with Kljuev's, but named Kljuev first. He did not want to be the disciple and revolted against Kljuev's authority.

Esenin had by now completely broken with his former leftist friends. Perhaps the example of Gorodeckij and Kljuev, who during the war turned more and more to the right, had influenced him. It is also possible that his fear of being drafted made him more careful in his choice of friends, but if so, his precautions were in vain. What he dreaded most, happened. He was drafted into the army. For the spoiled and undisciplined young poet this was a real tragedy. Again, as earlier in boarding school, he suffered agonies when his blond curls fell under the scissors of the military barber. He abhorred the dirty barracks which were full of vermin. The officers and sergeants made fun of him. He seemed utterly unfit for military drill.

Desperate letters to his acquaintances at last bore fruit. His friend, M. Murašev, decided to make an attempt to free Esenin from the barracks. He borrowed a colonel's uniform and presented himself at the barracks as Colonel Count Murašev. When the officer in charge received him, he boldly produced an order to the effect that Private Esenin henceforth would be attached to him personally. Sergej was called and a few minutes later he left the hated barracks. Of course, this was only a temporary respite, for the ruse could be discovered at any moment. Still his friends managed to arrange that Sergej be assigned to the "Commission of Trophies", where other writers, painters and musicians who served in the army were employed.[19] Now his worst sufferings were over. The work

[19]   See M. Murašev, "Esenin v Petrograde", *Sbornik S. A. Esenin* (1926), p. 52. Also G. Ustinov, "Gody vosxoda i zakata", *Sbornik pamjati Esenina* (1926), p. 85.

for the Commission was easy. He had to be there only a few hours a day.

He started to write again, spent less and less time on his job and soon stayed away altogether. This too flagrant neglect of his military duties drew the attention of his superiors. He was transferred to the Medical Corps and sent to a military hospital in Tsarskoe Selo near the residence of the Tsar. Even this was better than the Petrograd barracks. He was housed in a cold and somber room in an old fortress, but his duties occupied him only a few hours a day. One of his superiors, Colonel Loman, became interested in the young poet. He took Esenin under his protection and saw to it that he had enough free time to write. He liked to visit him and to listen to his poetry. Loman was attached to the court as an aide-de-camp of the Tsaritsa. He told her about Esenin and she expressed the wish to meet him. Sergej speaks about this visit to the court in his second autobiography. "Once, on the request of Loman, I read my poems to the Tsaritsa. After she had listened to them she told me that my poems were beautiful, but very sad. I answered that all Russia was like that. I stressed its poverty, the climate, etc." The princesses Maria and Anastasia were present at this visit.

There is no doubt that Esenin was flattered by the invitation of the Tsaritsa. It seems that he even dedicated to her a volume of poems he was then preparing for the press. Xodasevič mentions that he saw the proofs of this book with the dedication, but in the published volume it was omitted.[20] Although flattered by the attention of the court, Esenin did not feel happy about it. In his revolutionary days he had hated the Tsar and all he stood for. He evaded other interviews with the Tsaritsa and became more and more discontented with his life in Tsarskoe. Loman had eased his duties, but he supervised him strictly and only very seldom gave him permission to go to Petrograd to visit his friends. His dark and somber quarters and the boredom of his solitary life drove Esenin to drink. When he neglected his duties too flagrantly, Loman straightened things out for him. But even with ample free time it was hard for him to keep on writing without the crowds of admirers he had had in Petrograd.

The circumstances under which Esenin left Tsarskoe Selo have never been entirely clear. In the second autobiography he says: "The revolution found me at the front, in one of the disciplinary battalions where I was sent because I had refused to write poems in honor of the Tsar. I had refused after consulting Ivanov-Razumnik and asking for his help."

Esenin wrote this in 1923, when he wanted to please the authorities and give proof of his revolutionary convictions and he may well have embel-

[20]   See V. Xodasevič, "Esenin", *Sovremennye Zapiski*, XXVII (1926), p. 302.

lished the story. On the other hand, his friend Ustinov wrote that already in 1919 Esenin mentioned to him his disgrace and the disciplinary battalion.[21] Still, it seems rather improbable that a refusal to write poems would be punished in this way. Xodasevič considers it improbable that Esenin would have refused to write in honor of the Tsar when of his own free will he had dedicated poems to the Tsaritsa. One could argue that it was quite a different matter for him to dedicate poems he had already written to a woman, even though she was the wife of the Tsar, than to write on command to honor a man he had always despised or to glorify a war he abhorred. Whatever may have happened, Sergej was no longer in Tsarskoe Selo, nor in Petrograd, when in February 1917 the revolution broke out.

---

[21]   G. Ustinov, "Gody vosxoda i zakata", p. 85.

III

EARLY POEMS AND PROSE

1. *RADUNICA*

Already before 1917 Esenin was considered one of the most talented poets of the younger generation. Perhaps this fame was not due solely to his literary gifts, but also to his great personal charm and to the current interest in the poetic aspects of life in the country. A few of his poems, published in literary and political periodicals, had provoked some favorable comments. In 1916 a collection of his poems appeared under the title *Radunica*. Esenin explained that this was the name of a spring holiday when one meets the souls of one's ancestors. This little volume immediately received excellent reviews. It was a collection mostly of contemplative, lyrical poems, describing the nature and landscape of the region where the poet had spent his youth. They described his emotions during a beautiful sunset, a moonlit night or an early summer morning. Not only do they offer the idyllic and charming picture of country life which appealed most to the cultured readers of the time, but they tell of the kind of life he knew and loved. What attracted and touched him happened to coincide with his readers' taste. His descriptions ring true. They convince and charm by their sincere emotion, their freshness and directness.

One of the main themes of *Radunica* is the great love of the poet for his native country. We find numerous expressions of this love in his descriptions of nature. In one poem he says directly how he prefers his country to all the bliss of heaven:

> Если крикнет рать святая:
> "Кинь ты Русь, живи в раю!"
> Я скажу: "Не надо рая,
> Дайте родину мою".

> If the host of saints shouts:
> "Leave Russia, come live in paradise!"
> Then I'll say: "I don't need paradise,
> Give me my fatherland."[1]

[1] *Sobr. Soč.*, I, p. 130.

Or:

> Черная, потом пропахшая выть!
> Как мне тебя не ласкать, не любить?

> Black earth, drenched with the stench of sweat,
> How could I not caress, not love you?[2]

The mood of the majority of the poems is gay and happy. The poet feels contented to live in the beautiful countryside. He is glad to be young. He enjoys life. The melancholy and despair of his later work, the frequent mention of death, are nearly absent. Here and there only do we find a note of gentle melancholy, as in the following description of a summer evening:

> Лес застыл без печали и шума,
> Виснет темь, как платок, за сосной.
> Сердце гложет плакучая дума ...
> Ой, не весел ты, край мой родной.

> The forest has grown still, without sadness and noise,
> Darkness hangs, like a shawl, behind the pine trees.
> Weeping thoughts gnaw at my heart...
> O, you are somber, my native region.[3]

And in another poem:

> Где-то вдали, на кукане реки,
> Дремную песню поют рыбаки.
> Оловом светится лужная голь...
> Грустная песня, ты – русская боль.

> Somewhere far away, like the slaves of the river,
> Fishermen sing a sleepy song.
> The naked marshes glitter like tin...
> Sad song, you are the Russian pain.[4]

The somber poems in *Radunica*, however, are exceptions. Esenin's world still radiates happiness. The colors are light and gay: blues, whites, reds and greens predominate.

While most of the descriptions in his poetry are concrete and realistic, here and there a note of mystery and vagueness creeps in. Words like "someone", "something", "invisible", "with a quiet secret for someone", remind the reader of Aleksandr Blok's poetry, whose work Esenin had read long before he came to Petrograd. Blok's influence, as we shall see, was to become much stronger later, but is already clearly felt in the following four lines from one of the poems in *Radunica*:

[2] *Ibid.*, p. 142.
[3] *Ibid.*, p. 176.
[4] *Ibid.*, p. 142.

Все встречаю, все приемлю,
Рад и счастлив душу вынуть.
Я пришел на эту землю,
Чтоб скорей ее покинуть.

I greet everything, I accept everything,
I am glad and happy to abandon my soul.
I have come on this earth
To leave it soon.[5]

Blok's influence and that of other Petrograd intellectuals, would later draw Esenin towards a more mystical conception of religion. In *Radunica* this mysticism is still very rare, though more than a third of the poems are inspired by religious feelings.

It is not easy to define exactly what Esenin did believe at the time when he wrote the poems of *Radunica*. In later years he denied that he ever was deeply religious. In a preface to one of his later collections of poetry he wrote for instance:

The most ticklish stage (in my poetry) is my religiosity which is very clearly reflected in my early works. I do not consider that this stage, in a creative sense, belongs to me. It was conditioned by my upbringing and the surroundings where I grew up during the first period of my literary activity. My early poems show the strong influence of my grandfather. From my third year on he crammed the old patriarchal church culture down my throat. In my teens my grandmother dragged me to all the Russian monasteries. When I was 13–15 years old, the literary people around me believed about the same things as my grandparents, therefore my poems were received and understood with an enthusiasm which I now reject most emphatically. I am a realist... Mystics remind me of Jesuits. I would like to ask my readers to consider all my Jesuses, Mothers of God and Mikolas as the fairy figures in poetry. All these religious names should be considered as names which have become myths for us: Osiris, Zeus, Aphrodite, Athena, etc.[6]

And in his autobiography of 1921 he wrote: "I was early given to religious doubts. In my childhood I experienced abrupt transitions: now a period of prayer, then one of wantonness, when I wanted to blaspheme and utter profanities."[7] Of course, these passages were written after the revolution, when religion was in disrepute and Esenin may well have thought it advantageous to belittle his former beliefs. But the fact remains that many of the poems of *Radunica* have a religious content. Whether this religion should be called Christian is doubtful. Esenin does use the Christian terminology, but he applies this to half-pagan, pantheistic ideas. The images are often far removed from Christian content. For him the primary

[5] *Ibid.*, p. 119.
[6] G. Pokrovskij, *Esenin, Eseninščina, Religija*, 2nd ed. (Moscow, 1930), p. 52. Also: *Literaturnaja Ryazan'*, Al'manax, 1957, II, p. 267, 268.
[7] In S. Borisov, "K biografii S. Esenina", *Krasnaja Niva* (1926), no. 2.

source of religion is nature and even his Christ learns from nature. He expressed this most clearly in a poem, written in the style of a folksong, where an old peasant dreams how as a young man Christ asks the fishes to teach him wisdom. And a little fish answers:

> Ты иди учись в пустынях да лесах;
> Наша тайна отразилась в небесах.

> Go, learn in the deserts and the forests, –
> Our secret is reflected in heaven.[8]

Esenin's prayers are directed, not to God, but to nature:

> Позабыв людское горе,
> Сплю на вырублях сучья.
> Я молюсь на алы зори,
> Причащаюсь у ручья.

> Having forgotten human grief,
> I sleep on cut branches.
> I pray to the red dawn,
> I take communion at the stream.[9]

Esenin's religion is very different from that of the official Russian church. It is devoid of deep philosophical content, but remains concrete and close to the representation of God and the saints as we find them in Russian folk legends. His Mikola[10] is not the archbishop as shown in the Ortho- dox Church, clad in rich vestments, but a poor mendicant, like one of the itinerant monks who, sack on back and stick in hand, pass through the villages. Esenin's Mikola is very gentle and leads a simple life. In the morning he washes in the lake and the bark of a birchtree serves him as a towel. From the earth he converses with God who has opened the little window of his house in paradise.

Esenin's God is an old bearded man, who brings the wind and the rain, lives in a paradise which looks like an ideal village of the province of Rya- zan and often comes down to earth, dressed like a peasant, riding his little donkey. Then the trees bend their heads and shout "Hosannah!"[11] At any moment, he thinks, one might meet Christ and when the poet walks in the forest, he inspects every tree to see whether perhaps Christ is hidden behind it.[12]

There is, too, the charming little story in verse about the God-child who is eating while Mary has called the birds to the temple to pray. The

[8] *Sobr. Soč.*, I, p. 279.
[9] *Ibid.*, p. 132.
[10] *Ibid.*, pp. 89–93.
[11] *Ibid.*, p. 133.
[12] *Ibid.*, p. 123.

birds are hungry and after their prayer they tell the child that he has to feed them, since he has created them. Christ gives them all he has, but a little later he grows hungry and starts crying, begging his mother for something to eat. Mary calls the birds back and tells them to bring bread and grain. But the birds don't want to go out, they say that it is going to rain. While Mary has gone to look for food, a white stork comes, picks the little child up in his beak and takes him to his nest. When Mary returns and misses her son, she starts out through the world to look for him. Finally she sees him, riding on the stork's back. Then she punishes the birds who will have to collect food from now to eternity and the stork who must bring the babies to the peasant huts.[13]

While the religious content of this poem is superficial and light, there are a few poems in *Radunica* in which Esenin expresses deeper religious feelings. The following poem, quoted in full, is a good illustration:

Чую радуницу божью –
Не напрасно я живу,
Поклоняюсь придорожью,
Припадаю на траву.

Между сосен, между елок,
Меж берез кудрявых бус,
Под венком, в кольце иголок,
Мне мерещится Исус.

Он зовет меня в дубровы,
Как во царствие небес,
И горит в парче лиловой
Облаками крытый лес.

Голубиный дух от бога,
Словно огненный язык,
Завладел моей дорогой,
Заглушил мой слабый крик.

Льется пламя в бездну зренья,
В сердце радость детских снов,
Я поверил от рожденья
В богородицын покров.

I sense God's "radunica"
Not in vain do I live,
I bow at the wayside,
I prostrate myself on the grass.

Amidst the pine trees, amidst the firs,
Amidst the beads of the curly birches,
I see Jesus as in a dream,
Under a garland, a wreath of pine needles.

---

[13] *Ibid.*, pp. 229–232.

He calls me to the forest,
As to the kingdom of heaven,
And the woods, covered with clouds
Burn in lilac brocade.

The dovelike spirit of God,
Like a fiery tongue,
Has enveloped my road,
Has deafened my weak cry.

A flame shoots through the chasm of sight,
In my heart is the joy of childish dreams,
From birth I have had faith
In the protection of the Virgin.[14]

(1914)

In addition to the poems with religious content and those in which he expresses love of his country, we find in *Radunica* also a few descriptions of village life: a market day, pilgrims who pass through the village, a poor peasant's hut, a holiday. But there is never any mention of the daily work on the land or of the hardships of peasant life. Even one of the saddest events in the life of the farmers of Tsarist Russia, the departure of the young recruits, is depicted as a charming and idyllic occasion. Esenin's poems on village life are like genre paintings.

In their form and versification the poems of *Radunica*, written when their author was hardly twenty years old, show little originality. Esenin follows the example of the great Russian poets before his time. The influence of Kol'cov and Nekrasov is especially evident. For instance, Esenin's Mikola shows great similarity to Nekrasov's Vlas, not only in subject matter, but even in specific lines.

Nevertheless *Radunica* shows that Esenin already possessed a great mastery of the Russian language. The lines of his poetry flow easily and harmoniously. A too abundant use of regional expressions and specific peasant vocabulary was corrected in the second edition of *Radunica*, published in 1918. In this revised form the poems were included in the 1926 edition of Esenin's collected works.

2. THE INFLUENCE OF BLOK AND KLJUEV

Goluben', a second volume of poems by Esenin, was published in 1918. The influence of Aleksandr Blok's poetry is much more evident in this collection than in the earlier poems of *Radunica*. Not only do we recognize

[14] *Ibid.*, pp. 134–135.

the specific vocabulary Blok used in his early poetry, but the entire mood of the poems reminds one of Blok's melancholy and mysticism.

A few of the poems in *Goluben'* were written in 1914, but the majority in 1915 and 1916 during the first World War. About half of them have some religious content. During those years Esenin had broken with his revolutionary political past. Especially when he was in the army he felt lost and uncertain. He desperately needed something to believe in, something to hold on to and he thought that the religious mysticism of Blok and other Petrograd writers perhaps could give meaning to his life. But vague mystical beliefs were not enough to hide the ugly reality of a world torn by war. Esenin did not believe in the war and could not join in the patriotic glorification of a fighting he abhorred. Instead of the joy and radiance of so many of the poems of *Radunica*, a tone of sadness and melancholy now prevails. While he exclaimed in *Radunica*: "I don't need heaven. – Give me my native land", he now says, "I am only a guest, a chance guest – On your mountains, earth".[15]

Esenin's mysticism remains unconvincing so long as he imitates Blok too closely and uses expressions like "the invisible gates", "someone secret", "invisible fields", or the line "There is no name for external truth." But in most poems his mystical conceptions remain concrete. His "other world" is tangible. It has color and shape and its earthly flavor is evident in the images from peasant life that he uses for its description. Even the woman of his dreams is not as mysterious as Blok's "Beautiful Lady." She is not an extra-sensory apparition, but can be seen and described:

С алым соком ягоды на коже,
Нежная, красивая, была
На закат ты розовый похожа
И, как снег, лучиста и светла.

Зерна глаз твоих осыпались, завяли,
Имя тонкое растаяло, как звук,
Но остался в складках смятой шали
Запах меда от невинных рук.

With the red juice of berries on your skin,
Tender and beautiful, you were
Like a rosy sunset
And, like snow, sparkling and bright.

The seeds of your eyes fell and wilted,
Your slender name has melted, like a sound,
But in the folds of the rumpled shawl
Remained the honey smell of innocent hands.[16]

[15] *Ibid.*, p. 247.
[16] *Ibid.*, p. 204.

While the lack of realism and mysticism of his Petrograd friends were foreign to Esenin and left only a temporary mark on his poetry, their melancholy corresponded much more directly to his own feelings. Except for patriotic glorification of the war, this was the prevailing mood of much poetry at this time. In *Goluben'* Esenin's melancholy is still lyrical and sad rather than desperate, as it would become in his later life. But already in 1915, when he is twenty years old, he writes about the sadness of passing time, of growing old:

Я снова здесь, в семье родной,
Мой край, задумчивый и нежный!
Кудрявый сумрак за горой
Рукою машет белоснежной.

Седины пасмурного дня
Плывут всклокоченные мимо,
И грусть вечерняя меня
Волнует непреодолимо.

Над куполом церковных глав
Тень от зари упала ниже.
О други игрищ и забав,
Уж я вас больше не увижу!

В забвенье канули года,
Вослед и вы ушли куда-то.
И лишь по-прежнему вода
Шумит за мельницей крылатой.

И часто я в вечерней мгле,
Под звон надломленной осоки,
Молюсь дымящейся земле
О невозвратных и далеких.

Again I am here, with my own people,
My country, pensive and tender!
The curly twilight behind the hill
Beckons with its snow-white hand.

The greyness of the somber day
Floats rumpled past,
And the sadness of evening
Stirs me irresistibly.

Above the cupola of the church roof
The shadow of the evening glow fell lower.
O friends of games and play
I shall see you never more!

The years have sunk into forgetfulness,
And you also have gone somewhere.
Only the water, as before,
Swirls behind the winged mill.

And often in the evening twilight,
With the rustling of the broken reeds,
I pray to the steaming earth
Of those who are far and will not return.[17]

In another strangely prophetic poem, written in 1915, his melancholy has already turned into despair. In this poem, which was not included in *Goluben'*, he says that he is tired of living in the country. He will leave his hut and become a wanderer and a thief. His best friend will try to kill him. The girl he loves will chase him from her door. And then:

И вновь вернусь я в отчий дом,
Чужою радостью утешусь,
В зеленый вечер под окном
На рукаве своем повешусь.

Again I'll return to my father's house,
I'll console myself with the joy of others,
On a green evening, under the window,
I'll hang myself with my sleeve.[18]

The desire for suicide is once more expressed in a poem dated 1916, which was not published during his lifetime. It seems written in a moment of honesty toward himself, when he realized that the mysticism of the others remained for him an affectation, an empty playing with words. But if he did not believe in it, there was nothing left to live for. He expresses these thoughts with great simplicity in the following short poem:

Слушай, поганое сердце,
Сердце собачье мое.
Я на тебя, как на вора,
Спрятал в рукав лезвие.

Рано ли, поздно всажу я
В ребра холодную сталь.
Нет, не могу я стремиться
В вечную сгнившую даль.

Пусть поглупее болтают,
Что их загрызла мета;
Если и есть что на свете, –
Это одна пустота.

Listen, my rotten heart,
My dog's heart.
For you, as for a thief,
I have hidden a knife in my sleeve.

Sooner or later I'll stick
The cold steel into my ribs.
No, I cannot strive
Towards the eternal rotten horizon.

[17] *Ibid.*, pp. 206, 207.
[18] *Ibid.*, p. 200.

Let them prattle more stupidly,
That the dream is eating them;
If there is anything in the world, –
It is nothing but emptiness.[19]

While Blok's influence intensified Esenin's depressed mood, but otherwise remained superficial, another influence, that of Kljuev, touched him more deeply and proved to be more beneficial to his specific talent. We have already mentioned Kljuev's theories on the importance of the peasant, which attracted Esenin. At the same time, the tremendous popularity of Kljuev's poetry showed him that readers liked the descriptions of patriarchal peasant life and the images of the old folk-tales. This led Esenin to exploit more consciously than before the half-pagan religious imagery of the folk tales. He uses their representation of the Father, Mary and the Son as God, the earth and the harvest and their frequent identifications of nature with animals. The sun and the moon, evening and dawn become alive in this imagery which he develops. The moon, for instance, is often represented as a lamb. Esenin tells us how, like a lamb, the moon butts the lake with its horns, plays and tumbles through the grass.[20] The evening stoops over a brook and washes the toes of its blue feet in the white water.[21] Dawn is sitting on the roof and, like a cat, washes its face with its paw.[22] He describes a sunset in a flaming sky: "The sky, having calved, – Licks its red calf."[23] God is seen as an old man seated on a cloud. He throws stars down to the earth – they are the autumn seeds. When the grain is ripe the seeds, – human souls – fall in the forest.[24] This explanation of the origin of the human soul was not invented by Esenin, but he gave new life to the old images and developed them further. Along with these religious images he creates new ones. He compares, for instance, the peasant hut to an old woman who chews with the jaws of the threshold the odorous bread of silence.[25]

In a later period the use of images will become the main content of Esenin's poetry. In *Goluben'* we see how, under Kljuev's influence, he began to use them consciously in order to stress the peasant character of his writing.

From 1914 to 1917 Esenin lived most of the time in Petrograd or Tsarskoe Selo, but in no poem written during this period do we find a reflection

[19] *Ibid.*, V, p. 244.
[20] *Ibid.*, I, p. 202.
[21] *Ibid.*, p. 224.
[22] *Ibid.*, p. 204.
[23] *Ibid.*, p. 287.
[24] *Ibid.*, p. 183.
[25] *Ibid.*, p. 235.

of the city or of city life. Even the war is mentioned only indirectly, in two poems written in 1914, when Esenin was in Konstantinovo. In "Rus'"[26] he gives an idyllic description of the mobilized young men who are leaving the village. They are calm and willing to defend their fatherland. Their wives and mothers weep, but at last letters arrive from the front and they are proud to hear about the heroic deeds of their beloved ones. The other poem, "Us",[27] does not mention the war, but was evidently inspired by it. It is written in the old ballad style and describes how a young Cossack leaves his old mother to go to war. Years go by and he does not return. The mother weeps and prays before the ikon. She finds consolation when she suddenly notices that Christ on the ikon resembles her son.

After these two poems Esenin does not mention the war again. Soon he has lost any patriotic enthusiasm he may have had at the outbreak of war and refuses to write about it in a manner that would please the authorities. Other poets among his friends – Kljuev and Gorodeckij – adhere more and more to the official patriotism and glorify the war. Esenin turns away from real life and seeks refuge in mysticism. Only when the revolution starts in February 1917 would he again be able to include the real world in his poetry.

3. PROSE

Only three stories in prose have been published in the Collected Works of Esenin. They were written at about the same time as the poems of *Radunica*. Though they have attracted little attention, one of them shows us a different side of Esenin's talent and is important to a study of his literary development.

This story, "Jar",[28] is a long loosely-knit series of descriptions of forest life, held together by a rather fantastic plot. In 1915, when Esenin was writing it, he read avidly and was especially impressed by the works of Jack London. The influence of the American writer is clearly felt in the characters and also in the crudeness of certain scenes, in the descriptions of fights and killings. The hero, Karev, bears a great similarity to some of Jack London's characters. He is a passionate hunter who loves the primitive and difficult life in the forest. He is a strong man who values his freedom to such a degree that he even sacrifices the girl he loves and abandons her rather than lose his freedom. The other main character is the girl

[26]   *Ibid.*, pp. 144–148.
[27]   *Ibid.*, pp. 114–116.
[28]   *Ibid.*, IV, pp. 7–142.

Limpiada, who lives in the woods with her brother, a forest warden. Limpiada has never been touched by civilization. She has not gone to school, but knows every tree and animal in the forest.

The story is set in the country Esenin knew best: the villages, forests, lakes and river-shores of his native region. Most of the characters resemble the peasants with whom he grew up. The descriptions of the landscape and the characters are excellently done. They are vivid and realistic. Although several farmers figure in the story, their work is mentioned only occasionally. The only detailed descriptions we find are those of the tasks in which Esenin liked to participate: the milling of the grain, haying of the fields near the river and the threshing of the grain at the farm. Every little object used for hunting and the interiors of peasant homes are described in great detail, as well as the flora and fauna of the forest. The main characters are not interested in farming. Karev, a farmer's son, has become a hunter, Limpiada lives in the forest.

The story is continually interrupted by long descriptions, loosely connected by an irrational plot that is full of sudden, bloody events. It is evident that the author is young and inexperienced and that he uses the story only as a vehicle for his descriptions. The plot can be summarized as follows: Karev has ceased farming when he learns that his wife has been untrue to him. He leaves his house and fields and lives for a time by hunting and fishing. Then he starts working for an old miller and becomes a miller himself when the old man is killed in an accident in the mill. He meets Limpiada and they fall in love, but they cannot marry since Karev is already married. He suggests to Limpiada that they leave together and go far away where nobody will know whether they are married or not. Karev has become anxious to leave the mill. He does not want to settle down in one place, but Limpiada refuses to leave since she loves her forest, its plants and animals, too much. Then Karev decides to leave alone. When Limpiada finds that she is pregnant, she commits suicide. A peasant boy, who has fallen in love with her after Karev's departure, holds him responsible for her death. He follows Karev and kills him. Now the action shifts to Karev's parents, poor peasants who live with the wife he has abandoned. A false rumor convinces them that Karev was drowned in a river. Although the mother tries to accept his death with resignation as God's will, she languishes, does not want to eat and is very upset that her son has died without a priest's blessing. At last she decides to leave her house to visit the monasteries and pray for the soul of her son. Her husband does not hold her back. Quietly he prepares some provisions for her to take along. The description of the mother's departure is beautiful in its simplicity. Her husband and daughter-in-law accompany her. She is leaning on a heavy stick and the daughter-in-law carries her sack. At last they say goodbye. "You ... in any case ... come back home to die", says the husband. She walks away and for a long time they see her figure, disappearing and reappearing on the hills.

A little later the husband also decides to leave his farm. He does not want to stand in the way of his daughter-in-law, in case she should want to remarry. He goes to a monastery and becomes a monk.

Human characters and their doings form only a part of the story. At least as important are the descriptions of hunting scenes and of the life and death of animals. "Jar" starts with the description of a wolf hunt and of the joy one experiences killing a bear. Esenin recalls his early youth when he tells how the miller's young nephew swims after a wounded bird. Later the boy goes hunting for the first time. He shoots an elk and thinks he has killed him. But when he approaches it, the animal attacks the boy and kills him with his sharp antlers. Unable to free himself, the elk also dies. A charming scene of two deer grazing on an island in the river again ends when they are spotted by a hunter and killed.

Blood keeps running freely in this short novel in which seven people die, either killed by others or by suicide. The animals are shot by man or kill one another.

"Jar" was published in serial form in 1916 in the periodical *Severnye Zapiski* in Petrograd. The author never published it in book form, nor was it included in any of the later anthologies of his work.

"At the White Water",[29] published a few months later in a Petrograd newspaper and reprinted only in the Collected Works, tells about a young fisherman's wife, desperately longing for love when her husband has left her for a long fishing expedition. The story of her adventures with other men, her despair when the husband returns seriously ill, are again interwoven with excellent nature descriptions. The dialogues are in dialect and this may be one of the reasons why Esenin never republished it.

The last story is a short one for children. It is called "Bobyl' and Družok" and tells about an old beggar whose only friend is his dog Družok.[30] When the beggar dies, the dog refuses to leave his grave and dies there. The little tale is charmingly told, with great simplicity and gentleness, sad but never sentimental.

[29] *Ibid.*, pp. 142–152.
[30] *Ibid.*, pp. 153–156.

IV

THE RUSSIAN REVOLUTION

1. ESENIN AND POLITICAL EVENTS

In each of his autobiographies Esenin gives a different account of his attitude towards the Russian revolution and his activities at that time.

In the first, written in Berlin in 1922, he only states: "During the years of war and revolution fate threw me from one part of Russia to the other."

The second was written in 1924, after his return from Western Europe. There he says: "When the revolution started, I was at the front in one of the disciplinary battalions... During the revolution I left Kerenskij's army without permission and I became a deserter, collaborating with the Social Revolutionary party, not as a party member, but as a poet. When the party split into groups, I joined the left wing and in October I was in their militia. I left Petrograd with the Soviet government."

And in the last autobiography of October 1925 we read: "During the years of the revolution I was entirely on the side of October, but I accepted everything in my own way, from the peasant point of view."

It seems probable that Esenin exaggerated his revolutionary activities somewhat when he wrote about them in 1924. At that time – as we shall see later – he wanted to please the authorities and to be considered a good son of the revolution. Nevertheless, there is no doubt that he at first accepted the revolution with great enthusiasm.

In February 1917 Esenin was still strongly influenced by Kljuev's ideas about the future role of the peasants. When the Tsar fell and a provisional government was formed, he was convinced that now the golden age for the farmer would arrive. But his enthusiasm found expression only in his poetry. Esenin did not actively participate in the revolutionary events. Even if it were true that he deserted from the army, in itself this fact did not mean very much. After the February revolution many peasant soldiers left the army to go back to their villages, afraid that the land would be divided while they were away. Esenin did only what many others around him were doing.

Whether he deserted or not, Esenin was in Konstantinovo shortly after the February revolution. He observed what was happening, but remained a bystander, not taking an active part in the events. The revolution exalted him and he interpreted it in religious terms: now God would reign on the earth, all men would become brothers, would sing and rejoice together. In his less exalted moments he expected that the landowners would be dispossessed, that the land would be divided among the peasants and, above all, that the war would end. When none of this happened, he was greatly disappointed. Even the political party to which he had once belonged and still felt closest, the Social Revolutionary Party, seemed to have abandoned its principles and to have turned more and more to the right. With Kerenskij at the head, the provisional government, including several ministers of the Social Revolutionary Party, had neither divided the land among the peasants nor ended the war.

During the war years a small group of Social Revolutionaries criticized the politics of their party and were against continuation of the war. After the February revolution they formed a separate party in opposition to the government and in many issues on the side of the Communists. After the October revolution they formed a pact with the Bolsheviks which lasted till the peace-treaty of Brest-Litovsk. Their main difference with the Communists was that they believed that not the worker, but the farmer should be the backbone and driving force of the revolution. This, of course, appealed to Esenin who felt very close to these leftist Social Revolutionaries. When, however, after the peace of Brest-Litovsk they turned against the Communists and especially when the latter expropriated the landowners, divided the land among the farmers and ended the war, his sympathies – vague as they were – shifted towards the Communists.

The year following the October revolution was probably the happiest in Esenin's life. He had long since left his wife and child in Moscow and married a young woman who worked on a newspaper. Her name was Zinaida Rajx. Later she became a well-known actress and the wife of the famous theatrical director, Meyerhold. The young couple lived in two simply furnished rooms where at last Esenin found a home where he could write and read at ease. At this time he was an avid reader and most of all he liked to read the Bible and the *Slovo o Polku Igoreve*, an epic poem of the twelfth century, one of the earliest Russian literary works. During this year he drank little and wrote some of his best poems. He no longer needed to draw attention to himself by extravagant dress or behavior.

By now Esenin was known as a poet and had won his place among the Russian writers. But his desire to be the first among the poets remained as strong as ever. He had accepted the revolution and wanted now to be the only or at least the first, Russian poet to sing its praises. When Aleksandr Blok wrote "The Twelve", in which he showed a group of revolutionary soldiers led by Christ, Esenin criticized him severely. He maintained that Blok's poetry was not really Russian, that he did not understand the old expressions and had misused them. Blok had for long been considered the best living Russian poet. Esenin now felt strong enough to challenge his position.

2. POEMS INSPIRED BY THE REVOLUTION

The Russian revolution is represented in Esenin's works by a group of strangely mystical poems glorifying the events with joy and exultation. In the years 1917 and 1918, when these poems were written, he also continued his short lyrical pieces where the revolution and the changes it brought were hardly mentioned. We shall first consider his revolutionary poems and later return to the non-political works.

The volume *Goluben'*, published in 1918, contains one poem very different from the others in tone. It expresses joyful expectations of enormous changes to come. Although in the 1926 edition of Esenin's works 1916 is mentioned as the year in which it was written, later editions give the year as 1917. It seems very probable that it was written after the February revolution. Several other poems are dated incorrectly in the 1926 edition.

The poem starts with the following lines:

> О Русь, взмахни крылами,
> Поставь иную крепь!
> С иными именами
> Встает иная степь.

> O Russia, deploy your wings,
> Erect a new force!
> With other names
> Another steppe will arise.

The author describes how several poets are walking through the fields. First comes Aleksej Kol'cov, the nineteenth century poet whom Esenin considers his forerunner. Behind him walks Kljuev, who has just left the gates of a monastery. Then comes the author himself, curly-headed and gay, full of a brigand-like audacity:

> Долга, крута дорога,
> Несчетны склоны гор;
> Но даже с тайной бога
> Веду я тайно спор.

Сшибаю камнем месяц
И на немую дрожь
Бросаю, в небо свесясь,
Из голенища нож.

The road is long and steep,
Innumerable are the mountain slopes;
But secretly I even quarrel
With the secret of God.

I knock the moon down with a stone
And hanging in the sky
I pull my knife from my boot
And throw it towards the mute trembling.

A crowd of other poets, just as gay and audacious, follow him. They are now ready for action. The time of rotting and dreaming is over. Russia has awakened:

Уж повела крылами
Ее немая крепь!
С иными именами
Встает иная степь.

Its dumb force already
Has moved its wings!
With other names
Another steppe will arise.[1]

The February revolution had given Esenin a tremendous feeling of liberation. The Tsar had abdicated. The reign of the knout, cruel repression, of war and destruction seemed over. The people were fighting for liberty and a better world. Esenin lived in an atmosphere of general rejoicing and great expectations. In his poetry he tried to interpret the events and he did it in a very personal way, only vaguely understanding what was really happening around him.

In March 1917 he wrote a rather weak poem, "Comrade", in which for the first time his hero is not a peasant, but a worker's son, called Martin. Martin is a lonely boy who has only two friends, his cat and the Christ child on the icon. The revolution comes and there is a street battle near their house. There Martin's father fights for the revolution and is killed before Martin's eyes. The boy runs back into the house and addresses his friend on the icon:

"Исус, Исус, ты слышишь?
Ты видишь? Я один.
Тебя зовет и кличет
Товарищ твой Мартин!

---

[1] *Sobr. Soč.*, I, pp. 290–292. This edition also gives 1917 as the date of the poem.

Отец лежит убитый,
Но он не пал, как трус.
Я слышу, он зовет нас,
О верный мой Исус.

Зовет он нас на помощь,
Где бьется русский люд,
Велит стоять за волю,
За равенство и труд!..."

– Jesus, Jesus, do you hear?
Do you see? I am alone.
Your comrade Martin
Is calling you!

Father lies killed.
But he did not fall as a coward.
I hear – he is calling to us,
O, my faithful Jesus.

He is calling to us for help,
Where the Russian people are fighting.
He tells us to defend freedom,
Equality and work!

Then Jesus leaves the arms of his mother, steps out of the icon and goes with
Martin to the street to join the battle. A bullet hits him and he is killed.

Слушайте:
Больше нет воскресенья!
Тело его предали погребенью:
    Он лежит
На Марсовом
    Поле.

Listen:
There is no longer any resurrection!
His corpse was taken to be buried:
He lies
On the Field of Mars.

Martin, also wounded, crawls back to the house and dies.

Но спокойно звенит
    За окном,
То погаснув, то вспыхнув
    Снова,
Железное
    Слово:
"Рре-эс-пу-у-ублика!"

But quietly behind the window,
Now softer and then louder
Again resounds
The iron word:
"Republic!"[2]

²   *Ibid.*, pp. 265–267.

This poem was written in March 1917 before Aleksandr Blok published his "The Twelve", where Christ also sanctified the revolution by his participation. In Esenin's poem Jesus has become human by this action and will not be resurrected. Did he mean that the victorious revolution would sound the end of the Christian church? Or is this a first allusion to the identity of Christ and the revolution? Would the revolution and not the church bring the joys of heaven and a paradise on earth?

In "Singing Invitation",[3] written in April 1917, this identity of Christ and the revolution is expressed more clearly:

> О Родина,
> Мое русское поле,
> И вы, сыновья ее,
>   Остановившие
> На частоколе
> Луну и солнце, –
>   Хвалите бога!
>
> В мужичьих яслях
>   Родилось пламя
> К миру всего мира!
> Новый Назарет
>   Перед вами.
> Уже славят пастыри
>   Его утро.
> Свет за горами...

> ...O fatherland,
> My Russian field,
> And you, its sons,
> Who have halted
> The sun and the moon
> On the stakes of your fences, –
> Praise God!
>
> In the peasant mangers
> A flame was born
> For peace of the whole world!
> A new Nazareth
> Stands before you.
> Already the shepherds praise
> Its morning.
> There is light behind the mountains.

He then curses the monstrous English who are unable to understand the miracle that has happened in Russia. The poem ends with a hymn to peace, to the brotherhood of all men:

> Все мы – яблони и вишни
> Голубого сада.

[3] *Ibid.*, pp. 268–270.

Все мы – гроздья винограда
Золотого лета,
До кончины всем нам хватит
И тепла и света!

· · · · · · · · · · ·

Кто-то учит нас и просит
Постигать и мерить.
Не губить пришли мы в мире,
А любить и верить!

We are all apple and cherry trees
Of the blue garden.
We are bunches of grapes
Of the golden summer.
Till the end there will be
Enough warmth and light for all of us!

· ·

Somebody teaches us and asks us
To understand and measure.
Not for destruction have we come into the world,
But to love and to believe!

In "Father of the Earth",[4] written in June 1917, he glorifies the Russian peasant who holds the tender newborn baby – Christ-revolution – in his calloused hands. The peasant, who carries the world on his shoulders, will throw it into heaven and then everybody will be happy. There will be an abundance of food and drink and when the redheaded Judas embraces Christ there will be no tinkling of money.

3. THE YEAR 1918

In March 1918 Esenin moved to Moscow, "together with the Soviet government", as he says in his second autobiography. Very probably he did not go to Moscow because of his loyalty towards the government, but rather because he thought that from now on the cultural center of Russia would be in Moscow. He had many friends among the leftist group of Social-Revolutionaries, but did not participate in any political activities. Poetry remained his only serious occupation.

Xodasevič, who met Esenin in the spring of 1918, gives us the following picture of the poet: "Esenin made a pleasant impression. He was well built and moved quietly and with assurance. His face was not beautiful, but handsome. Most attractive was his gaiety, which was neither noisy nor rough. He was very well coordinated. He impressed you as a straight-

---

[4]   *Ibid.*, pp. 273–277.

forward fellow, probably an excellent friend. He frequented a bad crowd, mostly young leftist Social Revolutionaries and Bolshevists, rather ignorant people, cocksure that they would reconstruct the world. They philosophized continually and were extremists in everything. They ate little but drank a lot..."[5]

In Moscow Esenin sincerely tried to understand what was happening in his country. Certain aspects of the revolution filled him with great enthusiasm, but he abhorred the suffering and fighting he witnessed. To hide the reality of blood and misery he tried to envelop the events in a cloak of mysticism. He dreamt of an ideal world, a farmers' paradise on earth, where ugliness and poverty had disappeared and only beauty existed. To express his conception of the tremendous happenings he felt that a special language, a new poetic style, were necessary. In his search for it he began to make even greater use than before of the poetical image which for him became the very basis of poetry.

In Moscow he continued to write his optimistic, mystical poems about the future of Russia. He was intoxicated by the power of the people who had thrown off the chains of tsarism and whom he now believed capable of tremendous feats. Action on this earth alone would not be sufficient. From now on the whole cosmos would obey the will of man. Esenin sees himself as the personification of this powerful new giant. In one poem, "Oktoix",[6] his village, Konstantinovo, has become the center of the universe. With his own hands he will bring the sun to his village. His shoulders will shake the sky, his arms will rock the darkness and the stars will fall into the thin stalks of grain. Eternal lightning will find shelter in the house of his father and the universe will exist only to serve his country. God himself and the Virgin Mary will help Russia and take care of it. The trees and hills will echo with songs about paradise. Paradise is here, in his native land, where his grandfather is seated under an enormous oak tree, his fur coat shining with stars.

The mystical conception of the union of heaven and earth is still more clearly expressed in the next cycle of poems, "Transfiguration".[7] In "The Coming of the Messiah"[8] he gives an allegorical explanation of the revolution:

Jesus – the revolution – has descended on earth. Again He has to carry His cross, but this time He is not accompanied by apostles or disciples.

[5] V. Xodasevič, "Esenin", *Sovremennye Zapiski*, XXVII (1926), p. 311.
[6] *Sobr. Soč.*, I, pp. 280–284.
[7] *Ibid.*, II, pp. 13–17.
[8] *Ibid.*, pp. 7–12.

The Virgin Mary – Russia – is born from the sky and the stars. She has given birth to her son, the new Christ, among the sheep. Jesus will be beaten and tortured again, for the revolution is not yet victorious and everywhere fighting is raging. Here the allegory must end. There cannot be a crucifixion since that would mean that the revolution had been defeated. Esenin is not sure about the outcome of the civil war. He abhors the fighting of Russians against their brothers, but he wants frantically to believe that victory will soon come. And he says to God:

> Господи, я верую!...
> Но введи в свой рай
> Дождевыми стрелами
> Мой пронзенный край.

> Lord, I believe!
> But lead my country,
> Pierced by the arrows of rain,
> Into your paradise.

And:

> Лестница к саду твоему
> Без приступок.
> Как взойду, как поднимусь по ней
> С кровью на отцах и братьях?

> The stairs which lead to your garden
> Have no steps.
> How can I climb them, how can I enter
> With the blood of my parents and brothers on my hands?

But the poem ends in a tone of hope and confidence that the earthly paradise is bound to come:

> Холмы поют о чуде,
> Про рай звенит песок.
> О верю, верю – будет
> Телиться твой восток!

> В моря овса и гречи
> Он кинет нам телка...
> Но долог срок до встречи,
> А гибель так близка!

> The hills sing about a miracle,
> The sand rings about paradise.
> O, I believe, I believe,
> Your Orient will calve!

> Into the seas of oats and rye
> He will throw us the calf...
> But the time till the meeting is long,
> And ruin is so near!

In the following poems the same images are further developed. From the folk legends Esenin was familiar with the image of the cow as the symbol of fertility. Both heaven and earth are now represented as a cow: heaven, because it gave birth to Christ-revolution as God's calf; the earth, also born from heaven, which will produce the magnificent, abundant harvests of the earthly paradise. Love of the fatherland becomes identical with love of the cow. He has no intention to blaspheme when he exclaims in the first stanza of the poem, "Transfiguration":

> Облаки лают,
> Ревет златозубая высь...
> Пою и взываю:
> Господи, отелись!

> The clouds are barking,
> The gold-toothed heights are howling...
> I sing and implore:
> O Lord, calve!

Xodasevič, in his article on Esenin, has interpreted these lines as a parody of the lamb of the Lord: "While the lamb is killed on the altar, the calf is happy and well fed. It promises material abundance." It seems that actually no parody was intended. The calf, and the abundance it represented, simply symbolized the peasant ideal of the good life. Again happiness will result from the union of heaven and earth. This union will be accomplished as a result of the action of man, and the poet himself represents the power of this new humanity. He knocks at the gates of paradise and tells them to swaddle the calf – Russia – in stars. He reaches with his hand behind the clouds and the tempest will sing in his verse. He calls on his compatriots:

> Ей, россияне!
> Ловцы вселенной,
> Неводом зари зачерпнувшие небо, —
> Трубите в трубы.

> Под плугом бури
> Ревет земля.
> Рушит скалы златоклыкий
> Омеж.

> Hey, Russians!
> Fishermen of the universe,
> Who with the net of dawn have emptied the sky –
> Blow your trumpets.

> Under the plow of the storm
> The earth is howling.
> The golden-fanged plowshare
> Crumbles the rocks.

Then the transfiguration of the Lord takes place: the "luminous guest"
descends on earth. He will fill the days with milk.

> А когда над Волгой месяц
> Склонит лик испить воды, –
> Он, в ладью златую свесясь,
> Уплывет в свои сады.
>
> И из лона голубого,
> Широко взмахнув веслом,
> Как яйцо, нам сбросит слово
> С проклевавшимся птенцом.
>
> And when the moon above the Volga
> Bends its head to drink the water, –
> He, in his golden boat,
> Will drift away towards his gardens.
>
> And from his blue lap,
> Lifting the oar high up,
> He will throw us the word, like an egg
> With the little bird pecking the shell.

Esenin seems to announce in this poem the advent of a new religion when
the peasant paradise on earth has come.

It is clear from the passages we have quoted that Esenin's conception
of the revolutionary events was very different from that of the Communists. He exclaims in "The Dove from the Jordan":

> Небо – как колокол,
> Месяц – язык,
> Мать моя – родина,
> Я – большевик.
>
> The sky is like a bell,
> The moon is its clapper,
> My mother is my country,
> I am a Bolshevik.[9]

It is clear, however, that one should not take this last line too literally.
These words express only his belief that he was a revolutionary, that he
accepted the new state of affairs and was convinced of the great possibilities the revolution had opened. In 1918 Esenin was sincerely on the side
of the Communists. He believed in socialism and in the capacity of men
to create a better life on earth. At first he saw the events still in religious
terms. God and heaven are needed to bring this paradise on earth. But
gradually man becomes more and more powerful in his poetry, while God
becomes more human. Finally his confidence in the might of man becomes

---

[9] *Ibid.*, p. 55.

greater than his faith in God. Then God is no longer necessary. He will deny Him and blaspheme against all that had been holy. This happens in the last poem of the cycle, "*Inonija*".

4. "INONIJA"

When Esenin visited Konstantinovo in 1918, he was shocked by the lack of enthusiasm he found among the peasants. They seemed to accept the new government obediently, but to be entirely unconscious of the tremendous role they had to play. It seemed to him that with its preaching of resignation and humiliation, the Christian religion was the main cause of their lack of active participation in the creation of a new society. He realized that the peasant paradise would not come if those who should be its creators remained passive. In order to incite them to action, to clear the road for the new religion, it would first be necessary to destroy the Christian faith. The peasant should be made conscious of his force. He should be proud of the tremendous might of man, capable of changing the world. It was the poet's task to profess this faith in man, to inspire him with the confidence necessary for his task. Esenin saw himself as the prophet who dared to challenge God and who would show the way toward paradise on earth. This he did in his poem "Inonija".[10]

"Inonija", derived from the word "inoj" – other – is the name of this country that will be "otherwise". In the first lines the poet announces who he is:

> Не устрашуся гибели,
> Ни копий, ни стрел дождей, —
> Так говорит по библии
> Пророк Есенин Сергей.

> I shall not be afraid of perdition,
> Nor of spears, nor of arrows of rain, –
> Thus speaks, according to the Bible,
> The prophet Esenin Sergej.

Ivanov-Razumnik, who wrote a preface for "Inonija", gave the following commentary on these lines: "When Esenin says 'I' he does not speak of himself, but of the new universal world whose coming he feels in the world... The poet is always a prophet. For, I repeat, a prophet is an authentic poet and an authentic poet is a prophet."[11] Razumnik had expres-

---

[10]   *Ibid.*, pp. 36–44.
[11]   Ivanov-Razumnik, "Rossija i Inonija", *Naš Put'* (1918), no. 5, p. 20.

sed this idea about the prophetic role of the poet and Esenin knew about it. It appealed to him immensely and he accepted with exaltation this role of the spiritual leader of his people. He would lead the people away from the antiquated beliefs:

> Время мое приспело,
> Не страшен мне лязг кнута.
> Тело, Христово тело
> Выплевываю изо рта.
>
> Не хочу восприять спасения
> Через муки его и крест:
> Я иное постиг учение
> Прободающих вечность звезд.
>
> Я иное узрел пришествие –
> Где не пляшет над правдой смерть.
>
> My time has ripened.
> I do not fear the whistling of the knout.
> The body, the body of Christ
> I spit from my mouth.
> I don't want to accept salvation
> Through his suffering and cross:
> I've attained another doctrine
> Of the stars piercing eternity.
> I have seen another coming of the Messiah
> Where death does not dance on truth.

In a conversation with Aleksandr Blok, Esenin has said that he did not intend to shock the reader or to blaspheme. He told Blok: "I spit out the host not to make fun of holy things, but because I don't want any suffering, humility or crucifixion."[12] The old religion has to disappear before the new faith can triumph. In order to become conscious of his great power man must destroy what has kept him weak and humble. Man is greater than God and he must dare to challenge God:

> Даже богу я выщиплю бороду
> Оскалом моих зубов.
>
> Ухвачу его за гриву белую
> И скажу ему голосом вьюг:
> Я иным тебя, господи, сделаю,
> Чтобы зрел мой словесный луг!
>
> With my bare teeth
> I shall pull out even God's beard.
> I shall grab him by his white mane
> And I shall tell him with the voice of snowstorms:
> I shall make you different, Lord,
> So that the field of my word may ripen!

---

[12]   A. Blok, *Dnevnik. 1917–1921* (Leningrad, 1928), p. 91. According to Blok this conversation took place on 4 January 1918 and thus precedes the writing of *Inonija*.

He curses the holy cities of old Russia. He insults Christ and holy things, but only in order to erect a new faith which will bring happiness and abundance on earth:

Языком вылижу на иконах я
Лики мучеников и святых.
Обещаю вам град Инонию,
Где живет божество живых!
. . . .
Уведу твой народ от упования,
Дам ему веру и мощь,
Чтобы плугом он в зори ранние
Распахивал с солнцем нощь.

. . . .
Ныне ж бури воловьим голосом
Я кричу, сняв с Христа штаны:
Мойте руки свои и волосы
Из лоханки второй луны.
Говорю вам – вы все погибнете,
Всех задушит вас веры мох.

With my tongue I lick from the icons
The faces of the martyrs and saints.
I promise you the city Inonija
Where the godhead of the living dwells!
. . . .
I shall lead your people away from hope,
I shall give them faith and might,
So that, together with the sun
In early dawn it will plough up the night.
. . . .
Now with the oxen voice of the tempest
I shout, taking off Christ's pants:
Wash your hands and hair in the basin
Of the second quarter of the moon.
I tell you – you will all perish,
The moss of faith will smother you all.

But man can still be saved by the arrival of a new god. The poet is the prophet who announces this god and the might of the prophet has no limits:

Говорю вам – весь воздух выпью
И кометой вытяну язык.

До Египта раскорячу ноги,
Раскую с вас подковы мук...
В оба полюса снежнорогие
Вопьюся клещами рук.

Коленом придавлю экватор
И под бури и вихря плач
Пополам нашу землю-матерь
Разломлю, как златой калач.

I tell you – I shall drink all the air
And I'll stick out my tongue like a comet.
I shall spread my legs to Egypt
And take off your horseshoes of suffering...
With the pincers of my hands I shall grab
Both the snow-horned poles.
With my knee I shall press the equator
And under the storm and whirlwind of weeping
I shall break our mother the earth
Into two pieces, like a golden bread.

Then the poet turns to those who are against the new religion, especially America with its industrialization, its machines and electricity:

Не построить шляпками гвоздиными
Сияние далеких звезд.

You cannot build the glitter of far-away stars
With the heads of nails.

The final struggle will be against the Americans. But then the poet will force the universe to come to the aid of the new world. He will attach the sun and the moon as wheels to the axis of the earth. He will shake the mountains by their ears and with one sweep of his arm swipe away all fences and hedges like dust. In beautiful sonorous language he prophesies:

И вспашу я черные щеки
Нив твоих новой сохой;
Золотой пролетит сорокой
Урожай над твоей страной.

And I shall plow the dark cheeks
Of your fields with a new plow;
Like a golden magpie the harvest
Will fly over your country.

Finally the paradise on earth has come:

По тучам иду, как по ниве, я,
Свесясь головою вниз.
. . . .
Вижу тебя, Инония,
С золотыми шапками гор.

I walk on the clouds as on a field,
Hanging with my head down.
. . . .
I see you, Inonija,
With the golden caps of your mountains.

From above he looks down on the new world and there he sees his old mother sitting in front of her house, trying in vain to catch a ray of the

sun. Like a cat, the sun is playing with her knitting wool. From the
mountains comes the sound of a song, glorifying the new god:

> Кто-то с новой верой,
> Без креста и мук,
> Натянул на небе
> Радугу, как лук.
>
> Радуйся, Сионе,
> Проливай свой свет!
> Новый в небосклоне
> Вызрел Назарет.
>
> Новый на кобыле
> Едет к миру Спас.
> Наша вера – в силе.
> Наша правда – в нас!
>
> Somebody with a new faith
> Without cross and suffering
> Has stretched taut in the sky
> The rainbow, like a bow.
>
> Rejoice, Zion,
> Pour out your light!
> A new Nazareth
> Has ripened on the horizon.
>
> A new Savior on a mare
> Is riding towards the world.
> Our faith is in force.
> Our truth is in us!

Two other poems in the same style, written after "Inonija", complete the
cycle. In "The Celestial Drummer"[13] he again accepts the new society
with great joy: "Long live the revolution, on the earth and in heaven!"
The same confidence is expressed in the gigantic force of man. "The
white gorilla-troops" who attack the revolution will easily be defeated:

> Если это солнце
> В заговоре с ними, –
> Мы его всей ратью
> На штыках подымем.
>
> Если этот месяц
> Друг их черной силы, –
> Мы его с лазури
> Камнями в затылок.
>
> Разметем все тучи,
> Все дороги взмесим,
> Бубенцом мы землю
> К радуге привесим.

---

[13] *Sobr. Soč.*, II, pp. 71–74.

If that sun
Conspires with them, –
With our whole army
We shall lift it on our bayonets.

If that moon
Is a friend of their dark force, –
We shall chase it out of the sky
With stones thrown against it.

All clouds we'll sweep away,
All roads we shall pierce.
Like a little bell
We'll hang the earth on the rainbow.

In the last poem, "Pantokrator",[14] he reproaches the Lord that He has not taught him to pray, but to bark. He is waiting for the red horse which will be harnessed to the earth and draw it towards the country of happiness. The dead are already there and he sees his grandfather pushing the sun through the sky with a long fishing rod.

We have quoted at large from these poems written in 1917 and 1918 because they form an important stage in Esenin's development. They express the strongest confidence in the future of his country and sound an unusually joyful note in the work of a poet who is generally considered somber. Esenin felt happy in his role as a prophet. He believed that he, through the medium of poetry, was fighting with the others for the revolution.

The poems also show clearly that his optimism and confidence could be shattered very easily if the earthly paradise would not materialize, if the Russian farmers would not follow their prophet. This, of course, did happen and very soon Esenin's exaltation began to cool and he began to doubt his importance as the spiritual leader of his people.

5. OTHER POEMS

The other poems Esenin wrote during these years sound very different from his mystical ones about the revolution. He continues to sing about the idyllic life in the country, as if nothing had happened. In an article on Esenin,[15] Svjatopolk-Mirskij concludes from this that the cycle of revolutionary poems was insincere. We do not believe that this was the case. The great emotional tension which produced poems like "Inonija" could not be maintained all the time. There were quieter moments in Esenin's

[14]   *Ibid.*, pp. 82–85.
[15]   Svjatopolk-Mirskij, "Esenin", *Volja Rossii* (Praha, 1926), no. 5, p. 79.

life of those years, when he visited his village and was again moved by the idyllic beauty of the countryside.

When one compares these short poems with the lyrical ones from before the revolution, there are, nevertheless, noticeable differences. There are now only a few religious poems and these are inspired by his new faith. The mood of the great majority of the poems is happy. Sometimes a great joy is expressed, but more often the happiness is quiet and tinged with a sweet melancholy. Often great happiness and sadness are expressed in the same poem. A typical example is the following:

> О верю, верю, счастье есть!
> Еще и солнце не погасло.
> Заря молитвенником красным
> Пророчит благостную весть,
> О верю, верю, счастье есть.
>
> Звени, звени, златая Русь,
> Волнуйся, неуемный ветер!
> Блажен, кто радостью отметил
> Твою пастушескую грусть.
> Звени, звени, златая Русь.
>
> Люблю я ропот буйных вод
> И на волне звезды сиянье.
> Благословенное страданье,
> Благословляющий народ.
> Люблю я ропот буйных вод.

> O, I believe, I believe, happiness exists!
> Even the sun is still aflame.
> The evening glow, like a red prayerbook,
> Prophesies the blessed news.
> O, I believe, I believe, happiness exists.
>
> Resound, resound, golden Russia,
> Stir, impervious wind!
> Blessed is he who with joy has noticed
> Your shepherd-like sadness.
> Resound, resound, golden Russia.
>
> I love the murmur of turbulent water
> And the sparkle of a star on the wave,
> Blessed suffering,
> Blessing people.
> I love the murmur of turbulent water.[16]

One of the reasons for Esenin's happiness was the fact that he was now considered to be one of the most promising young poets. He proudly tells his mother about it in a poem where he asks her to wake him up early because he expects a guest whom he wants to meet:

[16]   *Sobr. Soč.*, II, p. 29.

Разбуди меня завтра рано,
Засвети в нашей горнице свет.
Говорят, что я скоро стану
Знаменитый русский поэт.

Воспою я тебя и гостя,
Нашу печь, петуха и кров...
И на песни мои прольется
Молоко твоих рыжих коров.

Call me early tomorrow,
Put a light in our room.
They say, that soon I'll be
A famous Russian poet.

I'll sing about you and our guest,
About our stove, the rooster and the roof...
And the milk of your red-brown cows
Shall flow over my songs.[17]

Though these poems are not as saturated with images as are the longer
ones, they do contain some interesting pictures:

Время – мельница с крылом
Опускает за селом
Месяц маятником в рожь
Лить часов незримый дождь.
Время – мельница с крылом.

Time – a mill with a wing
Lowers the moon like a pendulum
Behind the village in the rye
To pour the invisible rain of the hours.
Time – a mill with a wing.[18]

This same image of the mill is used in a poem where he reproaches Kljuev
for not understanding what is happening in Russia, ending with the lines:

Тебе о солнце не пропеть,
В окошко не увидеть рая.
Так мельница, крылом махая,
С земли не может улететь.

You will not sing about the sun,
You will not see paradise from your little window,
Thus the mill, flapping its wing,
Cannot fly away from the earth.[19]

Only one of the poems of these years is deeply melancholy and expresses
an even greater despair and lassitude than before. Written in a moment of
doubt when he no longer was sure of the importance of the poet-prophet,
a terrible fear took hold of him that he might be useless:

17   *Ibid.*, I, p. 295, 296.
18   *Ibid.*, II, p. 22.
19   *Ibid.*, p. 76.

Проплясал, проплакал дождь весенний,
    Замерла гроза.
Скучно мне с тобой, Сергей Есенин,
    Подымать глаза...

Скучно слушать под небесным древом
    Взмах незримых крыл:
Не разбудишь ты своим напевом
    Дедовских могил!
. . . .

Всколыхнет он Брюсова и Блока,
    Встормошит других.
Но все так же день взойдет с востока,
    Так же вспыхнет миг.

Не изменят лик земли напевы,
    Не стряхнут листа...
Навсегда твои пригвождены ко древу
    Красные уста.

The dancing and weeping of the spring rain is over,
    The thunder has died down.
I am bored to lift my eyes
    With you, Sergej Esenin...

I am bored to listen under the heavenly tree
    To the flapping of invisible wings:
You will not awaken with your song
    The graves of your forefathers.
. . . .

He will agitate Brjusov and Blok,
    He will stir others,
But the day will rise just the same from the East,
    The moment will flash up just the same.

Songs will not change the face of the earth,
    They will not shake the leaves.
Forever your red mouth
    Is nailed to the tree.[20]

Then he calls out to God with the words of Christ on the cross: "My God, my God, why have you abandoned me?"

Even in these relatively happy years the thought of suicide remained with him. An otherwise peaceful and gentle poem ends with the lines:

Может быть, к вратам господним
Сам себя я приведу.

Perhaps I'll lead myself
Towards the gates of the Lord.[21]

[20]   *Ibid.*, I, pp. 254, 255.
[21]   *Ibid.*, II, p. 61.

V

IMAGISM: 1919–1921

1. "THE KEYS OF MARY"

"The Keys of Mary"[1] is Esenin's only theoretical treatise. He wrote it in 1918, when Marxism and dialectical materialism were already the official credo of Soviet Russia. He had never understood, nor was he interested in the Communist theories, but, perhaps the fact that they existed urged him to define his conception of the world and, in particular, of poetry. It contains among other things a commentary on his mystical poems of the revolution and it expresses his mystical beliefs. This was probably one of the reasons why, after the original edition of 1920, Esenin never wanted to reprint "The Keys of Mary". He later seemed to be ashamed that he had written it and, when asked to include it in the edition of his complete works, he refused "because there was too much mysticism in it".[2]

Even though Esenin soon discarded the strange theories he formulated in this booklet, they throw an interesting light on his early revolutionary poems and are not without value for a real understanding of the poet. It is worthwhile including a brief summary of "The Keys of Mary", therefore. In a note Esenin explains the meaning of the title. Mary, he says, indicates the soul in the language of a certain religious sect.

The treatise starts out by giving a definition of the word "ornament". "Ornament", says Esenin, "is music." He tells us how extremely important the ornament was in old Russia. In nearly all its forms it conveyed the idea that we are only passing, travelling on the earth, and that the shore is waiting for us beyond our life on earth.

He explains the origin of the ornament and how it was influenced by the Orient, but the Russian ornament existed already before Byzantine and Greek influences touched it. The ornaments of old books and of minia-

---

[1] S. Esenin, *Ključi Marii*, ed. Moskovsk. Trud. Art. Xudožn. Slova (Moscow, 1920), 42 pp. Reprinted in *Sobr. Soč.*, V, pp. 27–54.
[2] G. Lelevič, *Sergej Esenin. Ego tvorčeskij put'*, ed. Gomel'skij Rabočij (1926), p. 38.

tures have often been the object of research, but nobody has studied those in the homes of Russian farmers or on their objects of everyday use. As an example he mentions the towels on which there is embroidery representing the family. That is a mystical image of man whose origin was a tree. Esenin quotes ancient legends to prove his point. Then he speaks of the different ornaments adorning the farmer's house, such as the wooden horse on the roof, the roosters and pigeons, the embroidered flowers on the towels and bedcovers. "All these are not only ornaments", he writes, "but also a great epic, explaining the origin of the world and the destination of man." In mythology the horse is often the symbol of impetuousness, but only the Russian peasant, according to Esenin, has thought of putting a horse on his roof and thus making his house similar to a cart. The pigeon on the roof is the symbol of hospitality. It invites you to enter the house. It is represented with spread wings, as if it wanted to fly into the soul of the person who entered the house.

In this interpretation of the symbolic value of ornaments Esenin is not original. He repeats what others had written before him. His former master, Kljuev, had also expressed the same ideas, when he wrote:

> ...The little horse on the roof
> Is a silent sign that our road is long.
> The hut is a cart, its corners are wheels,
> Seraphim will descend from the cloudy haze.
> . . . .[3]

Esenin then considers the alphabet and the art of writing. He admits that the Russian alphabet has come from the West, but maintains that without outside help a way of expression would just as well have been found. For in the old Russia signs were already used to indicate certain things. There was a "red corner" in the peasants' homes representing the dawn. The ceiling was the dome of the sky and the heavy beam in the ceiling represented the Milky Way.

Esenin's interpretation of metaphors in the Russian language, whereby he refers to often far-fetched and entirely false etymologies, is extremely weak. His examples are only valid when he speaks of images used in peasant speech and these explain many of the images he used in his poems. Man is a frightened being, he says, and wants to love in harmony with the world. He therefore tries to diminish the distance which separates him from the outside world by reducing everything to his own dimensions. Thus the sun seems to him like a big wheel, the clouds howl like wolves.

[3]   N. Kljuev, *Polnoe Sobranie sočinenij*, ed. Imeni Čexova (N.Y., 1954), vol. I, p. 344.

That is why the peasants say when it rains: "The wolves have devoured the sun."

His theories become completely fantastic when he tries to prove that the Russian alphabet reveals mystical secrets through the symbols of its letters. The letter "A", for instance, represents a man bent towards the earth; the Russian "B" (Ƃ) shows him standing erect; with the "V" ("B" in Russian), man has discovered his own center, the navel. The last letter of the alphabet, the letter "Ja" (an inverted "R"), shows man with his hand on his navel – the sign that he now knows himself – walking on the earth with uplifted head. He still has not found his aim in life and must keep on walking.

Esenin believed that in order to learn the secrets of our life and language, it was first necessary to understand the meaning of the symbols and images around us, of which we are no longer conscious. Only in the villages these symbols are still understood, in the cities people ignore their existence. "People, shouting like wild animals, a criticism which is completely ignorant, and the idiocy of the city population have exchanged this understanding for the stupid sound of American steel and for the facepowder on the vacant cheeks of the prostitutes of the metropolis."[4] Even the village, where the secret is still known, is partly destroyed by the different industries and divided by religious sects which contribute to its death.

But now comes the revolution like a whirlwind and shaves off the old world's beard. The revolution seems like an angel of salvation to a dying man. Art will now revive: "The art of the future will flower with all its possibilities, like a universal orchard, where man, when the dance is over, will rest in happiness and wisdom, shaded by the branches of a giant tree whose name is 'Socialism' or 'Paradise'." In peasant literature paradise is depicted as a country "where the fields cannot be sold, where the houses are new, covered with cypress wood, where decrepit time, wandering through the fields, invites all people to a feast ..."[5] Before man can share in this ideal life he must first relearn the forgotten signs. Esenin believes that this paradise of socialism will not be confined to the earth. The whole universe will take part in it. When man understands the symbolism of the alphabet, he will know that the last letters show the marriage of heaven and earth. Space will be vanquished. The roads in space will be marked by signs and man will come into contact with all the other planets. This will not happen immediately. First man has to pass through a period of long and intense preparation.

[4] *Sobr. Soč.*, V, p. 42.
[5] *Ibid.*, p. 43.

In the last chapter of "The Keys of Mary" Esenin speaks more concretely of the literary problems of the time. For him the very substance of creation is the image. Like man himself it is composed of three parts: soul, flesh and intelligence. He calls the image of the flesh "preposed"; that of the soul is "naval" and the image of intelligence is "angelic". A "preposed" image is like a metaphor, simply comparing one thing to another, such as, "the sun is like a wheel". In the "naval" image the "preposed" image is in motion and navigates on the water like a ship. Real creation begins with the "angelic" image. It breaks a window through the "preposed" or "naval" image, and then new images are formed which no longer use any direct comparison. Nearly all myths, says Esenin, are built around this "angelic" image.

He is convinced that Russian literature should make ample use of these three kinds of images. He severely criticizes his contemporaries because there are hardly any images in their works and he even finds fault with Kljuev's style for the same reason. His main wrath is directed against the group of Communist writers who had formed the semi-official organization, Proletkult, and wanted to promote a proletarian art. Esenin protests in the strongest terms against what he considers a stupid vulgarization of art: "... the shadows of men without reason, of those who are not born for the sacrament of listening to the sun within us, are now trying to smother every voice which goes from the heart to the intellect; but against them one must fight just as ruthlessly as against the old world. They want to choke us with the hands of the cursed fig tree, born to be fruitless.... We must tear this little body of our new era from their beastly hands. ... The human soul is too complicated to be enclosed in a definite circle of the sounds of one single melody or sonata of life".[6]

Esenin agrees with the writers of Proletkult that other forms of art must be created in the new revolutionary world. With the capitalist society the old art will disappear. Then a new art will arise, with new means of expression. According to him this change will take place within the realm of art without any help from outside. "Therefore", he says, "the hands of Marxist tutelage seem so disgusting when they touch the ideology of the essence of art. This tutelage, using workers' hands, is building a statue for Marx, but the peasants want to build a statue for the cow".[7]

The earth continues its voyage. Esenin compares it with the bird Noah released, which did not find what it sought. Only the dove will bring back the branch of olive, namely "the image whose wings are strengthened by

[6] *Ibid.*, p. 51.
[7] *Ibid.*, p. 52.

the faith of man, not because of his class consciousness, but because he is conscious of the temple of eternity around him".[8]

Thus, in the scant fifty pages of "The Keys of Mary" Esenin emphasizes three points. First, he stresses the importance of the ornament in art and gives an interesting commentary on the poems of the "Inonija" cycle. Next he speaks of the three kinds of images and formulates the theories that will lead him to participate in the Imagist school of literature. In the last part he formulates his political and religious convictions, whereby he clearly shows his ignorance of the social and economic theories of the Communists. He is only interested in what is happening in literature and here he openly rejects their theories. At that time, however, even many of the leading Communists did not agree with the literary theories of Prolet-kult and it was no serious crime to criticize them. Only where Esenin objects because they are building a statue for Marx, he might have been considered a counter-revolutionary, if he had been taken seriously. Perhaps this statement was one of the reasons why Esenin later refused to permit a new edition of "The Keys of Mary".

The mysticism he expressed was a last manifestation of the influences the Petrograd writers had exercised on him. In a conversation with his friend, Rozanov, Esenin once said that Andrej Belyj and Sergej Klyčkov had had a great influence on him. "For some time", he said, "I was a close friend of Sergej Klyčkov, a poet with whom I have much in common. That was when I was writing 'The Keys of Mary'".[9]

At the end of 1918, however, Esenin turned away form these friends. He was still exalted by the revolution and trying to find the new form of expression appropriate to a new revolutionary art. He could not understand and was irritated by the fact that they quietly continued to write as before. He was convinced that he would succeed in creating a new style. Since his break with Kljuev he did not want to accept another master. From now on he would form his own school and be a leader instead of a follower.

It was at this time that, with several other poets, he founded the imagist movement.

2. IMAGISM

In 1915 an article on the poets Ezra Pound and Wyndham Lewis was published in *Strelec*, a Russian Symposium of modern art and literature,

[8] *Ibid.*, p. 54.
I. Rozanov, *Esenin o sebe i drugix*, p. 16.

by Zinaida Vengerova.[10] She was very critical of these writers who loudly maintained that they were no futurists, but something entirely different: imagists in poetry. Vengerova, who had interviewed Ezra Pound, stated that their theories were nothing but empty words, for their work showed little evidence of their application.

Nevertheless, it was from this article that a group of Russian poets took over the name "Imagists". Ezra Pound – as quoted by Vengerova – had said: "Our task is centered on images which form the primary element of poetry, its pigment ..." This expressed exactly the ideas of the Russian poets and, if the English produced hardly any imagist poetry, the Russians who applied the theories created a school which has produced some valuable works. When in a letter to Ivanov-Razumnik Esenin wrote, "Z. Vengerova has introduced Imagism here by her essay in *Strelec* (on English futurism) and we have adopted it and changed it a little",[11] he can refer only to the English theories, since no poetry is quoted in her article and Esenin could not read English.

The Russian Imagist school of poetry was founded at the end of 1918, when Esenin met the poets, Šeršenevič and Mariengof, at a poetry-evening in the Polytechnic Museum in Moscow. They discovered that all three were convinced of the importance of the image in poetry and after long discussions decided to form a literary school with the name of "Imagism". Early in 1919 they published a manifesto in the periodicals *Sovetskaja Strana* in Moscow, and *Sirena* in Voronež. It contained a definition of their literary principles. They stated that they were against futurism and symbolism and that the image should be the only principle of poetry: "The only law of art, its only and incomparable method is to show life by means of images and by the rhythm of images."

But only Vadim Šeršenevič wrote his poetry entirely in accordance with the theory of imagism. He was a young poet who had had a great admiration for the Russian futurist, Majakovskij. Now, as an Imagist, he applied its theories to the extreme. His poetry had always made ample use of images, but now the image became for him the only content of the poem. In his essay "Two Times Two is Five" he says: "For the symbolist the image (or symbol) is a means for thought; for the futurist it serves to reinforce the visibility of the impression, for the Imagist it is an aim by itself... The image is not only not subordinated to grammar, but it fights with all its might against grammar and banishes it... Music is for

[10]   Z. Vengerova, "Anglijskie futuristy", *Strelec* (1915), no. 1.
[11]   See D. Blagoj, "Materialy i xarakteristiki S. Esenina", *Krasnaja Nov'* (1926), no. 2.

composers, ideas are for the philosophers, but for the poets there are only images and nothing but images".[12]

A poem, according to Šeršenevič, should be no more than a catalogue of images, and the reader should be able to enjoy it equally well if read from the end to the beginning. The content of the poem is unimportant, only the image counts. The poet should try to find the image, contained in every word, but which is now hidden, "devoured" by the current meaning. Notwithstanding – or perhaps because of – the application of these theories, Šeršenevič did not write poetry of any literary value.

The work of Anatolij Mariengof, who went a little less far, is of no greater importance, and he was better known as a friend of Esenin than as a poet. He was, like Šeršenevič, a poet of the city. For him the content of a poem still had a certain value. He defended and applied most vigorously the principle that the impure image should alternate with the pure image. This allowed him to include the most disgusting and horrible descriptions in his poetry. His work became more and more abnormal and he seems to have been temporarily insane and to have announced that he was the new Christ, or King Philip the Second of Spain.

Many other writers and artists joined the Imagist movement, but their work, at least at that period, was even less important than that of Šeršenevič or Mariengof. The whole movement might well have passed unnoticed, if two real poets had not attached their names to it. These were Kusikov and Esenin, who signed the numerous Imagist manifestoes with the others. Kusikov's Imagism went no further than that and it is not clear why he joined the group at all. Although Esenin took a more active part in the movement, he did not change his way of writing very noticeably after he joined it. Neither Kusikov nor Esenin ever agreed with the extreme pronouncements of Šeršenevič as he formulated them in his "Two Times Two is Five".

Among the numerous literary schools formed in the years after the revolution, all of which claimed to represent exclusively the new revolutionary art, the Imagists were the most vocal and probably the most extreme. They succeeded in drawing so much attention that finally Lunačarskij, at that time Commissar of Education, felt obliged to devote an article to Imagism in the January 1921 issue of *Pečat' i Revoljucija*. He sharply criticized the school, saying that it was nothing but "a group of charlatans who tried to mystify the public". The next issue of the periodical brought the answer of the Imagists in the form of a manifesto, signed by "The

---

[12]   V. Šeršenevič, *2 × 2 = 5. Listy imažinista*, ed. Imažinisty (Moscow, 1920).

Masters of the Central Committee of the Order of Imagists", Esenin,
Mariengof, Šeršenevič. Full of fury and indignation they demanded that
Commissar Lunačarskij "either cease this stupid persecution of a whole
group of poets who want to renovate poetry, or, if he really had expressed
his solemn conviction, banish them from Russia where their presence, as
charlatans, is offensive, where they are not needed and may even be harmful to the state". Neither of these alternatives, of course, was accepted
and the Imagists continued their work as before.

When Esenin went abroad in 1922, the movement gradually began to
decline. Several Imagist almanacs and a few volumes of poetry were still
published. In 1923 an Imagist periodical, "Hotel for Travelers in
the Magnificent", was started. Only four issues appeared and they contain the two last Imagist manifestoes. In the first, "Almost a Declara-
tion", the Imagists formulate a new definition of their literary theories.
They are now somewhat less extreme and concede that the small image
should be subordinated to the large one which composes the poem. They
admit that only a small part of their projects has been realized, but nevertheless, they exclaim: "Now the time has come for the creation of Man
and the Epoch".[13]

The second manifesto, "Eight Points", tries to defend Imagism against
the many accusations to which it had been exposed, but the defense is
weak and often completely unrealistic. It shows very clearly that these
Imagists, who aspired to be the artists of modern times, had not in the
least understood what was happening in their country. To the accusation
that they lacked class-consciousness they answered: "Yes, we have no
class-consciousness and we are proud of it, for we have already passed
through the period of classes and class struggle." When they were told
that their art was useless for the workers, they answered that this reproach
was unjust, even from a Marxist point of view: "One must not confuse the
working class with isolated workers. What is useless for a Sidorov or an
Ivanov may just be necessary for the working class. Only the workers of
the year 2124 will know what the workers of 1924 needed..."[14] The entire manifesto is written in this tone. One wonders why Esenin agreed to
sign it. In 1924 he had already broken with the Imagists.

The Imagist movement soon ceased to exist, when the attacks against
it became more violent and when its most talented member, Esenin, had
turned away from it.

[13]   *Gostinica dlja putešestvujuščix v Prekrasnom* (Moscow, 1923), no. 2.
[14]   *Ibid.* (1924), no. 1 (3).

3. MOSCOW: 1919–1921

At the end of 1918 Esenin's dream of being the first poet of Russia had not yet been realized. The critics continued to call him a second Kljuev or a peasant-poet. He no longer wanted to be considered only a young man from the village. The time had come for him to be a leader and no longer a follower of others. He wanted to show the world that he could write just as well about other things than the village. Mariengof and Šeršenevič attracted him first of all because they were the exact opposite of naive village boys. They were bred by the city and represented what at that moment he wanted to be. Of course, he would not have joined them if their ideas about poetry had not in many ways coincided with his own. He knew, however, that his talent was far greater than theirs. They would not overshadow him and he would remain the leader. Esenin underlined his new role by abandoning his peasant costume. He now began to dress like a city dandy. He wore an opera hat, kid gloves, patent leather shoes and carried a cane.

There was also another reason which led him to join the others and form a new literary school, namely, the difficulty of finding a publisher for his work. In 1919 the civil war was raging in the country. All the resources of the young republic were badly needed for the fight. If they could work at all, factories had to provide for the immediate needs of the population or for the war. There was not enough energy or paper to keep the presses going. Newspapers, propaganda tracts and textbooks were still published, but it became more and more difficult to bring out a volume of poetry. By creating a school of poetry, which claimed to represent the new art of the revolution, Esenin hoped to be able to overcome some of these difficulties. As a matter of fact, the Imagists did succeed in publishing a good number of their works, though often a great deal of ingenuity and disregard of the laws and regulations were needed.

In an article in memory of his friend written in 1926 after Esenin's death, Šeršenevič gives the following account of how they tried to overcome the difficulties:

In 1919 and 1920 only the State Publishing House was allowed to print books. Therefore, Esenin was at first very pleased when it offered to bring out a selection of his poetry. But to render him a service the editors crossed out every mention of God and other religious words from his poems. Esenin objected to these changes and took the manuscript back. The Imagists now decided to print the poems themselves. Therefore a permit from the State Publishing House and the war censorship was needed, which could not be obtained. Then Esenin found the following solution: the book was taken to just any printing shop and later the name of an arbitrary town, such as Kaluga or Vladivostok, was added. Since the communications were disrupted, it was impossible for the authorities to check whether the book had really been printed in that town. In this way – always according to Šeršenevič – twenty-three books were published. But then an order was issued forbidding the Imagists to print anything at all. Esenin refused to abide by this order. A critic had just written a book praising the Imagists and its publication seemed extremely important to them. Esenin decided to try to fool the authorities. Somewhere, he reasoned, people must ignore the fact that it was not permissible to publish the Imagists. So he sent Kusikov with a manuscript to the printing plant of the secret police (the Čeka) and there the book was, indeed, printed. The name of Revel was mentioned on the cover to make it appear that it had been published in that town. Just then an inventory was taken in the printing shop. Nobody knew how a book printed in Revel happened to be in the plant. Kusikov explained that it had really been printed in Revel and that only the cover had been made here. The trick succeeded and the book appeared. Later Esenin smuggled a volume of poems into the mobile printing plant attached to Trockij's train and had it printed there. Finally, the Imagists had to sign a paper, promising that they would not publish without the permission of the State Publishing House. But even then Esenin refused to give up. "If the State Publishing House does not let us publish, let's write on the walls", he said one evening. He and his friends spent a whole night covering the walls of the Strastnoj monastery in the center of Moscow with Imagist poetry. But only a few early citizens could read what they had written. The monks worked feverishly to clean the walls and soon every trace of the night's work had been effaced. Then the poets sent a request to the city council of Moscow to rename the streets with the names of the Imagists and when their request was refused, they took down the name plates themselves and replaced them with signs carrying the names of Esenin, Šeršenevič, Mariengof and others.[15]

Šeršenevič's account may be somewhat exaggerated, but in those chaotic times, when most Communists and workers were at the front, much of what he relates could well have happened.

When it had become entirely impossible to reach the public in print, the poets began more and more to appear in person to recite their new works.

[15] V. Šeršenevič, "O druge", Sbornik Esenin, žizn', ličnost', tvorčestvo (Moscow, 1926), p. 57.

This became a common practice and each group of writers had its own cafe where they organized literary evenings. The audience paid an entrance fee for the privilege of listening to the poets in person and of participating in a discussion of their work. These writers and the audience, which evening after evening crowded the cafes in Moscow, consisted of a rather Bohemian group of intellectuals who were on the whole anti-bourgeois and often inclined towards anarchism. This was especially true of the poets and writers, who opposed all rules and regulations and were convinced that, at last, the golden age of liberty had arrived. The Communist officials at that time did not interfere much with the activities of the artists and writers. Party members were either fighting in the civil war or fully occupied with the restoration of economic life in the country. They had no time to pay attention to the new trends in art. But for the writers the creation of a new art seemed of the utmost importance. Never before had there been an audience so avid for new forms, so willing to crowd any place where one could listen to a poet reciting his work. They expected the creation of a new revolutionary art and the poets and artists – the gifted as well as the less gifted – were driven into a frenzy of creation and tried to outdo each other in originality. Literary schools shot up like toadstools after a rain. In the different cafes one could listen to "Biocosmists", "Formlibrists", "Fouists", "Emotionalists", "Expressionists", "Luminists", "Nothingists", and of course the Imagists. This last was the only group to remain alive for even a few years.

For Esenin the Imagist school served as a platform from which he could make himself heard. How far he really did believe in the importance of the school is hard to ascertain, but there is no doubt that at first he felt very happy in his role as master. He knew that Imagism lived and was known mainly because of him, and was sincerely pleased to have found friends whose ideas coincided with his own. Imagism, however, did not have much influence on his writing and the work and ideas of his friends touched him very little. He was conscious of this and once, in a conversation with his friend Rozanov, with whom he often talked very openly and sincerely, he said: "Many people think that I am not an Imagist at all, but that is not true; from my first independent steps I have gone instinctively towards what I have more or less found in Imagism. But I have never forgotten that that is only one aspect of the thing, that it is only the outside. What is much more important is the poetical feeling".[16]

Esenin worked very seriously at this time and, because of his extraordi-

---

[16] I. Rozanov, *Esenin o sebe i drugix*, p. 5.

nary gift of reciting poetry, he always charmed his audience and made
many friends. The terrible cold and hunger from which the population
of Moscow suffered during these winters does not seem to have bothered
him. In his second autobiography he wrote: "The happiest time of my
life was the year 1919. At that time, in winter, we lived in a room temper-
ature of five degrees below zero. We didn't have a single piece of wood."
From 1919 to 1922 most of the time Esenin shared a room with his friend,
Anatolij Mariengof. In the latter's "Novel Without Lies" one finds many
details about the life of the Imagists during these years.[17] It was a strange
friendship between these two utterly different personalities. Mariengof
was a rather decadent cynic, always elegantly dressed, using all sorts of
cosmetics. Perhaps Esenin felt attracted to him just because of the contrast between this city dandy and the country boy he himself had been.
And, of course, he felt flattered by the sincere admiration Mariengof expressed for his work.

Xodasevič reports that early in 1919 Esenin had wanted to join the
Communist Party, but had not been accepted.[18] After this refusal he felt
justified in concentrating entirely on his poetry. If the party did not want
him, he would serve his country by writing poetry. But without publishers it became more and more difficult to make a living as a poet. The Imagists had become known all over Moscow, in great part by their extravagant behavior. The audiences remained enthusiastic and provided them
with some money, but it was insufficient and fame did not pay. Finally,
they decided to open two bookstores. The necessary permission was obtained and Esenin and Mariengof opened a store on the Nikitskaja Street
in the center of town. Šeršenevič and Kusikov worked in another bookstore. Though the store on the Nikitskaja was always crowded, the poets
and literary critics who came there did not buy very many books. They
came in order to read, to discuss literary matters, or simply to have a good
time. Nevertheless, Esenin felt very happy in their company and amidst
the books. He could read as much as he wanted and shared with Mariengof the living quarters behind the store.

Even during the most difficult times Esenin never seems to have suffered from hunger. He knew all sorts of people and always was able to
find the few places where one still could get a decent meal. This was often
the case in one of the little basement restaurants on the Tverskaja, such
as the "Stojlo Pegasa" or the "Domino", where the literary Bohemia met.
When these places no longer satisfied him, he became acquainted with a

[17] A. Mariengof, *Roman bez vran'ja*, p. 60–74.
[18] V. Xodasevič, "Esenin", *Sovr. Zap.*, CCVII (1926), p. 312.

certain Zoja Petrovna, a lady who still served excellent meals in her apartment. Unluckily, a group of people who conspired against the revolution also met at her place. Once the police raided the apartment and arrested all the guests. Esenin was among them and spent three days in prison after which he was released.

Towards the end of 1919 Esenin began to drink more heavily. His periods of drunkenness alternated with long weeks when he worked soberly and steadily. It has been said that his drinking was caused by the influence of his Imagist friends and this may be true to a certain degree. Esenin always adjusted himself to the surroundings in which he lived. In the cafes he met many heavy drinkers and his friends considered drunkenness as something quite usual. The example of his cynical friend Mariengof removed any scruples against drinking that Esenin still may have had. But there were also other and more basic reasons which drove him to drink as a means of forgetting his problems.

At the end of 1919 Esenin gradually began to become less and less certain of the importance of his work. He knew that he would be lost if he ever ceased to believe in his poetry, for he had dedicated his whole life to his writing. If he failed as a poet, life would no longer have any value for him. He knew that he had great talent, but that alone was not enough. He wanted to act by means of his art, to interpret the world, to be the one great poet of modern times. Little by little he began to realize that he was not aware of what was happening in the country, that the whole Bohemian group to which he belonged was no longer in the center of the revolution. And the revolution proved to be very different from what he had expected. In his poems he had spoken of universal love, of the peace and joy that would be the result of the revolution, but real life around him remained ugly and difficult. Russians were still fighting and killing each other in the civil war. Hunger and misery reigned in the streets of Moscow. During his now rarer visits to Konstantinovo he saw that his prophesies had not come true. There were no signs of an earthly paradise, with magnificent harvests and blissful farmers. On the contrary, even though the land had been divided, the villagers were still involved in violent struggles. The well-to-do farmers, to whom Esenin felt closest, were regarded as the enemies of the new system. The Communist thesis, that the city workers would lead the farmers toward the building of socialism, was contrary to his deepest convictions. For him the city with its paved streets, machines and electricity, was the worst enemy of the old peaceful village. He had vaguely hoped that the revolution would bring back the old traditions, but now he saw that the contrary was true. Machines, railroad tracks and telegraph poles were altering the countryside. That was the tangible result of the revolution he had glorified.

It was impossible for Esenin to retire to an ivory tower, to ignore what was happening around him and to continue to write for the people who admired him. The praise of his friends and the enthusiasm of the audiences to whom he read his poetry were not enough. He traveled through the country and recited his work in Xar'kov, Rostov and Batum. Everywhere the halls were crowded and he was frantically applauded. But he became more and more aware of the fact that the audiences were always composed of people who, on the whole, did not participate in the events that were changing the country. They were spectators who, like himself, lived on the fringe of society. He wanted to be known and admired by the whole country, by the workers and farmers and even the Communists. But these people did not come to the poetry evenings. They were busy with the civil war and the reconstruction of a ravaged country.

Esenin by now had lost the religious and mystical beliefs which had inspired his revolutionary poems. He realized that he had been a false prophet, that his interpretation of the events had been wrong. If he had been entirely logical in his thinking, he might well have turned against the revolution in the years 1920-1923. That he did not do so was probably not only because of the dangers it involved and because he loved his country too much to put himself in a position where he might be forced to leave it, but also because he was revolted by the idea of aligning himself with those who were fighting against the revolution. His sympathies were still with the revolutionaries, even though he could not understand why everything was so different from what he had expected.

It was this feeling of no longer being able to interpret and understand the events that drove Esenin to drink. It was the easiest way to forget his troubling thoughts, but in his sober moments he suffered from a strong feeling of guilt. He knew that his friends and the life he was leading were harmful for him and for his art and he believed that the city was the cause of his behavior. Several times he tried to return to the simple life of the village, but for that it was already too late. When he came to Konstantinovo, he became so nervous and so afraid of his thoughts that he could stay there no longer than a few days. Having lost his faith in God, uncertain about his attitude toward the revolution, he clung to his belief in his talent. He knew that his creative power was still growing, that he had not reached the limits of his art.

Esenin wrote only when he was completely sober. As long as he was working he felt happy. Then he was sure of his talent and felt that he still could be useful, but as soon as he stopped writing he became nervous and needed friends and alcohol to keep him from thinking. Even among his admiring friends he became more and more difficult and suspicious. The slightest criticism of his work made him furious. Everywhere he saw enemies. He was convinced that people wanted to insult him on purpose. Those who did not admire his work he immediately considered his enemies and never could forgive them.

Perhaps these were the first symptoms of a persecution complex from which he suffered later, but at the same time, it shows the beginning of doubt in his talent. He could not admit this doubt even to himself and had to suppress it, for he knew only too well that he would not be able to live without the conviction of the importance of his work. Therefore he shouted loudly to all those who would listen that he was the greatest poet of Russia and he accepted only the company of those who supported him in this opinion. More than ever he denied that anybody else would be able to write poems about the revolution with talent or originality. With great severity he turned against Majakovskij and the futurist school who represented the most talented group of revolutionary poets.

In 1919 Esenin wrote a poem entitled "Hooligan" which contained the following lines:

> Плюйся, ветер, охапками листьев, –
> Я такой же, как ты, хулиган.

> O wind, spit loads of leaves –
> I am a hooligan, just like you.[19]

The critics began to refer to him as the "hooligan", and once, when he recited this poem, the audience – according to Mariengof – applauded enthusiastically and shouted: "Hooligan, hooligan". Esenin was glad to accept this name. After the naive country boy and the city dandy, he would now become the good-for-nothing, the outcast of society. The romantic outlaw who feels himself above the law, who dares to commit crimes and even kill if necessary, had always attracted him. He liked to see himself as the proud and fearless man he had always wanted to be, although his decency and common sense prevented him, of course, from committing any real crime. His hooliganism existed mostly in his romantic imagination and manifested itself only in a few drunken pranks. Even if he wanted to revolt, he no longer knew exactly against what he should protest. To fight against the remnants of the old bourgeois society did not interest him, for that was permitted and could be done by anybody. Re-

[19]   *Sobr. Soč.*, II, p. 99.

volt against the government was dangerous and would put him in the camp of those he hated most. All he could do was ignore society and associate with the outcasts, the thieves, drunkards and prostitutes in the poorest taverns of Moscow. There he imagined himself to be one of them and, torn by feelings of guilt and self-pity, he asked himself what his relatives in the village would say if they could see how debased he had become. There was nothing left to steer him from the course he was taking. The party had refused his help. The village he loved was being devoured by the city. So he drowned his troubles in drink and read his verses to the dregs of society with whom he tried to identify himself.

4. THE IMAGIST PERIOD IN ESENIN'S WORK

We have seen how already in Esenin's early poetry and in the volumes, *Radunica* and *Goluben'*, the poetical image was used. In his theoretical essay "The Keys of Mary" he had tried to formulate the meaning of the image and its use in daily life and literature. Two of his poems, written in 1918 before the Imagist school was founded – "The Celestial Drummer" and "Pantocrator" – corresponded well enough to the Imagist conceptions to be included in a collection of Imagist poetry, "The Cavalry of Storms".[20] When Esenin did join Šeršenevič and Mariengof and the school of Imagism was founded, he did not have to change his style to put the theories of the school into practice. He never did agree with the more extreme pronouncements of his friends.

The Imagist poems Esenin wrote from 1919 to 1922 are not very numerous. They consist of about five short pieces, two longer ones and a drama in verse, *Pugačov*, of which we shall speak later. During the same years he also wrote many lyrical poems which have no particular Imagist characteristics. The difference between his Imagist and non-Imagist poems is not only that the former are even more saturated with images, but also that the image often seems forced which reduces the literary value of these poems.

The optimistic trend of his revolutionary poems had entirely disappeared. As we have seen, he had become disillusioned and no longer believed in his mission as a prophet. There are no longer any allusions to God or to a life hereafter, and the tone of his work is somber and melancholy. Man and the revolution have betrayed him and all he sees around

[20] *Konnica bur'*, ed. Moskovsk. Trud. Art. Xudožn. Slova, vols. I and II (Moscow, 1920).

him is misery and suffering. In one of his best Imagist poems, "Song about the Grain", he pretends to have found the reason for all that is wrong in his world:

> Вот она, суровая жестокость,
> Где весь смысль – страдания людей!
> Режет серп тяжелые колосья,
> Как под горло режут лебедей.

> Here it is, the stern cruelty,
> The whole sense of the suffering of people!
> The scythe cuts the heavy ears of grain,
> As they cut the swan's throat.

Then the sheaves of grain, lying in the fields, are compared to yellow corpses. On carts like hearses they are brought to the threshing floor:

> А потом их бережно, без злости,
> Головами стелют по земле
> И цепами маленькие кости
> Выбивают из худых телес.

> Никому и в голову не встанет,
> Что солома – это тоже плоть!...
> Людоедке-мельнице – зубами
> В рот суют те кости обмолоть.

> And then carefully, without malice,
> They spread them with their heads on the ground,
> And with flails they beat the little bones
> Out of their thin bodies.

> It even doesn't occur to anybody
> That grain is also flesh!...
> They shove the bones to the man-eating mill
> To crush them with its teeth.

Bread and cakes are baked from this flour. Like white poison they invade the human body to lay their eggs of evil:

> И свистят по всей стране, как осень,
> Шарлатан, убийца и злодей...
> Оттого что режет серп колосья,
> Как под горло режут лебедей.

> And through the whole country, like autumn,
> The charlatan, killer and criminal are whistling...
> Because the scythe cuts the ears of grain,
> As they cut the swan's throat.[21]

Esenin's love and tenderness turned more and more away from people and toward plants and animals. He wrote little about the misery of men,

---

[21]   *Sobr. Soč.*, II, pp. 105, 106.

but the sight of a dead horse in a street inspired him to one of his most Imagist poems, "The Ships of the Mare". Šeršenevič has described how once in 1919, when he took a walk with Esenin, they suddenly noticed the corpse of a white horse in one of the main streets of Moscow. Black crows, their wings spread out like sails, were eating its flesh. For Esenin the horse symbolized the bloodiness and horror of the civil war and at the same time it awakened his fears of growing old and deteriorating. The poem begins with a highly imaginistic and impressionist description:

Если волк на звезду завыл,
Значит, небо тучами изглодано.
Рваные животы кобыл,
Черные паруса воронов.

Не просунет когтей лазурь
Из пургового кашля-смрада;
Облетает под ржанье бурь
Черепов златохвойный сад.

Слышите ль? Слышите звонкий стук?
Это грабли зари по пущам.
Веслами отрубленных рук
Вы гребетесь в страну грядущего.

Плывите, плывите в высь!
Лейте с радуги крик вороний!
Скоро белое дерево сронит
Головы моей желтый лист.

If the wolf has begun to howl toward a star,
That means that the sky has been devoured by clouds.
Torn bellies of mares,
Black sails of crows.

The blue sky will not stick its nails
Out of the coughing stink of the snowstorm; –
The golden-leaved garden of skulls
Flies away under the howling of storms.[22]

Do you hear? Do you hear that loud noise?
It is the rakes of dawn in the dense forest.
With oars from amputated arms
You are rowing toward the country of the future.

Sail, sail toward the heights!
Pour from the rainbow the crow's cawing!
Soon the white tree will drop
From my head the yellow leaves.

His country has become unrecognizable and in despair he asks: "My Russia, who are you? Who?" And: "Dogs with hungry mouths are suck-

[22] Esenin often uses the comparison of his head with a tree or a garden. His hair is then compared to the leaves.

ing the edge of dawn on the roads." Everything he sees has become hor-
rid and obscene. No longer can he hope for a paradise on earth and he
exclaims bitterly: "Evidently, to fool myself did I sing the song of the
wonderful host."

Although terribly disappointed by the results of the revolution, Esenin's
despair is not yet lasting. Within the poem his mood changes. Disgusted
with man, he turns to the animals to seek consolation, for they are innocent and have done no harm:

> Звери, звери, приидите ко мне,
> В чашки рук моих злобу выплакать!
> . . . .
> Сестры-суки и братья-кобели,
> Я, как вы, у людей в загоне.
> Не нужны мне кобыл корабли
> И паруса вороньи.
>
> Если голод с разрушенных стен
> Вцепится в мои волоса, –
> Половину ноги моей сам съем,
> Половину отдам вам высасывать.

> Animals, animals, come to me,
> To cry out evil into the cups of my hands!
> . . . .
> My sisters, the bitches and my brothers, the male dogs,
> I am persecuted by man, like you.
> I don't need the ships of the mare,
> Nor the sails of the crows.
>
> If hunger from the ruined walls
> Seizes me by the hair –
> I shall eat half of my leg myself,
> And half I'll give you to suck.

If death is inevitable he prefers to die together with the animals, far from
the world of humans.

The last part of the poem is less desperate and even expressed the desire to accept life as it is:

> Буду петь, буду петь, буду петь!
> Не обижу ни козы, ни зайца.
> Если можно о чем скорбеть,
> Значит, можно чему улыбаться.
>
> Все мы яблоко радости носим,
> И разбойный нам близок свист.
> Срежет мудрый садовник осень
> Головы моей желтый лист.
> . . . .
> Все познать, ничего не взять
> Пришел в этот мир поэт.

I shall sing, sing and sing!
I shall offend neither goat nor hare.
If one can be grieved about something,
That means one can also smile.

We all carry an apple of joy,
And the whistling of the criminal is close to us.
The wise gardener – autumn
Will cut the yellow leaf from my head.
. . . .
The poet has come into this world
To learn everything, but to take nothing.[23]

His love and sympathy for animals is closely connected with his longing
to return to the village which still represents for him all that is pure and
good in his life. In "The Confession of a Hooligan" he expresses this
longing, knowing very well that it is no longer possible to leave the city
where he needs his friends and admirers. Only in the city are his drunken
scandals possible and only in the city can he gain the publicity which he
craves. But the admiration of his audiences cannot drown the feeling of
guilt which is always present. He exaggerates his own degradation and
sees himself as an outcast, a good-for-nothing, persecuted and vilified by
the critics and officials. In reality, though some critics did judge him
rather severely, Esenin was never persecuted and even the police were extremely lenient toward him when he was drunk and disorderly. Nevertheless, he sees in those who criticize him – and in the city itself – the
cause of his downfall, while even the animals in the city represent to him
the village, where they still know and love him as the innocent boy he
once was. This he expresses in "The Confessions of a Hooligan" which
begins in the Imagist manner as follows:

Не каждый умеет петь,
Не каждому дано яблоком
Падать к чужим ногам.

Сие есть самая великая исповедь,
Которой исповедуется хулиган.

Я нарочно иду нечесаным,
С головой, как керосиновая лампа, на плечах.
Ваших душ безлиственную осень
Мне нравится в потемках освещать.
Мне нравится, когда каменья брани
Летят в меня, как град рыгающей грозы,
Я только крепче жму тогда руками
Моих волос качнувшийся пузырь.

[23] *Sobr. Soč.*, II, pp. 87–90.

Так хорошо тогда мне вспоминать
Заросший пруд и хриплый звон ольхи,
Что где-то у меня живут отец и мать,
Которым наплевать на все мои стихи,
Которым дорог я, как поле и как плоть,
Как дождик, что весной взрыхляет зеленя.
Они бы вилами пришли вас заколоть
За каждый крик ваш, брошенный в меня.

Бедные, бедные крестьяне!
Вы, наверно, стали некрасивыми,
Так же боитесь бога и болотных недр.
О, если б вы понимали,
Что сын ваш в России
Самый лучший поэт!
. . . .
А теперь он ходит в цилиндре
И лакированных башмаках.

Not everyone is able to sing,
Not to everyone was it given to fall
Like an apple before stranger's feet.

This is the very greatest confession,
Confessed by a hooligan.

On purpose I go uncombed,
With my head, like an oil lamp, on my shoulders.
I like to light up in the dark
The leafless autumn of your souls.
I like it when the stones of insults
Hit me, like hail in a howling storm.
I only press more firmly then with my hands
The rocking bubble of my hair.

It is so good then to remember
The overgrown pond and the hoarse noise of the alder tree,
That somewhere my father and mother are living,
Who despise all my verses,
To whom I am dear, like the field and the fruit,
Like the rain in spring rustling the leaves.
They would come impale you on their hay forks
For every shout you throw at me.

Poor, poor farmers!
You probably have become ugly,
You are just as afraid of God and the deep swamps.
O, if you only could understand
That your son is in Russia
The very best poet!
. . . .
And now he wears a top hat
And patent leather shoes.

He assures them that he has not changed. He is still the eager boy, full of mischief:

> Каждой корове с вывески мясной лавки
> Он кланяется издалека.
> И, встречаясь с извозчиками на площади,
> Вспоминая запах навоза с родных полей,
> Он готов нести хвост каждой лошади,
> Как венчального платья шлейф.

> From afar he bows
> To every cow on a butcher's signboard.
> And when he sees a horse-cab on the square,
> Remembering the smell of manure on the fields,
> He would like to carry each horse's tail
> Like the train of a marriage gown.[24]

The poem then continues in a more simple style with only a few images. He recalls the village as it was when he was a boy and says that he still loves his fatherland as much as ever. The tone of the poem is tender and melancholy, but Esenin does not mention his fear about the development of the revolution

This fear, namely that the cynical, mechanized city will vanquish the village, is expressed with great force in one of his most beautiful Imagist poems, "Sorokoust". The first part of the poem contains many extremely crude images and announces the catastrophe which threatens the village. The enemy with his iron belly will smother the plains and nobody will be able to hide or to escape. The old mill and the bull in the courtyard have smelled the coming disaster and the accordion at the edge of the village plays only sad songs. The wooden huts are trembling at the approach of electricity and steel. The unequal struggle between city and village is then symbolized by a little colt, trying to overtake a train:

> Видели ли вы,
> Как бежит по степям,
> В туманах озерных кроясь,
> Железной ноздрей храпя,
> На лапах чугунных поезд?

> А за ним
> По большой траве,
> Как на празднике отчаянных гонок,
> Тонкие ноги закидывая к голове,
> Скачет красногривый жеребенок?

> Милый, милый, смешной дуралей,
> Ну куда он, куда он гонится?
> Неужель он не знает, что живых коней
> Победила стальная конница?

[24]   *Ibid.*, pp. 101–104.

Have you seen
How on its steel paws
A train rushes through the steppes,
Hiding in the mist of the lakes,
Snorting through its iron nostrils?

And behind it
Over the high grass
As in a festive, desperate horse race,
Throwing its legs up toward its head
A little red-brown colt is galloping?

Dear, dear, funny stupid one,
Where, o where is he running?
Does he really not know that the large steel horse
Has defeated the live horses?[25]

Nothing can prevent the victory of the iron horse and Esenin regrets "that it was not drowned in its youth, like a pail dropped in the well".

The little incident Esenin witnessed and which inspired him to write this poem is described in a letter he wrote to a girl. Since the letter shows the mood and thoughts of the poet at that time in greater detail than the poem, it is quoted here without significant omissions:

Dear, dear Ženja:

For God's sake don't think that I want something from you, I don't know myself why I remind you once more of my existence. Of course, there are all kinds of illnesses, but they all pass. I think that this one also will pass. This morning we left Kislovodsk to go to Baku and when I saw this Caucasian landscape from the train I felt ill at ease and oppressed. This is the second time that I am here and I can't understand at all how it could impress the people who have created for us the pictures of the Terek, Kazbek, the Darial, etc. I must say that I was richer with the Caucasus in the province of Ryazan than here. A while ago I began to think how harmful traveling is for me. I don't know what would become of me if by chance I had to make a trip around the world. Obviously, if it were not the revolver of Junker Schmidt, in any case there would be something to destroy the feeling of the size of the world. It is already so terribly boring and crowded on this earth. Evidently, man sometimes takes a jump, as in the transition from horse to train, but that is only acceleration or convexity. All this gets known much faster and in a much richer way by allusion. In these things I feel only sadness for what is going, for what is dear, near and wild, and the indestructible force of the dead and mechanical thing.

I'll give you a simple example. We were traveling from Tixoretski to Pyatigorsk, suddenly we heard shouting, we looked out of the window and what did we see: a little colt was galloping as fast as he could behind the engine. From the way he was running we understood immediately that it was his intention to outdistance the locomotive. He ran for a long time, but at last he got tired and they caught him at a little station. It was an episode, meaningless for other people, but it meant a great deal to me. The steel horse has vanquished the living horse and this little colt was for me the simple, dear and dying image of the village. It was like the personality of

[25]   *Ibid.*, pp. 93–96.

Maxno.[26] In our revolution both are very similar to this little colt, because there is also a rivalry between the living force and the iron force.

Once more, forgive me, my dear, for troubling you. I am very sad at this moment, for history goes through a difficult period of murder of the personality, as far as it is alive. For this is not at all socialism as I had expected it to come, but a determined and deliberate socialism, like a sort of St. Helena's Island, without glory and without dreams. In this socialism the living person feels hedged in. He who is building a bridge towards the invisible world feels hedged in, because these bridges are torn down and blown up from under the feet of the future generations. Of course, he to whom all will be revealed, will *then* see these bridges already covered with mould, but it is always a pity when a house is built and nobody lives in it, when the boat has been hollowed out and nobody sails it.[27]

Mariengof has quoted this letter in his "Novel Without Lies". The ideas it expresses – Esenin's disillusionment with the turn the revolution has taken, his hatred of the city, his regret for what was lost – are the same as those we find in some of the poems of this time. Esenin's sympathies turn more and more toward the underdog, the loser, but only toward those who fight tenaciously till they are crushed by superior forces. That was the case with the colt. In another poem it is a wolf, hunted and slain by man. This poem, written in 1921, first describes the agony of the village:

> Мир таинственный, мир мой древний,
> Ты как ветер, затих и присел.
> Вот сдавили за шею деревню
> Каменные руки шоссе.

> Mysterious world, my ancient world,
> You have grown silent, calmed down like the wind.
> Look, the stone hands of the highway
> Are choking the village's neck.

The frozen fields are crushed by the telegraph poles. But the poet greets the black ruin and goes out to meet it. "What does it matter? Not for the first time are we shaken and do we have to perish". Then he compares the village – and himself – with the wolf, wounded by hunters and harassed by their dogs. He cannot escape, but before he dies, he jumps on one of the hunters and kills him. Esenin feels like this wolf – "chased from everywhere I go among my iron enemies" – and he also wants to taste their blood before he dies.[28]

This poem, with "Ships of the Mare" and "Sorokoust" – as well as an unfinished drama in verse, "The Country of Scoundrels", which was written two years later – expressed Esenin's most hostile feelings toward the revolution. His very real disappointment with the outcome of the revol-

---

[26] Maxno was a Russian peasant who in the years 1918–1921 had organized a group of peasants to fight against the government.

[27] In Mariengof, *Roman bez vran'ja*, pp. 93, 94, and *Sobr. Soč.*, V, pp. 139, 140.

[28] *Sobr. Soč.*, II, pp. 111, 112.

ution was, however, not the only cause of his hostility and despair. They were also the result of his feeling of guilt about his own betrayal of the village, his drinking and his life in the city. It was much easier to blame the revolution for his behavior than himself.

Esenin was much too intelligent not to be aware of the fact that his poems did not and could not influence the political events and that he was ignored ·by those active in building the new society. He saw how everything was changing while he and his dreams were left behind. Although he is only twenty-five, he speaks more and more frequently of growing old, of his thinning hair. and how his poetry will soon be outmoded and nobody will listen to him:

> Скоро мне без листвы холодеть,
> . . . .
> Без меня будут юноши петь,
> Не меня будут старцы слушать.
>
> Новый с поля придет поэт,
> В новом лес огласится свисте.
>
> Soon I shall grow cold without leaves,
> . . . .
> Without me the young people will sing,
> And not to me will the old ones listen.
> A new poet will come from the field,
> The forest will echo with a new whistling...[29]

This feeling of being superfluous haunts him continuously. No longer can he enjoy nature. The outside world now fills him with an unreasonable fear. Perhaps these fears were the result of his heavy drinking, or they may have been early signs of the persecution complex from which he suffered later. In a poem of 1921 he speaks of the street lights which look to him like horrible heads without lips. Afraid to look at them he closes his eyes tight:

> Так немного теплей и безбольней,
> Посмотри: меж скелетов домов,
> Словно мельник, несет колокольня
> Медные мешки колоколов.
>
> Thus it is a little warmer and it hurts less.
> Look: among the skeletons of the houses,
> Like a miller, the bell tower
> Carries the copper bags of its bells.

But even then the street lights still wink at him and laugh with their lipless mouths. Only death can hide all this horror and he whispers:

[29] *Ibid.*, p. 92.

If Esenin had intended, as seems to be the case, to write a historical tragedy which would depict the events more realistically than Puškin had done, his *Pugačov* is a complete failure. Nowhere does he even approach a true description of the events. Historical allusions are rare and no details of the life of the peasants are mentioned. Neither do we find any facts about the campaigns of Pugačov or the dimension of the revolt. What interests Esenin above all, and this is described at great length, is Pugačov's thoughts and feelings and the emotions of the peasants who were led by him. The story of the revolt serves only as a loose frame for nature descriptions and lyrical outpourings. Pugačov himself is described as the romantic hero of Esenin's daydreams and has very little in common with the real eighteenth century rebel. It is clear that the author has identified himself with his hero and has made him the mouthpiece for his own thoughts and feelings.

The poem begins with Pugačov's arrival in a little Cossack village in the Urals. The suffering of the oppressed population has drawn him toward this region. The situation seems ripe for a revolt. Two officers of the tsarist army have arrived in the village and have ordered the Cossacks to pursue a tribe of Kalmuks who have fled toward Mongolia to escape the domination of the Russians. The Cossacks, who do not hate the Kalmuks but rather pity them, refuse to obey the order and kill one of the officers. Not knowing how to continue their revolt, they then turn to Pugačov and ask him to be their leader. Pugačov accepts, but he knows that he will need the support of the poor peasants whose sufferings are so great that they are ready to revolt if he can gain their confidence. But how to go about it? He hears that they believe that Tsar Peter III, who had died not long ago, had been a good and kind ruler and that all their difficulties were caused by his successor, Catherine II. Rumors have been circulated that Peter has come to life again and Pugačov's friends advise him to impersonate Peter. According to Puškin, Pugačov answered this suggestion with the following words: "For several days you have been asking me to take the name of the dead Tsar; I have hesitated a long time ..." These words are developed by Esenin as follows:

> Братья, братья, ведь каждый зверь
> Любит шкуру свою и имя...
> Тяжко, тяжко моей голове
> Опушать себя чуждым инеем.
> Трудно сердцу светильником мести
> Освещать корявые чащи.
> Знайте, в мертвое имя влезть –
> То же, что в гроб смердящий.
> Больно, больно мне быть Петром,

Когда кровь и душа Емельянова.
Человек в этом мире не бревенчатый дом,
Не всегда перестроишь наново...

Brothers, brothers, after all each wild beast
Loves its own skin and its name...
It is terrible, terrible for my head
To adorn itself with the frost of another.
It is difficult for my heart to light
The rugged forests with a lamp of vengeance.
You know, to crawl into the name of a corpse
Is like crawling into a stinking coffin.
It hurts, it hurts me to be Peter
When I have the blood and soul of Emel'jan.
A man in this world is not like a wooden house,
You can't build it anew every time...[35]

Another episode mentioned by Puškin and described in detail by Esenin is the story about the bandit, Xlopuša. When this robber and murderer had been caught and imprisoned, he was offered freedom if he would find Pugačov and deliver him into the hands of the government. Xlopuša accepted, but instead of betraying Pugačov he became one of his most faithful friends. This episode appealed strongly to Esenin and he gave it a prominent place in his poem.

The period of Pugačov's greatest power, of his many victories, evidently does not interest Esenin and he hardly mentions it. There are in the whole poem only a few lines where the siege of Orenburg is mentioned and where the reader is told that a third of the country is in the hands of the rebels. But the decline of the revolt and Pugačov's tragic end are described in detail and more than a third of the poem is devoted to the betrayal of Pugačov by his own comrades. The first signs of the disaster are vague rumors that have begun to circulate among the people. While one of Pugačov's commanders speaks proudly of the victories they have won, a soldier interrupts him:

Стоп, Зарубин!
Ты, наверное, не слыхал,
Это видел не я...
Другие...
Многие...
Около Самары с пробитой башкой ольха,
Капая желтым мозгом,
Прихрамывает при дороге.
Словно слепец, от ватаги своей отстав,
С гнусавой и хриплой дрожью
В рваную шапку вороньего гнезда
Просит она на пропитанье

[35] *Sobr. Soč.*, IV, p. 177.

У проезжих и у прохожих.
Но никто ей не бросит даже камня.
В испуге крестясь на звезду,
Все считают, что это страшное знамение,
Предвещающее беду.
Что-то будет.
Что-то должно случиться.
Говорят, наступит глад и мор.

Wait, Zarubin!
You probably haven't heard,
I did not see it myself...
Others...
Many...
Near Samara an alder tree with broken crown,
Dripping its yellow brain,
Is limping at the roadside.
Like a blind man, left behind the horde,
With a hoarse and nasal trembling
It is begging those who pass for alms
With the torn hat of a crow's nest.
But nobody throws it even a stone.
Crossing themselves with fear toward a star,
All think that this is a frightening sign,
Prophesying evil.
Something will happen.
Something must happen.
They say that hunger and pest are coming.[36]

And indeed, the peasants who had followed Pugačov began to get tired
of the fighting. They had lost their confidence in a victory and the signs
of disaster trouble them. With great lyrical force Esenin describes the
struggle in the heart of the peasants between their loyalty to Pugačov –
whom they still believe to be Tsar Peter – and their desire to return to their
farms. While they are still hesitating they hear that Pugačov's army has
suffered a crushing defeat. The Cossack Čumakov, who had been able to
escape the slaughter, has come to bring the bad tidings:

Мертвые, мертвые, посмотрите, кругом мертвецы,
Воп они хохочут, выплевывая сгнившие зубы.
Сорок тысяч нас было, сорок тысяч,
И все сорок тысяч за Волгой легли, как один.
Даже дождь так не смог бы траву иль солому выссчь,
Как осыпали саблями головы наши они.

Что это? Как это? Куда мы бежим?
Сколько здесь нас в живых осталось?
От горящих деревень бьющий лапами в небо дым
Расстилает по земле наш позор и усталость.
Лучше б было погибнуть нам там и лечь,

[36] Ibid., pp. 183, 184.

Где кружит воронье беспокойным, зловещим свадьбищем,
Чем струить эти пальцы пятерками пылающих свеч,
Чем нести это тело с гробами надежд, как кладбище!

Corpses, corpses, look, everywhere corpses,
There they lie grinning, spitting out their rotten teeth.
Forty thousand we were, forty thousand,
And all forty thousand lay down at the Volga, like one.
Even rain could not beat down grass or grain
As they have cut our heads with their sabres.
What is it? How could it be? Whither are we running?
How many of us have remained alive here?
The smoke from the burning villages, clawing at the sky with its paws
Spreads our shame and tiredness over the earth.
It would have been better for us to perish there and be slain,
Where the crows are circling in a restless and sinister wedding,
Than to spread these fingers like five flashing candles,
Than to carry this body with coffins of hope, like a graveyard![37]

One of the Cossacks, Burnov, who has heard this tragic news, suddenly
feels an immense desire to live. His whole life passes before his eyes, his
youth and his childish fantasies when he believed that the lantern-lighter
in Tambov also lighted the moon, and that the stars were yellow butter-
flies who flew toward the flame of the moon. When Čumakov tries to convince him that the end really has come for them and reminds him of the
evil omen – birds screaming in the sky, with wings like black crosses – Burnov answers him in beautiful lines, expressing his love of life and of the
beauty of nature. It is as if we hear Esenin trying to convince himself that
the time to take his life has not yet come:

Нет, нет, нет! Я совсем не хочу умереть!
Эти птицы напрасно над нами вьются.
Я хочу снова отроком, отряхая с осинника медь,
Подставлять ладони, как белые скользкие блюдца.
Как же смерть?
Разве мысль эта в сердце поместится,
Когда в Пензенской губернии у меня есть дом?
Жалко солнышко мне, жалко месяц,
Жалко тополь над низким окном.
Только для живых ведь благословенны
Рощи, потоки, степи и зеленя.
Слушай, плевать мне на всю вселенную,
Если завтра здесь не будет меня!
Я хочу жить, жить, жить,
Жить до страха и боли!
Хоть карманником, хоть золоторотцем,
Лишь бы видеть, как мыши от радости прыгают в поле,
Лишь бы слышать, как лягушки от восторга поют в колодце.
Яблоневым цветом брызжется душа моя белая,

В синее пламя ветер глаза раздул.
Ради бога научите меня,
Научите меня, и я что угодно сделаю,
Сделаю что угодно, чтоб звенеть в человечьем саду!

No, no, no! I absolutely do not want to die!
In vain those birds are circling over us.
I want again as a boy, shaking the copper from the aspen tree,
To hold up my hands, like white slippery saucers.
How can you speak about death?
Can that thought find a place in my heart
When I have my home in the province of Penza?
How wasted the sun, how wasted the moon,
And the poplar tree near the low window.
For the woods and streams, the steppes and meadows
Are blessed only for the living.

Listen, I spit on the whole universe,
If tomorrow I'll no longer be here!
I want to live, live, live,
To live till it hurts and frightens!
Be it as a pickpocket, a rowdy,
If only I can see how the mice jump from joy in the field,
If only I can hear how the frogs sing from delight in the well.
My white soul is sprayed with apple blossoms,
The wind has blown my eyes into a blue flame.
For God's sake, tell me what to do,
Tell me, and I'll do what you say,
I'll do whatever you say, to ring in the human garden![38]

Tvorogov, who had been one of Pugačov's best friends, but who now, when the situation has become hopeless, turns against him, tries to exploit Burnov's desire for life. He gives a vivid description of the certain death which awaits those who remain true to Pugačov, and reveals his plan to capture him and deliver him to the authorities. Only in this way will they be able to save their lives. "We live only once, only once", he repeats. And: "Emel'jan's head is for us as a boat for him who is drowning in a whirling river".

The poem ends with a tragic scene when Pugačov tries in vain to convince the peasants that they should follow him. He knows that the uprising has not succeeded and he can only suggest that they should flee together toward Asia, but his words are of no avail. The peasants are tired of the hopeless struggle and want to return to their villages. At first Pugačov cannot understand what is happening. He tries to command his men to follow him and when they refuse, he kills one of them. Then the others throw themselves upon him. They knock him down, bind him and begin to mock him. Still Pugačov cannot understand why those for whom

[38]   *Ibid.*, p. 189.

he was fighting have turned against him. Only in his last speech does he
see that the end has come. Powerless and sad he complains:

> Где ж ты? Где ж ты, былая мощь?
> Хочешь встать – и рукою не можешь двинуться!
> Юность, юность! Как майская ночь,
> Отзвенела ты черемухой в степной провинции.
> Вот всплывает, всплывает синь ночная над Доном,
> Тянет мягкою гарью с сухих перелесиц.
> Золотою известкой над низеньким домом
> Брызжет широкий и теплый месяц.
> Где-то хрипло и нехотя кукарекнет петух,
> В рваные ноздри пылью чихнет околица.
> И все дальше, все дальше, встревоживши сонный луг,
> Бежит колокольчик, пока за горой не расколется.
> Боже мой!
> Неужели пришла пора?
> Неужель под душой так же падаешь, как под ношей?
> А казалось… казалось еще вчера…
> Дорогие мои… дорогие… хор-рошие…

> Where are you then? Where are you, former might?
> You want to get up – and you can't move a hand!
> Youth, youth! Like the May night
> You have ceased to flower like a wild cherry in the steppes.
> Look, the blue of the night is rising, rising over the Don,
> A soft odor of burning comes drifting from the dry glades.
> The large and mild moon sprinkles
> Golden lime over the low house.
> Somewhere a rooster is crowing hoarsely and reluctantly.
> The outskirts of the village are sneezing from dust in their torn nostrils.
> And always farther and farther, alarming the sleepy fields,
> The bell tower is running away, till it is hidden behind the hills.
> My God!
> Has the moment really come?
> Can you really be crushed under your soul like under a burden?
> And it seemed… it seemed only yesterday…
> My dear ones… my dear… my friends…[39]

When *Pugačov* was published in 1922 Esenin waited with impatience for
the praise of readers and critics. His friends, and especially Mariengof, to
whom he had dedicated his drama, had been very enthusiastic when he had
read his poem to them, but to his great disappointment the critics showed
no appreciation of what he considered his masterpiece. Nearly all of them
called the poem a complete failure as a historical drama. This, for instance, is how Jakubovskij, one of the critics, wrote about it:

Esenin is a lyrical poet only. That is the reason why his *Pugačov* proved to be a
failure. It is clear that the poem, written in a purely lyrical style, does not give the
slightest picture of the period. There is nothing of the movement of the masses, nor

[39]   *Ibid.*, p. 196.

of the inner motives of this movement. One must admit that all this was foreign to the poet. He did not understand it and could not feel it. The historical theme, without dramatic action, is filled with an extreme lyricism. There is in *Pugačov* a complete lack of conformity between the subject and its artistic form. The energy of the lyrical form is lost because the artistic essence of the poem seems not to be the historical action, but rather the state of mind of the poet, his feelings, combined with a contemplation of the Russian landscape. This does not mean, however, that the poem does not contain fragments of literary value...[40]

Jakubovskij's criticism contained a great deal of truth. It had indeed been Esenin's intention to write a historical drama which should give a more accurate picture of the revolt than Puškin had done, but his poem lacks completely any historical characterization. Pugačov and his friends speak the language of the Imagists of the twentieth century and, were it not for the names of the characters, the reader would be unaware of the fact that the events described took place in the eighteenth century. Everybody speaks the same flowery language, rich with images, and there is little differentiation between the characters. If Esenin had limited the use of images to Pugačov's speeches, there might have been some justification for it. It is a historical fact – and Puškin has also mentioned it – that Pugačov did make frequent use of metaphors. When, however, all the characters speak in images, the effect is stilted and sometimes ridiculous, as when the bandit Xlopuška says that Governor Rejnsdorp entered his prison cell "like a fluttering leaf". And if Pugačov often did talk in metaphors, we doubt that he ever would have described the dawn in the following words:

> Клещи рассвета в небесах
> Из пасти темноты
> Выдергивают звезды, словно зубы,...

> The pincers of the dawn in the sky
> Pull the stars like teeth
> From the mouth of darkness.[41]

The Soviet critics had expected from Esenin a realistic description of historical events. Since he was not able to do this, as a historical drama *Pugačov* is indeed a failure. If, however, one considers the poem as a collection of loosely connected lyrical pieces, it contains many beautiful passages which can be included among the best examples of the Imagist school.

---

[40] G. Jakubovskij, "Poèt velikogo raskola. O lirike S. Esenina", *Oktjabr'* (1926), no. 2, p. 132.

Sobr. Soč., IV, p. 163.

VI

MARRIAGE AND TRAVEL ABROAD: 1921–1923

1. ESENIN AND ISADORA DUNCAN

When he was not writing, Esenin hated to be alone. He needed the company of friends and admirers and was a frequent guest at the many parties and gatherings of the literary Bohemia in Moscow, where he was especially appreciated for his great talent in reciting poetry.

In the autumn of 1921, during a party at the studio of his friend Jakulov, he met Isadora Duncan who had come to Russia to give a series of dance recitals. She was already in her forties, a tall, rather heavy woman who looked her age. As usual, she arrived late at the party where most of the guests were unknown to her. Looking around, she noticed Esenin who impressed her as a charming young man with golden-blond hair, blue eyes and a slender, well-proportioned body. She smiled at him, stretched out on a couch and begged him to come and sit at her feet. She then stroked his hair, kissed him and said in Russian: "Zolotaja golova" (golden head). Since she spoke only a dozen Russian words, everybody was amazed that she should know just these. Esenin did not know any English, but evidently this did not interfere with the attraction they held for one another. In the early morning Isadora left the studio accompanied by Esenin who from then on stayed in her apartment.[1]

It seems doubtful that Esenin ever loved Isadora with whom he could hardly communicate. When his friend Ustinov once asked him why he lived with her, Esenin first seemed embarrassed, then said defiantly and with irritation: "You don't understand anything! She has had more than a thousand men and I am the last!..."[2] Of course, this answer probably was not quite sincere and though seventeen years older than Esenin, Isadora still had great charm and other qualities which attracted him, but

---

[1] See Mariengof, *Roman bez vran'ja*, p. 125.
[2] G. Ustinov, "Gody vosxoda i zakata", *Sbornik pamjati Esenina* (Moscow, 1926), p. 83.

the fact that she was famous throughout the whole world undoubtedly increased her charm for Esenin. He had wanted to meet her as soon as he had heard about her arrival in Moscow and he must have felt very flattered when he attracted her attention and was chosen by her as her lover. She seems really to have adored the handsome poet who could sing folksongs, play the accordion and dance Russian dances. She had wanted the love of a Russian while she was in their country and the blond young man with his typically Slavic face, who called himself a peasant but was dressed with the elegance of a dandy, was exactly the person she had hoped to meet.

At first, Esenin seemed pleased to live with Isadora in the house on the Prečistenka Street which had been put at her disposal. Every night – and a great part of the day as well – people gathered at her house to sing, dance and above all, to drink. Innumerable bottles of champagne and expensive wines were always available. Esenin, who never lost his peasant feeling toward money and for whom every cent counted, was dazzled by this carefree waste of money. He felt proud to be considered the master of this household and, especially when his friends were present, to order around Isadora who was only too happy to obey the man she adored.

Soon his friends realized that this atmosphere was extremely harmful for Esenin. He could hardly ever be alone in her house and did not have the time or desire to do any serious work. Hoping to lure him away, they arranged a trip to Persia for him. Esenin agreed to go and did leave Moscow, but in Rostov he changed his mind and returned to Isadora.

As the novelty of his new surroundings began to wear off, Esenin became more and more dissatisfied with his life in Isadora's house. Although he still felt flattered by the adoration of the older woman and succumbed to her charm and though he did enjoy the material wel-being and luxury he had never experienced before, he knew as well as his friends that this kind of life harmed him as a poet and he suffered because he was unable to write. Several times he decided to leave. He packed his few belongings and returned to the rooms he had shared with Mariengof. His friends received him with open arms and he felt relieved and happy to be among them. A few hours later a letter would come from Isadora, begging him to come back to her. He remained firm and refused coldly. Then Isadora's secretary, a Mr. Schneider, would arrive and plead with Esenin who would still not give in. Finally, usually toward evening, Isadora herself came to talk to him. Close to tears, she sank down at his feet, kissed his hands an implored him to come back. Then Esenin would collect his suitcases and once more move to her house.[3] This happened several times and each time Esenin despised himself more for his weakness and tried to drown his conscience in drink. He felt that by living with Isadora he was betraying not only his poetry, but also his old revolutionary feelings. What he noticed of the results of the New Economic Policy only added to his feelings of disillusion and he no longer even tried to understand what was happening. When the luxury of his surroundings became too oppressive, he went into town and visited the taverns where he drank with the poorest drunkards and beggars.

During this time Esenin never went back to his village. Was he perhaps afraid that the village would have changed, that he would notice the increasing influence of the city? That might destroy his conviction that at least somewhere there was an ideal place where life was peaceful and where he really belonged. Or did he fear to revisit the places where he had dreamt of such a different life for himself?

In February 1922 he went with Isadora to Leningrad where they stayed at the Hotel Angleterre. The drunken parties continued as before. After a few weeks they returned to Moscow where Isadora had founded a dancing school. The Soviet government had agreed with the principles of the school, but could not provide all the money it needed. Therefore, Isadora decided to interrupt her stay in Russia and give a series of dance recitals in Europe and America to collect the necessary money. She wanted Esenin to accompany her on the trip, but realized that difficulties would arise, especially in America, if they were not officially married. Thus, on the second of May, 1922, Esenin became the first and only legal husband of Isadora Duncan.[4]

Esenin was excited at the prospect of going abroad and visiting Western Europe and America, not so much in order to see new landscapes and cities, but more because he could now show himself and become known in other parts of the world, where he expected to find a new audience. This, at least, was what he told his friend, Šeršenevič, before his departure.[5] The fame he enjoyed in his own country did not satisfy him. Certainly, he was one of the best known modern poets. The halls were always crowded when he recited his poetry. His books were sold in all the bookstores. But this was not enough for him. He knew that those who read and admired him were only a small minority of the population.

[3] See Mariengof, *Roman bez vran'ja*, pp. 131–133. Also in Irma Duncan and Allan Ross Macdougall, *Isadora Duncan's Russian Days and her Last Years in France* (London, 1929).
[4] Esenin's marriage with Zinaida Rajx had ended in divorce.
[5] V. Šeršenevič, "O druge", p. 58.

The most important citizens, the leaders of the party and the government, either ignored him or were very critical of his work. It seemed that he could not increase the circle of his admirers in his own country. Knowing very little about Western Europe and America, he imagined that the general level of culture would be higher and that the interest in poetry would be much greater there. Only there, he hoped, would he find the appreciation he deserved as the foremost poet of Russia.

On May 10 the Esenins flew from Moscow to Berlin where they took rooms in the Adlon Hotel. Esenin enjoyed his first plane trip and was pleasantly surprised by the luxury and elegance of the hotel. Many Russian refugees who lived in Berlin knew Esenin personally and received him enthusiastically. He was invited to read his poetry in public and had, as usual, tremendous success. This time, however, he did not feel flattered by the admiration of his audience. He despised these refugees who had left his beloved Russia. In their company all his old revolutionary feelings were revived. He provoked quarrels, tried to shock them by singing Communist songs and was nearly constantly drunk.

Maksim Gorkij met the Esenins in Berlin at the home of A. N. Tolstoj and was shocked by the appearance and behavior of the poet. He had met Esenin once before, in 1914, but now he could hardly recognize him. Only his eyes, wrote Gorkij, were about the same, but even they had lost their sparkle. His glance shifted from one person to the other, he looked contemptuous and defiant, then, suddenly, seemed uncertain and nervous.

Gorkij was especially disturbed by Esenin's attitude toward Isadora. They communicated only by gestures. When she danced, he looked at her and frowned. It was, says Gorkij, as if he regarded his wife as a nightmare to which he was used, that did not scare him any more, but still oppressed him. Several times he shook his head, like somebody bothered by a fly. Then Duncan, tired from dancing, knelt down at his feet and looked at him with a tired, half-drunken smile. Esenin put his hand on her shoulder, but turned abruptly away from her.[6]

From Germany Esenin wrote to I. Schneider, who was the director of Isadora's dancing school in Moscow:

The atmosphere in Berlin made me go to pieces. My nerves are so on edge that I hardly can walk. I am taking a cure in Wiesbaden. I don't drink any more and am beginning to work. If only Isadora were not so crazy and would allow me to settle down somewhere, I could make a lot of money... Isadora's affairs are in a terrible mess... The famous Paul Boncour ... even has refused to sign the papers for a visa to go to Paris... As if nothing were the matter she rushes by car now to Lubeck,

[6]   M. Gorkij, *O pisateljax. Sergej Esenin* (Moscow, 1929), pp. 97, 100.

now to Leipzig, now to Frankfort, now to Weimar. I follow her in silent obedience for she becomes hysterical whenever I disagree with her.[7]

Finally, they left Berlin and traveled through Germany and Belgium, but Esenin's mood did not change. In Mariengof's "Novel Without Lies" he quotes some of the letters which Esenin wrote to the author and to Saxarov. They show Esenin's profound despair and immense disgust with everything he saw in the countries he visited. From Dusseldorf he wrote to Saxarov:

What can I tell you about this horrible ruling of the petty bourgeoisie which borders on idiocy? There is nearly nothing here except the foxtrot. People eat and drink and then the foxtrot starts again. Up till now I haven't met one human being and I don't know where to find one. Mister Dollar is most fashionable, but they don't give a damn for art; the highest you can find is the music hall. I didn't even want to publish books here, although paper and translations are very cheap. But nobody reads books. If Europe is the book market and L'vov-Rogačevskij the critic,[8] then it is stupid to write poetry to please them and to their taste. Everything here is well ironed, smoothed out and combed down like Mariengof's hair. The birds sit where they are allowed to sit. Where then should we go with our unseemly poetry? You know, that's just as impolite as Communism. Sometimes I would like to let it all go to the devil and rush back to Russia. We are poor, there is a famine and cold, men have eaten each other, certainly, but we have a soul which here they have rented out because it was useless. Of course, somewhere we are known, somewhere there are translations of my poems and of Anatolij's,[9] but what is the use, since nobody reads them? Just now I have an English magazine on my table with Anatolij's poems and I don't even want to send it to him. It is a very good publication, but on the cover you read: "Printed in 500 copies." That is the largest circulation here.[10]

From Ostend he wrote to Mariengof:

How I would like to leave this nightmarish Europe and return to Russia, to our young extravagances and all our ardor. There is such a spleen here, such a tepidness without talent... At the moment I am in Ostend. A mangy sea and the stupid pigheads of the Europeans. Thanks to the abundance of wine in these countries I have stopped drinking and take only mineral water.... In Moscow it seemed to us that Europe offered the greatest opportunity to spread our ideas and our poetry, but from here I see: my God, how rich and magnificent is Russia for that! It seems to me that there never has been and never will be such a country. As for my impressions of what I have seen since my departure, here everything is well ordered and smooth. Perhaps at first you would like that, but I think that you also would start to stamp your feet and to bare your teeth like a dog. It is an endless graveyard. All those people who move faster than lizards are not people, but worms who eat the dead; their houses are coffins and the continent is the grave. Those who did live here have died long ago and only we remember them. For worms don't have a memory... In Berlin I made, of course, many scandals and a lot of noise. My opera hat and the coat I had made by a Berlin

[7] V. Belousov, "Sergej Esenin za granicej (Novye materialy k biografii)", *Oktjabr'*, 1958, no. 5, pp. 182–191, and *Sobr. Soč.*, V, pp. 156–157.
[8] A Soviet critic who had severely criticized Esenin.
[9] Anatolij Mariengof.
[10] Mariengof, *Roman bez vran'ja*, p. 138. Also *Gostinica dlja putešestvujuščix v Prekrasnom* (Moscow, 1922), no. 1, and *Sobr. Soč.*, V, pp. 158, 159.

tailor made everybody furious. They all thought that I had come as a spy or agitator, paid by the Bolsheviks. That cheered me up and amused me...[11]

In his second letter to Mariengof he wrote:

No, you don't know Europe. My God, what an impression, how my heart is beating... O no, you don't know Europe. First, my God, such dirt, such monotony, such neglect of the soul that you feel like throwing up...[12]

It is, of course, possible that Esenin wrote to his friends only in his blackest moods of despair and that at other times he may have enjoyed some aspects of his trip, but he never mentioned that he noticed anything good or valuable in Europe. He does not seem to have visited a single museum or church. From Ostend Esenin and Isadora went to Paris, made a short trip to Venice and then back to Paris. They always lived in luxury hotels where Esenin only saw the rich or those who liked to live as if they were rich. Sometimes he visited some artists or poets with whom he could get drunk and who shared his hatred of the Philistine burghers. His scorn for the Russian refugees remained as great as ever. In Paris he was greatly amused when the Russian counts and princes who earned their living as waiters in the cafés and restaurants had to obey him, the poor little peasant, when he shouted his orders at them. His only serious work in Paris was with the French writer Franz Hellens and his wife who prepared a translation of his work.

At the end of September 1922 Isadora and Esenin embarked on the "Paris" for their trip to the United States. Again he was impressed by the luxury of their first class accomodations and by the number of trunks they took along. In an article he wrote later about his trip, published in the newspaper "Izvestija", he tried to describe the impression the ocean made on him. But he was unable to find an image to convey its immensity:

Forgive me that I have no image for a comparison; I wanted to say – like an elephant, but this is about ten thousand times bigger than an elephant. This immensity is an image in itself. An image without anything with which you can compare it. At that moment I felt very clearly that the Imagism my friends and I have advocated is drying up...[13]

On board his days were mostly spent in the bar and he looked forward to his arrival in the United States, hoping that there he would finally find the recognition he craved.

---

[11] Mariengof, *Roman bez vran'ja*, pp. 135, 136. Also *Gost. dlja put. v Pr.* (1922), no. 1, and *Sobr. Soč.*, V, pp. 160, 161.
[12] *Ibid.*, p. 166.
[13] "Železnyj Mirgorod", *Izvestija*, 1923, no. 187. Also *Sobr. Soč.*, IV, pp. 257, 258.

His first impressions on arrival were excellent. When the boat had docked, reporters surrounded Esenin and his wife. They were interviewed and photographed like celebrities. Because they came from Russia the authorities were afraid that they might have been sent as spies or to make propaganda for Communism; they were therefore not allowed to enter the country, but were detained on Ellis Island. Luckily Isadora had some influential friends and soon they were set free and could go to New York. In the Waldorf Astoria, where they went to stay, they were again surrounded by reporters. Great publicity had been given to the fact that the famous dancer had been detained on Ellis Island and many people wanted to meet the couple just returned from a Communist country.

At first Esenin felt happy and flattered by the attention he drew. He had been extremely pleased, for instance, when he saw an American illustrated weekly with his portrait on the first page. Soon he was bitterly disappointed when the text accompanying the photo was translated for him. It only said: "Sergej Esenin, Russian poet, husband of the famous dancer, Isadora Duncan". He realized the Americans were not interested in him because he was a famous poet, but only because he was Isadora's husband. The people he met seemed even less interested in art and poetry than the Germans and French had been. When they asked him what he did for a living and when he answered that he was a poet, they would think he was joking and say, "But that's not a job! What else do you do?"

Esenin arrived in the United States during the time of prohibition, but that did not prevent him from drinking more and more heavily. On the contrary, the fact that it was illegal to buy drinks became an added attraction for him. He loved the tricks one had to use – the introductions, the special knocks on doors of bars, the back entries. Drinking had become a sport and Esenin mastered it very quickly.

When he was not with Isadora, he seems to have spent most of his time in New York in the company of a young Negro with whom he visited the bars and took long walks. Perhaps he considered this a protest against race discrimination, or perhaps he was simply attracted to this man who, because of his color, belonged to the oppressed for whom Esenin always felt great sympathy.

During the months he spent in the United States Esenin became more and more melancholy and his longing for his native land grew stronger. His health suffered from the often harmful alcohol he drank and he began to hate the luxury of the hotels where they stayed.

Isadora also had less success than she had expected. During her performances she used to make a speech to the audience, telling them about her trip to Russia. In one of her dances she used a red scarf which angered the audiences who protested and called her a Communist. Finally she decided to cut her trip short and to return to Europe. She also realized that it would be harmful for Esenin to stay any longer in the United States. Several times already he had had severe nervous attacks, probably as a result of bad whiskey he had drunk. Early in 1923 the couple left New York and sailed to France.

In Paris Esenin's condition did not improve. He had become extremely nervous and irritable and his behavior became more and more abnormal. Once, to shock the elegant guests, or perhaps in an attack of insanity, he walked naked through the corridors of the Hotel Crillon where he was staying. He often made terrible scenes with Isadora. There were even rumors that he beat her and several times he had destroyed the furniture in their room. Finally the management of the hotel called the police. Esenin was arrested but soon released when Isadora intervened. They were, however, forced to leave the hotel and rented a private apartment elsewhere.

Esenin's sickness only manifested itself from time to time. There were many periods when he seemed normal, when he worked or visited friends and, on the whole, he seemed to feel less unhappy in Paris than in the United States, but his hatred of the Russian refugees and of many of Isadora's friends became violent and dangerous. Isadora was advised to have him committed to a mental hospital. She discussed it with Esenin and finally he consented to enter one of the best hospitals in Neuilly. Rumors published at the time in French and American newspapers that she had sent him there against his will because he beat her are quite unfounded.[14]

In the hospital Esenin's condition improved rapidly, but he refused to stay long enough for complete recovery. Both he and Isadora thought that his return to Russia might be better for him. They decided that he would leave immediately while Isadora would follow him a few weeks later. This was the end of their marriage. When Isadora did come to Moscow some time later, Esenin refused to return to her.

2. "MOSCOW THE TAVERN CITY"

When Esenin returned from abroad, he brought with him a number of poems which had been written partly before his departure, partly during his trip. Some of these had been published in Berlin in 1923 under

[14] See Duncan and Macdougall, *Isadora Duncan's Russian Days*.

the title *Stixi Skandalista* (Poems of a Brawler). In 1924 they appeared in Moscow in a volume entitled *Moskva Kabackaja* (Moscow the Tavern City). Several of these poems immediately had tremendous success and are still among the best known works of Esenin. In these poems he writes about the poorest taverns of Moscow where he used to get drunk in the company of thieves and prostitutes and describes the most negative and decadent aspects of Soviet life during the period of the New Economic Policy. While these poems held a great appeal for certain groups of Soviet readers, the critics were unanimous in their condemnation of what they considered extremely harmful literature. The Communists among them especially resented the fact that one of the best poets should have chosen precisely the most negative side of Soviet life as the subject of his poems. They considered it useless and even harmful to show what they called "the survivals of the worst outgrowths of capitalism". Especially after Esenin's suicide these poems were quoted as an example of his decadence.[15] However, nearly all critics did recognize the literary value of the poems of "Moscow the Tavern City" but this, they said, made them all the more dangerous for young people. It is true that after Esenin's death there was a wave of suicides among young men and women who had been avid readers of Esenin. The Communists wanted a literature which would encourage and help the younger generation to rebuild and mechanize their country, destroyed by war and revolution. No wonder that they considered most of Esenin's work, and "Moscow the Tavern City" in particular, highly undesirable.

Esenin's friends defended him, stressing the fact that he never glorified the underworld or drunkenness, that, on the contrary, every line of these poems expressed his loathing for himself and others like him. However true this may be, it cannot be denied that the tavern seemed to Esenin the only refuge for a man who no longer could understand what was happening around him. Even if he did abhor the bars and their customers, he nevertheless continued to go there. Perhaps it was partly because he needed the company of thieves and prostitutes to counteract the luxury of his life with Isadora, but it was also his way of demonstrating his disillusion with the revolution, as one can clearly see from the following stanzas from one of these poems:

[15]   See, for example, A. V. Lunačarskij, *Upadočnoe nastroenie sredi molodeži* (Moscow, 1927). K. Radek, "Ne Termometr vinovat", *Komsomolskaja Pravda* (Moscow), 27 March, 1926. N. Buxarin, *Zlye zametki*, ed. Priboj (n.d.). V. Ermilov, *Protiv meščanstva i upadočničestva* (Moscow, 1927).

Снова пьют здесь, дерутся и плачут
Под гармоники желтую грусть.
Проклинают свои неудачи,
Вспоминают московскую Русь.

И я сам, опустясь головою,
Заливаю глаза вином,
Чтоб не видеть в лицо роковое,
Чтоб подумать хоть миг об ином.

Что-то всеми навек утрачено.
Май мой синий! Июнь голубой!
. . . .

Again they are drinking here, fighting and crying
Under the yellow sadness of the accordion.
They are cursing their failures,
And recall Muscovite Russia.

And I myself, with hanging head,
Drown my eyes in wine,
So as not to look fate in the eyes,
To think at least a moment about other things.

They all have lost something forever.
My blue May! Azure June!
. . . .[16]

In the same poem he says how these people pity the young who have ruined their lives in their youthful enthusiasm and how the October Revolution has betrayed them.

This is the only poem in which the political situation is mentioned as
one of the causes of his despair. More often he blames his break with the
village and the bad influence of city life for his misery and his drinking,
as in the following poem, one of the best of this group, which is quoted
in its entirety:

Да! Теперь решено. Без возврата
Я покинул родные поля.
Уж не будут листвою крылатой
Надо мною звенеть тополя.

Низкий дом без меня ссутулится,
Старый пес мой давно издох.
На московских изогнутых улицах
Умереть, знать, судил мне бог.

Я люблю этот город вязевый,
Пусть обрюзг он и пусть одрях.
Золотая дремотная Азия
Опочила на куполах.

[16] *Sobr. Soč.*, II, p. 123.

А когда ночью светит месяц,
Когда светит... черт знает как!
Я иду, головою свесясь,
Переулком в знакомый кабак.

Шум и гам в этом логове жутком,
Но всю ночь напролет, до зари,
Я читаю стихи проституткам
И с бандитами жарю спирт.

Сердце бьется все чаще и чаще,
И уж я говорю невпопад:
"Я такой же, как вы, пропащий,
Мне теперь не уйти назад".

Низкий дом без меня ссутулится,
Старый пес мой давно издох.
На московских изогнутых улицах
Умереть, знать, судил мне бог.

Yes! Now it is certain. Without return
I have left my native fields.
No longer with their winged leaves
Will the poplars rustle above me.

The low house will stoop without me,
My old dog has died long ago.
On the curved streets of Moscow
God must have destined me to die.

I love this tortuous city,
Even though it is flabby and senile,
Golden, drowsy Asia
Has fallen asleep on its domes.

And when at night the moon is shining,
When it shines ... the devil knows how!
I am going, with hanging head,
Through the alley to the well-known tavern.

There is noise and uproar in this frightful den,
But the whole night through, till dawn,
I read poems to the prostitutes
And drink alcohol with the bandits.

My heart beats faster and faster,
And already I am saying at random:
"I am just as lost as you are,
I can't go back anymore".

The low house will stoop without me,
My old dog has died long ago.
On the curved streets of Moscow
God must have destined me to die.[17]

In this group of poems we find several lyrics where Esenin speaks of his
love for a woman, a theme which from now on will appear more and more

[17]   *Ibid.*, pp. 121, 122.

frequently in his work. Here he is evidently referring to his relations with
Isadora. Revolted by his purely sensual love for the older woman with
whom he could not communicate on any other level, he at first insults
her in the crudest terms. But this only increases his misery and finally,
ashamed of himself, he cries:

> Дорогая, я плачу,
> Прости ... прости ...
>
> My dear, I am crying,
> Forgive me ... forgive ...[18]

And in the following poem:

> Пой же, пой. На проклятой гитаре
> Пальцы пляшут твои в полукруг.
> Захлебнуться бы в этом угаре,
> Мой последний, единственный друг.
>
> Не гляди на ее запястья
> И с плечей ее льющийся шелк.
> Я искал в этой женщине счастья,
> А нечаянно гибель нашел.
>
> Я не знал, что любовь – зараза,
> Я не знал, что любовь – чума.
> Подошла и прищуренным глазом
> Хулигана свела с ума.
>
> Sing, come on, sing! On the damned guitar
> Your fingers are dancing in a semi-circle.
> I would like to be drowned in this revelry,
> My last, my only friend.
>
> Don't look at her bracelets
> And at the silk slipping from her shoulders.
> I sought happiness with this woman,
> And by accident I found my ruin.
>
> I didn't know that love is an infection,
> I didn't know that love is the pest.
> She came and with narrowed eyes
> She drove the hooligan to insanity.

He felt that he had not only betrayed his peasant origin by his life in the
city, but that he had still further degraded himself by his love for this
foreign woman. In a masochistic frenzy of self-pity he sought the company of the lowest dregs of society with whom he wanted to identify himself. When he was asked to read from his works in public, he liked to recite precisely these three poems. His wonderful diction, the sincere emotion he expressed, the real suffering one felt behind the crude expressions,

---

[18]   *Ibid.*, p. 126.

moved even those critics who has most loudly protested against their decadence and immorality.

In the other short lyrics of this period Esenin expresses only great discouragement and sadness:

> Нет любви ни к деревне, ни к городу,
> Как же смог я ее донести?
>
> I feel no love for village nor city
> How could I have kept it?[19]

He suffers because he has lost all his ideals. There is nothing more in which he can believe, not even in himself. He cannot understand what has happened to him and asks the question which he is unable to answer:

> Отчего прослыл я щарлатаном?
> Отчего прослыл я скандалистом?
>
> Why was I known as a charlatan?
> Why was I known as a brawler?[20]

All his love and tenderness now go out to the animals. He writes how the dogs in the streets of Moscow know him and how the horses lift their heads when they see him:

> Для зверей приятель я хороший,
> Каждый стих мой душу зверя лечит.
>
> For the animals I am a good friend,
> Each of my verses heals the soul of an animal.[21]

Conscious of the contradictions within himself, where the good and gentle are continually fighting against his bad qualities and his need to shock others, he says:

> Розу белую с черною жабой
> Я хотел на земле повенчать.
>
> I have wanted to marry on earth
> The white rose with the black toad.[22]

Long ago his faith in God had helped him, but:

> Стыдно мне, что я в бога верил.
> Горько мне, что не верю теперь.
> . . . .
> Но коль черти в душе гнездились –
> Значит, ангелы жили в ней.

[19] *Ibid.*, p. 117.
[20] *Ibid.*, p. 119.
[21] *Ibid.*
[22] Probably an allusion to Garšin's "Tale of the Toad and the Rose".

I am ashamed that I believed in God,
I am sad that I don't believe now.

. . . .

But if devils are nested in my soul –
That means angels have lived in it.[23]

At the end of this poem he asks those who will be with him during his last moments to let him die under the icons, dressed in a Russian blouse.

When Esenin was abroad, his thoughts frequently turned toward the village and he wrote some nostalgic poems in which the village seemed to him the only place where, perhaps, he could have been happy. He realized that it was too late for him to return to this simple life and that he could not live there now.

The poems of "Moscow the Tavern City" are written in clear and simple language. Since Esenin had completely broken with Imagism, the use of images is reduced to a minimum. More and more his verse approaches the clarity of Puškin's style, while here and there the influence of Blok is still evident. Not only do the harmony and rhythm of Esenin's verse show a great similarity with some of Blok's poems, but even the subject matter is sometimes the same. The following stanza from a poem by Blok sounds very similar to what Esenin wrote:

Гость бессонный, пол скрипучий?
Ах, не все ли мне равно!
Вновь сдружусь с кабацкой скрипкой,
Монотонной и певучей!
Вновь я буду пить вино!

A sleepless guest, a creaking floor?
Oh, what do I care!
Again I make friends with the tavern-violin,
Monotonous and singing!
Again I shall drink wine![24]

This influence of Puškin and Blok will be even more evident in Esenin's later works, as will be seen in the following chapter.

3. "THE BLACK MAN"

The nervous attacks Esenin suffered while abroad are clearly reflected in the long poem "The Black Man" which describes a hallucination he had had, a typical symptom of severe alcoholism. In the Collected Works

[23]   *Ibid.*, pp. 131, 132.
[24]   A. Blok, *Sočinenija*, I (Moscow, 1955), p. 405.

this poem is dated November 1925, but a first version had been written during his trip abroad. Mariengof mentions in his book that Esenin read this poem to him in the autumn of 1923 when he came back from abroad, but did not want to publish it at that time and did not show it to anybody else. It also seems probable that Isadora Duncan is the woman of over forty years old whom Esenin mentions in the poem. He did not refer to her again in this way in his later poems.

"The Black Man" is written in free verse. Short lines of five syllables alternate with longer lines. Esenin shows a great mastery in the use of this form and the poem, which proves how completely he recognized his physical illness and how he suffered from it, has a strong emotional tension. One can easily understand that he did not want to publish it at first, afraid that others might realize how sick he was.

The poem begins with the desperate cry of the poet, terrified by the effect of his drinking, but unable to stop his habit:

> Друг мой, друг мой,
> Я очень и очень болен!
> Сам не знаю, откуда взялась эта боль.
> То ли ветер свистит
> Над пустым и безлюдным полем,
> То ль, как рощу в сентябрь,
> Осыпает мозги алкоголь.
> . . . .
> Черный человек,
> Черный, черный,
> Черный человек
> На кровать ко мне садится,
> Черный человек
> Спать не дает мне всю ночь.

> My friend, my friend,
> I am very, very sick!
> I don't know myself from where this sickness has come.
> Is it the wind whistling
> Over the empty and lonely field,
> Or is the alcohol scattering my brain,
> Like leaves in September?
> . . . .
> A black man,
> Black, black,
> A black man
> Sits down on my bed,
> The black man
> Doesn't let me sleep all night long.

The black man then takes a book and reads aloud from it about the life of a miserable scoundrel. It is a vile description of Esenin's own life. With complete sincerity he sees what he has done in his life and, above all, what

he has failed to do. He hates himself for his failures and can only see bad
or mediocre qualities. He knows that what the black man reads to him is
true, although he never had dared to confess it so openly:

> Был он изящен,
> К тому ж поэт,
> Хоть с небольшой,
> Но ухватистой силою,
> И какую-то женщину,
> Сорока с лишним лет,
> Называл скверной девочкой
> И своею милою.
>
> Счастье, – говорил он, –
> Есть ловкость ума и рук.
> Все неловкие души
> За несчастных всегда известны.
>
> He was elegant,
> Moreover, a poet,
> Perhaps not with a great,
> But with a catching force,
> And some woman who was
> More than forty years old,
> He called a nasty girl
> And his darling.
> Happiness – he said –
> Is the cunning of mind and hands.
> All clumsy souls
> Have always been known as unhappy.

The black man does not stop talking. He provokes and insults the poet
and becomes more and more ugly and frightening:

> Черный человек
> Глядит на меня в упор.
> И глаза покрываются
> Голубой блевотой, —
> Словно хочет сказать мне,
> Что я жулик и вор,
> Так бесстыдно и нагло
> Обокравший кого-то.
>
> The black man
> Stares at me.
> And his eyes are covered
> With blue vomit –
> It is as if he wants to tell me
> That I am a crook and a thief,
> That I have shamelessly and brutally
> Robbed somebody.

Finally the poet cannot stand the torment any longer. He lifts his stick
and strikes the black man in the face:

... Месяц умер.
Синеет в окошко рассвет.
Ах, ты, ночь!
Что ты, ночь, наковеркала?
Я в цилиндре стою.
Никого со мной нет.
Я один...
И разбитое зеркало...

... The moon has died.
The dawn is blue in the window.
Oh, you, night!
How you have distorted things!
I stand with my opera hat on my head.
There is nobody with me.
I am alone...
And the mirror is broken...[25]

Thus ends this most morbid of Esenin's poems, written during one of the darkest hours of his life, when the black man – his other self – saw him as the alcoholic wreck he had become, a man who could no longer believe in the greatness of his talent, who had not fulfilled what he had once hoped to accomplish.

4. "THE COUNTRY OF SCOUNDRELS"

After *Pugačov* Esenin tried once more to write a drama in verse, but this time he chose a subject from more recent history and the action takes place during the civil war after the revolution. The hero is again a peasant who leads a revolt, but this time the revolt is directed against the Communists. This peasant, called Nomax in the poem, is clearly inspired by the historical figure of Maxno, who led a group of farmers against the Communists during the civil war.

This drama was written in the years 1922 and 1923, partly while Esenin was abroad and partly immediately after his return to the Soviet Union. From a literary point of view it was a complete failure and Esenin seems to have realized this, for he did not finish it and during his lifetime only a few fragments were published. If one compares "The Country of Scoundrels" with *Pugačov*, the contrast is striking. He now used hardly any images and instead of the expansive lyricism of *Pugačov* he wrote in a cold and rather crude realistic style. Only here and there, as if by chance, do we find a little of the old warmth and lyricism. "The Country of Scoundrels" is nevertheless an interesting document, since it shows Esenin's attitude toward the government in the years 1922 and 1923. At

[25]   *Sobr. Soč.*, III, pp. 209–214.

that time he had completely lost his early enthusiasm for the revolution and his sympathy was clearly with the hero of his poem who was in revolt against the Soviet system.

The plot of the drama is rather simple: the attack of Nomax and his men on a gold transport, Nomax's arrest and his final escape. The action begins near a small railway station somewhere in the Urals. Red guards, exhausted and nearly desperate from hunger and cold, have to protect the line against attacks by Nomax and his men who are operating in the neighborhood. Čekistov, one of the guards, a German Jew, complains bitterly about the lack of hygiene and modern conveniences in Russia. Evidently Esenin himself had realized abroad how backward his country was in this regard compared to Western Europe and America. Zamaraškin, another guard who takes over his watch, had been Nomax's friend when they were boys. Nomax now appears and talks to him as to an old acquaintance. In a long speech he explains why he has become a bandit. A proud man, he enjoys the sensation of hatred. He was bored by ordinary life and believed that the Communist state was not so different from Tsarism. He had heard how Čekistov had mentioned Hamlet and justifies his actions by saying that Hamlet also would have been a bandit if he had lived now:

И если преступно здесь быть бандитом,
То не более преступно,
Чем быть королем...
Я слышал, как этот прохвост
Говорил тебе о Гамлете.
Что он в нем смыслит?

Гамлет восстал против лжи,
В которой варился королевский двор.
Но если б теперь он жил,
То был бы бандит и вор.
Потому что человеческая жизнь
Это тоже двор,
Если не королевский, то скотный.

And if it is a crime to be a bandit here,
It is not more criminal
Than to be a king...
I heard how that villain
Spoke to you about Hamlet.
What does he understand about him?
Hamlet rose up against the lie
In which the royal court was wallowing.
But if he had lived now,
He would have been a bandit and a thief.
Because human life is also a court,
If not for a king, then for cattle.[26]

[26]   *Sobr. Soč.*, IV, pp. 204, 205.

Then he tells Zamaraškin what he wants from him. During the night a train will pass carrying gold from the mines in Siberia. He intends to stop the train to steal the gold, but for this he needs the red lantern the guard is carrying. Zamaraškin refuses to give it to him, and, after many threats and insults, Nomax takes it away from him by force. Now the action shifts to one of the compartments of the train, where Communist commissars of the gold mine, who accompany the transport, are talking. Rasvetov, who formerly had been a gold prospector in America, tells his comrades anout his adventures in the goldfields. Although he speaks in loosely rhymed verse, his language is completely without lyricism, even rather dry and precise. He tells about the tricks you have to use in America in order to become rich, tricks at the expense of the little man. He himself used them, he explains, because he hated the small capitalists as much as the big ones and after all, one has to live. In Rasvetov's long monologue Esenin has tried – for the first and only time – to describe in verse his impressions of America. Rasvetov speaks about cities built of steel and concrete. He tells how a whole network of railroad lines covers the country and describes the marvelous dustless roads where trains and cars, for whom each second counts, speed along noiselessly. Then he continues:

> Места нет здесь мечтам и химерам,
> Отшумела тех лет пора.
> Все курьеры, курьеры, курьеры,
> Маклера, маклера, маклера.
> От еврея и до китайца,
> Проходимец и джентльмен,
> Все в единой графе считаются
> Одинаково – business men.
> На цилиндры, шапо и кепи
> Дождик акций свистит и льет.
> Вот где вам мировые цепи,
> Вот где вам мировое жулье.
> Если хочешь здесь душу выржать,
> То сочтут: или глуп или пьян.
> Вот она – мировая биржа!
> Вот они – подлецы всех стран.

> There is no room here for dreams and phantasy,
> The time of those years is gone.
> Nothing but messengers, messengers, messengers,
> Stock-brokers, stock-brokers and stock-brokers.
> From the Jew to the Chinaman,
> The swindler and gentleman,
> They all come under one heading,
> All are equally – businessmen.
> On the homburgs, caps and opera hats

A rain of shares pours and whistles.
There you have the fetters of the world,
There you have the swindlers.
If there you cry out about your soul,
They will think you are either stupid or drunk.
There you have the world's stockmarket!
There you have the scoundrels of all lands.[27]

Then one of the others says that in Russia the stock-brokers are also busy again, that the heavy taxes imposed on the farmers have caused hatred toward the government and that sympathy for bandits like Maxno is growing. Rasvetov answers that Russia needs only one thing: a network of roads and railroads.

At this moment a frightened guard enters to tell them that they have been attacked and robbed. Nomax had stopped the train with a red lantern, detached the locomotive and the car containing the gold, and had fled with his rich booty.

The next scene shows Nomax in a little bar where liquor and drugs are sold clandestinely. The owner is a former society lady who complains about the hard times and cries with her friends about all the good things the revolution has taken from them. Nomax at first feels save and at home here, but then he hears that a prize of 10,000 rubles has been offered for his head. He tells a friend who accompanies him that he plans to go to Kiev, where it will be safer, and that he will take part of the gold with him. This conversation is overheard by a Chinese, disguised as a drug-peddler, but in reality a government agent who has been sent to find and capture Nomax. In order to catch him with the gold he decides to follow him to Kiev.

The scene in the bar was evidently used by Esenin to show the contrast between the decadent aristocrats, who do nothing but drink, use drugs and complain, and Nomax and his group, who hate the government just as much, but are able to act and want to overthrow the government. Nomax himself, however, has no intention of taking over the government. Esenin wants us to believe that Nomax is primarily driven by his love of a good and bloody fight, for the hero says:

Я не целюсь играть короля
И в правители тоже не лезу,
Но мне хочется погулять
И под порохом и под железом.
Мне хочется вызвать тех,
Что на Марксе жиреют, как янки.
Мы посмотрим их храбрость и смех
Когда двинутся наши танки.

[27] *Ibid.*, p. 217.

> I do not aim at playing the king
> And I have no desire to govern,
> But I want to walk around
> Amidst gunpowder and iron.
> I want to rouse those people,
> Who grow fat on Marx, like Yankees.
> We shall see their courage and laughter
> When our tanks approach them.[28]

The last scene takes place in a room in Kiev, where Nomax is hiding. The Chinese agent who followed him knows where he is staying. While his men surround the house, he enters Nomax's room to arrest him, but the bandit overpowers him, ties and gags him, puts on the agent's clothes and, disguised as a Chinaman, he escapes unnoticed.

Before he leaves Nomax explains once more in a long monologue why he has become a bandit. In his youth, he says, he believed in love, heroism and joy, but later he understood that they were all lies. One is strongly reminded of Lermontov's heroes in his early romantic plays when Nomax exclaims:

> Я верил... я горел...
> Я шел с революцией,
> Я думал, что братство не мечта и не сон,
> Что все во единое море сольются,
> Все сонмы народов
> И рас и племен.

> I believed... I was burning...
> I went with the revolution,
> I thought that brotherhood was not a dream and a fancy,
> That everything would flow together in one ocean,
> All the crowds of people,
> Races and tribes.[29]

Now he is disillusioned and nothing remains but "blood, brains and hatred".

"The Country of Scoundrels" was the last poem where Esenin expressed a negative attitude toward the revolution. Though his sympathies were with Nomax and he clearly identified himself with him, he portrayed the Communists as sensible people who have reason on their side. He liked the undisciplined individualists like Nomax much better than the cool and matter-of-fact Communists, but he understood that bandits have no place in a civilized society and are doomed to failure.

Esenin did not want to glorify only what was doomed to disappear. When he realized that the Soviet government was firmly entrenched and

[28] *Ibid.*, p. 237.
[29] *Ibid.*, pp. 248, 249.

that the new generation supported it, he tried to understand this new Russia, to become its poet and write about the positive aspects of the new state. With "The Country of Scoundrels" one period of his development was closed. To what extent Esenin would be able to write for the new generation will be seen in the next chapter.

VII

POET OF THE NEW RUSSIA: 1923–1925

1. NEW IMPRESSIONS

When Esenin returned from abroad, his friends could hardly recognize him. He looked ill and pale, his eyes had lost their sparkle, his voice was hoarse and dull. Somber and irritable, he seemed extremely nervous and upset. His sick appearance contrasted with the elegance of his clothes; from abroad he had brought several trunks with new suits, shirts, ties, socks, silk underwear and different kinds of powder and scents.

When his friends asked him about the countries he had visited, Esenin hardly replied. He seemed not to want to think about his travels, or perhaps he really had little to tell. Nevertheless, his impressions of foreign countries made him see Russia with different eyes. Since he had tasted the luxury and comfort of first class hotels and ocean liners, he could no longer deny that industrialization – which he had hated so much – did have some very useful and pleasant results. He had to admit that it was good to have plenty of electricity and running water and that he liked the cleanliness and the little luxuries so common in Western Europe and America, but still nearly unknown in the Soviet Union.

In his third autobiography he speaks of these changes in his attitude toward Russia and says:

After my trip abroad I look differently at my country and at the events that have taken place here. I do not like our nomadic life which has hardly taken any definite form, but what I do like is civilization. Still, I don't like America at all. It is permeated by a terrible stench in which not only art perishes, but, in general, all the best efforts of humanity.

Even if he hated what he had seen in the capitalist countries, did that mean that now he should accept and approve the Soviet regime which represented everything he had resented so much before he went abroad? Esenin could not see clearly and felt more uncertain than ever. He realized that the old patriarchal way of life which he had formerly idealized had to disappear and that the city with its industry must play the leading role in the development of the country. Recognizing its necessity did not yet mean that he really desired and approved of it. When he was in Berlin he had told Kusikov: "I love Russia. It doesn't recognize anything but the Soviet authorities. Only abroad did I understand how great are the merits of the Russian revolution which has saved the world from a horrible spirit of Philistinism."[1] In his third autobiography he said: "But, if today one wants to follow the example of America, I would rather prefer our grey skies and our landscape with the old peasant huts ... "

A. Voronskij, who was then editor of the literary magazine *Krasnaja Nov'* met Esenin in his office in the autumn of 1923. Esenin seemed very quiet and spoke little, but just before he left, he suddenly said: "We'll work together and be friends. But take care. I know you are a Communist. I am also for the Soviet authorities, but I love Russia. I do everything in my own way. I will not allow myself to be muzzled and I'll say what I want." He spoke with a smile, half jokingly and half seriously.[2]

More than ever, Esenin now seemed preoccupied with the problem of his attitude toward the Soviet state. He could not fail to notice that many things had changed during his absence. Life seemed quieter in Moscow and the bohemian artists and intellectuals no longer set the tone. As a literary school, Imagism no longer existed. In 1922 Kusikov had emigrated to Berlin, Šeršenevič no longer wrote poetry but devoted himself to the theater. The friendship between Esenin and Mariengof had cooled off considerably. Although he did not break openly with Imagism, Esenin no longer adhered to its theories.

When he crossed the frontier on his return from abroad, Esenin had been moved by a great love for his fatherland. He had kissed the Russian earth and had felt extremely happy to be home again among his own people. These feelings had very soon disappeared. Moscow seemed inhabited by a new kind of people whom he did not know and whose poet he could not be. They were mostly the young people, returned to the city from the civil war, energetic and active young men and women who clamored for a vigorous and revolutionary art. Always extremely sensitive to public opinion, Esenin would have liked to write the kind of poetry they wanted, but he felt incapable of doing so. It is true that he still was famous and could draw a large and enthusiastic audience when he recited his works, but he suffered from the thought that he might become what

[1]   A. V. (Vetlugin), "U. S. A. Esenina (beseda)", *Nakanune* (Berlin, 1922), no. 47.
[2]   A. Voronskij, *Literaturnye portrety. Iz vospominanij o Esenine*, III (Moscow, 1928).

he feared most: a poet past his prime, superfluous, unwanted by his compatriots.

In order to drown his fears and unhappiness, Esenin continued his drinking. He knew perfectly well that he was not only ruining his health, but his reputation as well, by his excesses and drunken behavior, but why should he spare himself, he thought, when his country did not need him? Much has been written, especially after Esenin's death, about the drunken brawls in which the poet and his friends were involved during this period. Whe shall mention here only one case, which had rather serious consequences and great repercussions in the Soviet press of those days.

At the end of November 1923 Esenin was accused of anti-Semitic feelings because during a drunken fight at a studio party he had insulted and beaten up a Jewish artist. What exactly did happen and whose fault it was has never been clearly stated, for the witnesses, all more or less drunk, contradicted one another. Some have maintained that the Jewish artist had started the fight, but it seems that the day after the event, in a telephone conversation with the Communist poet, Dem'jan Bednyj, Esenin again expressed anti-Semitic feelings. This affair was considered so serious that Esenin and his friends, Orešin, Klyčkov and Ganin (all of whom were involved), were called before the court of the Central Bureau of the Workers of the Press, where they were accused of anti-Semitic manifestations. Although they got off with a serious reprimand, the many articles in the Soviet press which blamed the court for its excessive leniency clearly showed that public opinion no longer tolerated this kind of bohemian misbehavior.[3] Esenin began to realize that he might well lose the sympathy of his more serious admirers if he did not change his conduct. It had already happened several times that at one of his recitals the audience had become impatient and angry, had even demanded its money back when Esenin had arrived drunk and had begun to talk incoherently about himself. But always, when he finally recited some poems from "Moscow the Tavern City", the hall became silent and when he finished, there was tremendous applause. Esenin, however, was no longer satisfied with easy successes. He realized that these poems of tragedy and despair were becoming outdated and that he had to write differently in order to be the great poet of his time.

Just at this time something happened to strengthen Esenin's desire to improve his behavior and to lead a more normal life. He fell in love with a woman who seems to have had a very good and steadying influence on

[3]   See V. Èrlix, *Pravo na pesn'* (Leningrad, 1930), p. 23. *Pravda* (Moscow), 30 November, 1923. *Rabočaja Moskva* (Moscow), 18 December, 1923.

him. His marriage with Isadora Duncan was definitely broken, if not legally, then, in fact. When she had come to Russia some time after his return, he had at first refused to see her. Later he once visited her, but came back completely resolved to break off all relations. Nothing is known about his new love, except the fact that seven love poems are dedicated to a certain Avgusta Miklaševskaja. From these poems, most of which were included in the volume, "Moscow the Tavern City," it seems evident that their love was passionate and sincere, although short-lived. The tone of the poems is very different from the desperate mood of the others in "Moscow the Tavern City". The poet now says that for him the time of drinking and drunken brawls is over:

> В первый раз я запел про любовь,
> В первый раз отрекаюсь скандалить.
> . . . .
> Разонравилось пить и плясать
> И терять свою жизнь без оглядки.
> . . . .
> Я б навеки забыл кабаки
> И стихи бы писать забросил,
> Только б тонко касаться руки
> И волос твоих цветом в осень.

> For the first time I've begun to sing about love,
> For the first time I repudiate scandals.
> . . . .
> I no longer like to drink and to dance
> And to squander life without looking back.
> . . . .
> I would forever forget the taverns
> And I would give up writing verse,
> Only softly to touch your arm
> And your hair, the color of autumn.[4]

What he loves about her, above all, is that she is Russian, that she loves the Russian landscape, that she looks like a Russian icon. She seems to have been younger than Isadora, but probably somewhat older than Esenin. The word, 'autumn', with all its associations of color and smell is used frequently, and he compares both her and himself to the time of year when the flowers wither away and the leaves are falling. Through her love he has found peace and a willingness to accept life:

> Теперь со многим я мирюсь
> Без принужденья, без утраты.
> Иною кажется мне Русь,
> Иными – кладбища и хаты.

[4] *Sobr. Soč.*, II, p. 133, 134.

> Now I am at peace with many things
> Without constraint, without a loss.
> Russia seems different to me,
> And different are the graveyard and peasant huts.[5]

Even when he realizes that their love is fading, there is no despair, but only resignation and regret for the many mistakes he has made in his life.

The last poem dedicated to Avgusta Miklaševskaja was written in a hospital where he had gone for treatment. Still the tone is hopeful and tender and he remains grateful for the love she has given him:

> Может, завтра больничная койка
> Упокоит меня навсегда.
>
> Может, завтра совсем по-другому
> Я уйду, исцеленный навек,
> Слушать песни дождей и черемух,
> Чем здоровый живет человек.
>
> Позабуду я мрачные силы,
> Что терзали меня, губя.
> Облик ласковый! Облик милый!
> Лишь одну не забуду тебя.

> Perhaps tomorrow the hospital bed
> Will take me to rest forever.
>
> Perhaps tomorrow, quite differently
> I shall leave, forever healed,
> To listen to the songs of rains and wild cherry trees,
> As a healthy man lives.
>
> I shall forget the somber forces,
> That have torn me and ruined me.
> Gentle face! Dear face!
> Only you I shall not forget.[6]

When Esenin left the hospital, he again had not completely recovered from his nervous disorders, but he seemed much better and more able to cope with life. Finally, in the early summer of 1924, he felt strong enough to pay a visit to his native village, where he had not been since his trip abroad. His impressions are described with great simplicity in the poem "Return to my Native Land" which, both in tone and content, is completely different from his tavern verses, as well as from his former lyrics about the village. It is as if, recovered from a severe illness, he sees the country with new eyes. For the first time the changes the revolution has brought are seen as something positive. He now accepts the new developments as inevitable and necessary, even though he still regrets the disappearance of the village he knew so well.

[5]   *Ibid.*, p. 138.
[6]   *Ibid.*, p. 145.

The tone of the poem is rather sad. The poet at first feels lost in his village where nobody recognizes him and where he has to ask his way to the house of his parents, destroyed by a fire in 1922. When he asks an old man for directions, it turns out to be his grandfather. The old man complains loudly about the changes in the village and about his granddaughters who have joined the Young Communists Organization. He is upset because they have removed the icons from the room and also because the cross has been taken from the church tower. While the poet is walking with his grandfather toward his parents' house, he begins to feel happy when he sees the well-known landscape that has not changed. His tears flow freely when he enters the poor little hut where his parents and sisters are now living. In the corner of the room where the icons should have been a large portrait of Lenin is hanging:

Здесь жизнь сестер,
Сестер, а не моя, –
Но все ж готов упасть я на колени,
Увидев вас, любимые края.
. . . .

Ах, милый край!
Не тот ты стал,
Не тот.
Да уж и я, конечно, стал не прежний.
Чем мать и дед грустней и безнадежней,
Тем веселей сестры смеется рот.

Here is my sisters' life,
My sisters', but not mine –
But still I want to kneel down,
Seeing you, my beloved country.
. . . .

Oh, dear country!
You are no longer the same,
Not the same.
But, of course, I also am no longer as before.
The sadder and more hopeless grandfather and mother are,
The gayer laughs my sister's mouth.[7]

Esenin feels closer to the older generation and, although he does not believe any more, nevertheless before he sits down he bows toward the corner where the icons should be. His sisters speak about Marx and Engels and tell him about books he has never read. He is amused by the superior tone his little sister adopts toward him.

The poem is written in a very simple, straightforward language. Especially the beginning, but also several other lines, show great similarity

7 *Ibid.*, p. 162.

with Puškin's poem about his visit to his former school in Tsarskoe Selo. As an example the first lines of both poems are quoted. Puškin wrote:

> ...Вновь я посетил
> Тот уголок земли, где я провел
> Изгнанником два года незаметных.
> Уж десять лет ушло с тех пор – и много
> Переменилось в жизни для меня,
> И сам, покорный общему закону,
> Переменился я...

> Again I have visited
> That little corner of the earth, where I spent
> As an exile two inconspicuous years.
> Ten years have gone by since, and much
> Has changed in life and for me.
> And I myself, obedient to the general law,
> Have changed...[8]

Esenin's poem starts as follows:

> Я посетил родимые места,
> Ту сельщину,
> Где жил мальчишкой...

> I have visited my native regions,
> That village,
> Where I lived as a boy...

Esenin's interest in Puškin and his desire to emulate him are also very evident in a short lyric he wrote at this time. In "To Puškin"[9] he identifies himself so much with the great poet that he describes him as very blond! He compares Puškin's often rakish behavior with his own hooliganism and he feels very pleased that Puškin nevertheless is still famous. If he could share that fate, he would die of happiness, says Esenin.

In three other poems of this time, in which he developed his impressions of the village and his attitude toward the Soviet state – "Soviet Russia", "Homeless Russia", and "Departing Russia", – Puškin's influence is again strong. It is this time no longer a simple imitation, but a sometimes very successful attempt to approach the beauty and purity of Puškin's verse. The most beautiful of the three poems is "Soviet Russia". It reflects the inner tragedy of the poet who feels too old to change and fears to be left behind by the younger generation. Its grave and simple rhythm expresses the sincerity and seriousness of thought. Although in translation the beauty of the verse cannot be rendered, this poem should be

---

[8]   A. Puškin, *Sočinenija*, ed. Vengerov (S. Petersburg, Brockhous-Efron, 1910), IV, p. 38.
[9]   *Sobr. Soč.*, II, pp. 164, 165.

quoted since it shows so clearly Esenin's attitude at this time toward the
Soviet regime:

Тот ураган прошел. Нас мало уцелело.
На перекличке дружбы многих нет.
Я вновь вернулся в край осиротелый,
В котором не был восемь лет.

Кого позвать мне? С кем мне поделиться
Той грустной радостью, что я остался жив?
Здесь даже мельница – бревенчатая птица
С крылом единственным – стоит, глаза смежив.

Я никому здесь не знаком.
А те, что помнили, давно забыли.
А там, где был когда-то отчий дом,
Теперь лежит зола да слой дорожной пыли.

А жизнь кипит.
Вокруг меня снуют
И старые и молодые лица.
Но некому мне шляпой поклониться,
Ни в чьих глазах не нахожу приют.

И в голове моей проходят роем думы:
Что родина?
Ужели это сны?
Ведь я почти для всех здесь пилигрим угрюмый
Бог весть с какой далекой стороны.

И это я!
Я, гражданин села,
Которое лишь тем и будет знаменито,
Что здесь когда-то баба родила
Российского скандального пиита.

Но голос мысли сердцу говорит:
"Опомнись! Чем же ты обижен?
Ведь это только новый свет горит
Другого поколения у хижин.

Уже ты стал немного отцветать,
Другие юноши поют другие песни.
Они, пожалуй, будут интересней –
Уж не село, а вся земля им мать".

Ах, родина! Какой я стал смешной.
На щеки впалые летит сухой румянец.
Язык сограждан стал мне как чужой,
В своей стране я словно иностранец.
. . . .
С горы идет крестьянский комсомол,
И под гармонику, наяривая рьяно,
Поют агитки Бедного Демьяна,
Веселым криком оглашая дол.

Вот так страна!
Какого ж я рожна
Орал в стихах, что я с народом дружен?
Моя поэзия здесь больше не нужна,
Да и, пожалуй, сам я тоже здесь не нужен.

Ну что ж!
Прости, родной приют.
Чем сослужил тебе, и тем уж я доволен,
Пускай меня сегодня не поют –
Я пел тогда, когда был край мой болен.

Приемлю все.
Как есть все принимаю.
Готов идти по выбитым следам.
Отдам всю душу октябрю и маю,
Но только лиры милой не отдам.

Я не отдам ее в чужие руки,
Ни матери, ни другу, ни жене.
Лишь только мне она свои вверяла звуки
И песни нежные лишь только пела мне.

Цветите, юные! И здоровейте телом!
У вас иная жизнь, у вас другой напев.
А я пойду один к неведомым пределам,
Душой бунтующей навеки присмирев.

Но и тогда,
Когда во всей планете
Пройдет вражда племен,
Исчезнет ложь и грусть, –
Я буду воспевать
Всем существом в поэте
Шестую часть земли
С названьем кратким "Русь".

That hurricane has gone. A few of us were spared.
At the roll call of friendship many were absent.
Again I have returned to the bereaved region,
Where for eight years I had not been.

Whom shall I call? With whom should I share
This sad joy that I've remained alive?
Here even the mill – like a bird of timbers
With an only wing – stands with eyes closed.

Here nobody knows me,
And those who remembered have long since forgotten.
And there where once the house of my father stood,
Lie now some ashes and a layer of dust.

But life is seething.
Around me emerge
Old and young faces.
But there is no one I can greet,
And in no eyes do I find shelter.

And in my head a swarm of thoughts arise:
What is the fatherland?
Is it then only dreams?
For nearly everybody here I am a somber pilgrim,
God knows from what far region.

And that am I!
I, the citizen of a village,
Which only thereby will be famous,
That once a peasant woman bore here
A dissolute Russian poet.

But the voice of thought says to my heart:
"Consider! Why do you feel insulted?
It's only a new light that burns
Of another generation in the huts.

You have already begun to show signs of age,
Other young men are singing other songs.
Perhaps they will be more interesting –
No longer the village, but the whole earth is their mother."

Oh fatherland! How ridiculous I've become.
On sunken cheeks a dry blush spreads.
The speech of my compatriots has become strange to me,
In my own country I am like a foreigner.

. . . .

The village komsomols[10] come down from the hills,
And with accordion playing loudly
They sing the propaganda songs of Demian Bednyj,
The valley is ringing with their gay shouts.

So that's what the country is like!
Then why the devil
Have I shouted in my verses that I'm the people's friend?
My poetry is here no longer needed,
And neither am I needed here.

Well, what of it?
Forgive, refuge where I was born.
With what I've done for you – with that I am contented.
So let them not sing my verses today –
I sang at the time when my country was ill.

I'll accept everything.
I accept everything as it is.
I am ready to go along the beaten path.
I'll give my whole soul to October and May,
But only my dear lyre I will not give.

[10] Members of the Young Communists Organization.

I will not give it into the hands of strangers –
Not to my mother, nor friends, nor wife.
Only to me has it entrusted its sounds,
And only for me did it sing its tender songs.

Flourish, young ones! And be healthy in body!
You have another life, you have another song.
But I shall go alone toward unknown regions,
Having quieted forever my rebellious soul.

But even then,
When on the whole planet
The enmity of races shall have disappeared,
When lies and sadness are no more –
Then I shall sing
With all that is in me as a poet
Of the sixth part of the earth
Which bears the short name "Rus'."[11] [12]

This poem shows clearly that Esenin understood that he would have to write differently if he wanted to remain the poet of modern Russia. He knew that to do this he had to understand the new way of life, that he had to write for the vigorous and optimistic young people who had accepted the new conditions and had no nostalgic longing for what was disappearing. At this moment he sincerely wanted to change his way of writing, but he was honest enough to know that he would be unable to write good poetry if he should try to write on command. He was too individualistic to submit himself to party discipline and he refused to lend his lyre to anybody who would tell him what to write.

In "Departing Russia" he tried to explain why it was so difficult for him to take part in the new Soviet life, why there was such a great distance between him and the young generation. He wished to be like them and envied their joy of life:

Друзья! Друзья!
Какой раскол в стране,
Какая грусть в кипении веселом!
Знать, оттого так хочется и мне,
Задрав штаны,
Бежать за комсомолом.

My friends! My friends!
How the country is split,
What sadness in the gay seething!
That is why I would like so much,
With rolled-up trousers
To run after the komsomols.

[11] An old name for Russia.
[12] *Ibid.*, pp. 168–171.

While it is impossible for him to join them, he feels nothing but scorn for those who cannot accept the new conditions and who are fated to disappear. He complains that he finds himself between the young and the old and that this is the cause of his drinking. But why can't he be inspired by the lyricism of the revolution, by the heroic struggle of the Communists, by enthusiasm for the new life? It is, he says, because he had not participated in the battles of the civil war:

> Советскую я власть виню,
> И потому я на нее в обиде,
> Что юность светлую мою
> В борьбе других я не увидел.
> · · · · · · · · · · · · · · · ·
> Я человек не новый!
> Что скрывать?
> Остался в прошлом я одной ногою,
> Стремясь догнать стальную рать,
> Скольжу и падаю другою.

> I accuse the Soviet power
> And I am angry at it
> Because I did not see
> My shining youth in the fight of the others.
> · · · · · · · · · · · · · · · · · · ·
> I am not a new man!
> Why should I hide it?
> I've remained with one leg in the past,
> And trying to overtake the steel army,
> I slip and fall with the other.

He refuses to identify himself with the old. He is convinced that those who do not want to accept the new order are still more unhappy than he is: "their eyes are sadder than the eyes of cows", and "their blood is moldy like a pond". These people are rotting away. They are like living corpses. Since his visit to the village Esenin also feels that he no longer belongs to the farmers. It is true that they are drawn toward the future, that in general they are for the Soviet state, but when he listens to their conversations he sees that they are interested only in food, or in getting a piece of cloth or a few nails. He cannot identify himself with these people who are interested only in the material side of life. What he would have liked to be was one of those who fought for an ideal:

> Я тем завидую,
> Кто жизнь провел в бою,
> Кто защищал великую идею.
> А я, сгубивший молодость свою
> Воспоминаний даже не имею.

> I envy those
> Who spent their life in battle,
> Who defended a great idea.
> But I, having ruined my youth,
> Do not even have memories.[13]

The third poem of this group, "Homeless Russia",[14] contains little auto-biographical material. It was inspired by Esenin's pity for the abandoned children, mostly orphans of the civil war, who wandered in bands through the country and cities.

After his visit to Konstantinovo, Esenin saw that he no longer was the poet of the village. More and more often he asked himself who needed his poetry, for whom he was writing. He told his friends: "It seems to me that I am writing my poems only for my friends. I would do better not to write and publish at all."[15] His friends suggested a trip through Russia to see new sights and perhaps be inspired by the reconstruction of the country. Esenin followed their advice and in the autumn of 1924 he visited the Caucasus where he had been once before his trip abroad. Then the southern landscape had not made a great impression on him, but this time his trip proved more fruitful. He worked seriously and wrote some of the best works of his last period during his stay in Batum and Tiflis, where he found many new sources of inspiration. It is true that, like everywhere else, he found in the Caucasus several bohemian friends just as willing to drink with him as his Moscow acquaintances. He also met and became friendly with some local Communists who took great trouble to explain Marxism and the Soviet system to him. Esenin tried sincerely to understand. He read books on Communist theory and even tried to read Marx, but this proved to be too difficult and he soon gave up his attempts to read *Das Kapital*. He later told his friends that the winter of 1924–1925 spent in Tiflis was one of the happiest periods of his life. Besides many lyrics he now tried also to write longer poems in which he spoke positively about the revolution and its results.

2. "SONGS ABOUT THE REVOLUTION"

When in 1917 Esenin had written about the revolution, he had seen himself as a prophet predicting the future and had been convinced that this was the task of the poet. In 1924 he no longer predicted, but turned to the

[13]   *Ibid.*, pp. 195–198.
[14]   *Ibid.*, pp. 199–202.
[15]   V. Šeršenevič, "O druge", p. 61.

past to sing about the Russian revolution, trying to describe what had really taken place. The first of these poems, "Song about the Big Campaign", was written in the summer of 1924, shortly after his trip to Konstantinovo. He evidently hoped that this would be the kind of poetry the younger generation and the Communists would appreciate.

This poem is written in the style of the old folk-legends, in short lines of five syllables each. Just like the old minstrels, he speaks directly to his audience, interrupting his story now and then to ask his listeners for a drink. The same device was used by Lermontov in his "Song about the Merchant Kalašnikov". The popular rhythm of Esenin's verse is also the same as that of the "častuška", short songs the workers and peasants improvised on some current topic. Some of the real "častuška's" of the twenties were used by him.

The poem begins by exhorting the audience which has come to listen to the bard. They are evidently poor people, gathered in some market place, for the poet addresses them as follows:

> Русь нечесаная,
> Русь немытая.
> Вы послушайте
> Новый вольный сказ,
> Новый вольный сказ
> Про житье у нас.
> Первый сказ о том,
> Что давно было.
> А второй – про то,
> Что сейчас всплыло.

> Uncombed Russia,
> Unwashed Russia,
> Listen
> To the new free tale
> To the new free tale
> About our life.
> The first tale is about
> What was long ago.
> And the second about
> What has now begun.

He then tells the story of a poor little clerk at the time of Peter the Great who had dared to criticize the Tsar. He is arrested and brought to the court in Petersburg. When the Tsar hears what the clerk has said about him, he becomes so angry that he kills the clerk with a blow of his fist. This is only one little example of the might of Tsar Peter:

> Это только, ребята,
> Начало.
> Ой, суров наш царь,

Алексеич Петр.
Он в единый дух
Ведра пива пьет.

This, fellows, is
Only the beginning.
Oh, grim is our Tsar
Alekseič Pëtr.
In one draught he drinks
A whole pail of beer.

But this mighty Tsar is often afraid. In his dreams he sees the skeletons of those who died in the marshes while building the city of Petersburg. Those skeletons lie buried under the granite buildings of the city, but some day, he fears, this army of corpses will arise and shout: "We are the Tsars of everything." They all hate Peter and he hears their threats:

Поблажал ты знать
Со министрами,
На крови для них
Город выстроил.
Но пускай за то
Знает каждый дом –
Мы придем еще,
Мы придем, придем!
Этот город наш,
Потому и тут
Только может жить
Лишь рабочий люд.

You have connived
With the ministers,
On blood you built
The city for them.
But let now
Every house know –
We shall come again,
We shall come, shall come!
This city is ours,
And therefore here
May only live
The working people.

During the two centuries after Peter's death these subterranean voices were always audible. Finally, their prediction comes true: with the revolution the workers take over the city.

In the second part of the poem some events of the civil war are described, especially the attitude of the peasants during the struggle. Their sympathies says Esenin, are with the Communists, because they have given them the land and have ended the war against Germany. When during the civil war the armies of Vrangel', Denikin and Kolčak were fighting the Reds, many peasants joined the Communists. They fought for their piece of land, for their harvests and the life of plenty they expected to come. The Whites are depicted as enemies of the people: their troops trample the harvests, they violate the wives and daughters of the peasants, they want to avenge themselves for the loss of their estates. No individual heroes are depicted in the poem. The masses of peasants are led by anonymous Communists, "men in leather jackets", who "are ready to live and die for the poor", who never seem to sleep at night but guard their camp, always ready to lead their men into a new battle.

Esenin first describes a battle near Petrograd which lasted ten days. When the Whites are finally defeated, the "men in the leather jackets" move to the Don to help the peasants in their fight. They arrive when the White armies have already suffered one defeat. Their soldiers are seeking consolation in the bars of a town they still hold. The Reds are resting in their camp, ready for the next battle:

> В красном стане храп,
> В красном стане смрад,
> Вонь портяночная
> От сапог солдат.
> Завтра, еле свет,
> Нужно снова в бой.

> In the red camp they snore,
> In the red camp it stinks,
> With the stench of leg-wrappings
> And of soldier boots.
> Tomorrow, when it is hardly light
> They must again go into battle.

The poet tells the story as if he himself had been one of the red soldiers. In the morning, he says, the man in the leather jacket addresses the soldiers:

> Братья, если здесь
> Одолеют нас,
> То октябрьский свет
> Навсегда погас.
> Будет крыть нас кнут,
> Будет крыть нас плеть,
> Всем весь век тогда
> В нищете корпеть.

> Brothers, if here
> they vanquish us,
> Then the October light
> Will go out forever.

> The knout will beat us,
> The whip will lash us,
> And we all will then
> Remain in misery.

Then follows a little realistic episode which is very reminiscent of similar details in Lermontov's "Valerik":

> С горьким гневом рук,
> Утерев слезу,
> Ротный наш с тех слов
> Сапоги разул,
> Громко кашлянув,
> "На, – сказал он мне, –
> Дома нет сапог,
> Передай жене".

> With bitter anger
> Wiping off a tear,
> Our commander then
> Took off his boots,
> Loudly coughing,
> "Here," he said to me –
> "There are no boots at home,
> Give them to my wife."

The battle finally ends with a victory for the Reds:

> Вот и кончен бой,
> Машет красный флаг.
> Не жалея пят,
> Удирает враг.
> Удивленный тем,
> Что остался цел,
> Молча ротный наш
> Сапоги надел.
> И сказал: "Жене
> Сапоги не враз,
> Я их сам теперь
> Износить горазд".

> Now the fight is over,
> The red flag is waving.
> Showing his heels
> The enemy is fleeing.
> Amazed by the fact
> That he remained alive,
> Quietly our commander
> Put on his boots.
> And said: "For my wife
> These boots are too large,
> I shall instead now
> Wear them out myself."[16]

---

[6]   *Sobr. Soč.*, III, pp. 145–164.

The story ends with this victory. A short epilogue in which the phantom of Peter the Great roams through the streets of modern Petrograd concludes the poem.

"The Song of the Great Campaign" shows great mastery of the short verse and contains some excellent passages. Esenin, who had thought this poem would satisfy the Soviet critics was deeply disappointed when nearly all of them were highly critical of the poem because, according to them, it did not give a true picture of the civil war. If some names of Communist leaders had not been mentioned, they said, the whole action could just as well have taken place during one of the pre-revolutionary peasant revolts. They also criticized the author for not having shown the leading role of the workers in the civil war. Even those critics who praised the literary qualities of the poem still preferred Esenin's shorter lyrics, the poems of his "Moscow the Tavern City" and even the early ones about the village.

One group of people, however, did prefer this poem to Esenin's other works. Their judgment would have made him extremely happy, but it became known only several years after his death. In 1930 a little book was published, "Farmers About Writers", by A. M. Toporov, in which the author quoted the remarks made by an audience of farmers after a story or poems by different writers had been read to them. Some of Esenin's poems were included in the recital. In general the farmers did not like his work, but when they had heard "The Song of the Great Campaign", they were unanimous in their praise. One farmer is quoted as saying: "Esenin was wallowing in the mud with many of his former poems, but now, with this one, he has come out of the mud. With this poem he makes good all his bad verses." Another one said: "I praise the poet for his thoughts, his harmony and everything, everything! The conversations in this poem are completely right. Every farmer from Ryazan, Kursk, Tambov or Siberia understands it completely."[17]

Perhaps, if Esenin could have known the praise of the farmers, he would have tried to write other poems about the events of the civil war, but discouraged by the negative reviews, he wrote only once more about this period. This was "The Ballad of the Twenty-six"[18] where he describes how the English in 1918 executed twenty-six Communists near Baku. The language and content of this poem are extremely weak. No explanation is given for the execution and although Lenin, the proletariat and the blessings of Communism are mentioned, real pathos and conviction are absent.

[17] A. M. Toporov, *Krest'jane o pisateljax* (Moscow, 1930), p. 240.
[18] *Sobr. Soč.*, II, pp. 178–184.

Of greater literary value is the "Poem of the Thirty-six" about the adventures of a group of revolutionaries arrested after the revolution of 1905 and sent to Siberia. Here was a subject that could appeal to the modern reader and at the same time one that was dear to his heart. Already in 1915 he had written about a convoy of criminals who were taken to Siberia. Now they were revolutionaries, but for Esenin both groups represented the romantic heroes he loved. He describes the men who march along the endless roads to Siberia:

> Каждый из них
> Сидел
> За то, что был горд
> И смел,
> Что в гневной своей
> Тщете
> К рыдающим в нищете
> Большую любовь
> Имел.

> Each of them
> Had been imprisoned
> Because he was proud
> And daring,
> Because in his futile
> Anger
> He had nursed
> A great love
> For those who cry in misery.

In the course of the somewhat involved story the prisoners are not individualized. Some of them escape on the way, others reach Siberia and suffer in the Siberian goldmines until liberated by the revolution of 1917. Nearly the only thing we know about them is that they all came from the village:

> В каждом кипела
> Месть.
> Каждый оставил
> Дом
> С ивами над прудом.

> In each of them
> Vengeance was seething.
> Each had left a house
> With willows over the pond.

In short lines and simple language a beautiful description is given of their long march through Russia. The first lines set the scene for the endless journey through the somber winter landscape:

Много в России
Троп.
Что ни тропа –
То гроб.
Что ни верста –
То крест.
До енисейских мест
Шесть тысяч один
Сугроб.

In Russia there are many
Paths.
On every path
There is a grave.
At every mile
There stands a cross.
On the road to the Enisej River
There are six thousand and one
Snowdrifts.[19]

Again the critics could not approve of Esenin's conception of the revolutionaries. They remained unreal, somewhat sentimental rebels, who pitied the poor, and protested against the injustice and misery of their time. According to the critics, they were not true Marxists fighting against the capitalist system.

Finally, Esenin decided to write about a subject that, he thought, could not fail to be approved by the critics. He started a poem devoted to the memory of Lenin. But the personality of this Communist leader had so little in common with the figures of his romantic heroes that the task proved too difficult for him and he could not finish it. The fragment that has been published shows the poet's dilemma in the naive and often unintentionally amusing way in which he approaches his subject:

Суровый гений! Он меня
Влечет не по своей фигуре.
Он не садился на коня
И не летел навстречу буре.
С плеча голов он не рубил,
Не обращал в побег пехоту.
Одно в убийстве он любил –
Перепелиную охоту.
. . . .
И не носил он тех волос,
Что льют успех на женщин томных, –
Он с лысиною, как поднос,
Глядел скромней из самых скромных.
Застенчивый, простой и милый,
Он вроде сфинкса предо мной.

[19]   *Ibid.*, III, pp. 165–181.

Я не пойму, какою силой
Сумел потрясть он шар земной?
Но он потряс...

Stern genius! He does not
Attract me by his figure.
He was not seated on a horse
And did not rush toward the storm.
He did not chop off heads
And did not turn soldiers to flight.
The only time he liked to kill
Was when he hunted quail.

. . . .

And he did not have the hair
That impresses languid women –
With a bald spot like a platter,
He looked like the most modest of men.
Shy, simple and dear,
He stands like a sphinx before me.
I can't understand by what force
He succeeded in shaking the earth.
But he did shake it...[20]

Esenin's admiration for Lenin may well have been sincere, but he was completely unable to understand this type of person. His words of praise remain abstract and the poem lacks all warmth of feeling.

3. THE FELLOW-TRAVELER

When, during his stay in the Caucasus, Esenin decided to write for the new generation, he had thought that he would enter a new period of his creative life. He believed that he had finished for good with his Bohemian debauches and might still write his best works. In his poem "In the Caucasus", written in 1924, he compares his fate with that of Puškin, Lermontov and Griboedov, who had all visited the Caucasus, fleeing from their friends or enemies. So, he says, has he fled Bohemia to become the great epic poet of his time. He is full of scorn for other Soviet poets, such as Majakovskij, "who sings about the corks sold in the Soviet stores", or his old friend Kljuev, whom he now calls "the little priest from Ladoga-lake", and: "when yesterday I read his verses aloud/My canary bird fell dead in its cage". The other modern poets are, according to him, even more incompetent. Only he himself will be capable of singing about modern Russia and the Caucasus will inspire him:

[20]   *Ibid.*, pp. 141–144.

Чтоб, воротясь опять в Москву
Я мог прекраснейшей поэмой
Забыть ненужную тоску
И не дружить вовек с богемой.

So that, when I return to Moscow
I could with a magnificent poem
Forget my unnecessary spleen
And nevermore befriend Bohemia.[21]

To what extent Esenin believed these boastful predictions is hard to say. He certainly did try to understand the greatness of the time and in *Stanzas* he tries to formulate his new, positive attitude toward the Soviet state. His strongest feeling, he says there, is love of his fatherland. He is willing to study the theories of the Communists:

Давай, Сергей,
За Маркса тихо сядем,
Понюхаем премудрость
Скучных строк.

Come on, Sergej,
Let's quietly study Marx,
Let's smell the wisdom
Of the boring lines.[22]

But when one of his Communist friends praises the beauty of the oil wells and Esenin agrees that they are more beautiful than churches and that he prefers the street lights in Baku to the stars and the moon, he is less convincing, even though he says that he is "ready to swear with a pure heart" that this is true. Voronskij was right when he severely criticized this poem and told Esenin not to try to be too much of a Marxist.[23]

A much better poem, and more sincere, is "Letter to a Woman", perhaps addressed to his former wife, Zinaida Rajx, who had married the theater director, Meyerhold. Again he tries to explain to her why he drank and misbehaved while the Communists were fighting to defend the revolution. He tells her that she left him because she feared that he would disgrace himself more and more by his drinking and scandalous behavior. He reproaches her for not understanding him. He drank only because he could not understand what was happening around him. He compares Russia shortly after the revolution to a ship during a storm. Somebody is steering the ship to safety, but the passengers do not know that and he says:

[21] *Ibid.*, II, pp. 175-177.
[22] *Ibid.*, pp. 191-194.
[23] A. Voronskij, "Na raznye temy, II. O Marksizme i ploxix stixax", *Al'manax Naši dni*, 1925, no. 5.

Ну кто ж из нас на палубе большой
Не падал, не блевал и не ругался?
Их мало, с опытной душой,
Кто крепким в качке оставался.

Well, who among us on the large deck
Did not fall, did not vomit and curse?
There were but few who with experienced soul
Remained firm during the rolling.

In order not to see the disgusting state of the others he went down into the hold of the ship:

Тот трюм был –
Русским кабаком.
И я склонился над стаканом,
Чтоб, не страдая ни о ком,
Себя сгубить
В угаре пьяном.

This hold was
The Russian tavern.
And I sat bent over a glass,
To ruin myself
In drunkenness,
Not suffering for anyone.

Since then the years have gone by. He now thinks and feels differently, for now he understands the greatness of the helmsman and proudly he tells his former wife:

Любимая!
Сказать приятно мне:
Я избежал паденья с кручи.
Теперь в Советской стороне
Я самый яростный попутчик.

Beloved!
I am glad to tell you:
I have evaded the fall from the slope.
Now in the country of the Soviets
I am the most fervent fellow-traveler.[24]

But, however sincerely Esenin may have wanted to accept the new Russia, it remained impossible for him to be part of it and to find there the subject matter for his work. He still had little personal contact with what was new and positive and his conversations with his Communist friends in the Caucasus impressed him only temporarily. The rare letters he received from his relatives in Konstantinovo seem to have touched him much more deeply. By far the best poem he wrote at this time was the "Letter from

[24] *Sobr. Soč.*, II, pp. 203–206.

my Mother", which with the poems from "Moscow the Tavern City" has contributed most to his fame. Without a trace of sentimentality it expresses the naive and simple complaint of an old peasant woman whose son has left his parents to become a poet. Bad rumors have reached her about the life he is leading in the city and he has never brought or sent them any money. Now she feels old and lonely, but if her son had stayed at home she would have a daughter-in-law and grandchildren:

> Мне страх не нравится,
> Что ты поэт,
> Что ты сдружился
> С славою плохою.
> Гораздо лучше б
> С малых лет
> Ходил ты в поле за сохою.

> I don't like it at all
> That you are a poet.
> That you have embraced
> Bad fame.
> It would have been better
> If from your young years
> You had walked in the fields behind the plough.

Once she had hoped that he would become rich by writing poetry, but even if he has made some money, he has never supported his parents:

> Теперь сплошная грусть,
> Живем мы, как во тьме.
> У нас нет лошади.
> Но если б был ты в доме,
> То было б все...

> Now there is nothing but sadness,
> We live as if in darkness.
> We have no horse,
> But if you had been home
> We would have everything...[25]

In the next poem, "Answer", Esenin responds rather feebly to the reproaches of his mother. "The time will come", he says, "when everything will be better." She would never be able to understand how he lives and why it is impossible for him to live in the village. He is afraid of the winter storms when it sounds as if thousands of priests are singing his death song and when his bed resembles a narrow coffin. This fear of death is again mentioned in "Letter to My Grandfather"[26] where he asks him if he

---

[25]   *Ibid.*, pp. 211–214.
[26]   *Ibid.*, pp. 229–233.

would dare to take the train if his grandson were dying far away from Ryazan.

Written toward the end of 1924, these poems show how already Esenin's optimism was being replaced by the reappearance of his old fears.

4. PERSIAN MOTIFS

While in the Caucasus Esenin wrote a cycle of short lyrics, published under the title "Persian Motifs". They do not express any of his new faith in the Soviet state, but are simple love lyrics, addressed to different Persian girls and were probably inspired by some superficial love affairs he had had in the Caucasus. Esenin had never been in Persia and his attempt to create a Persian background does not succeed very well and is limited to some general remarks about an abundance of flowers and many beautiful, mysterious women. From a purely technical point of view these poems are excellent, although they miss the directness and sincerity of the "Letter From my Mother". The poet's love for the beautiful Lalas or Šaganè's does not go very deep, and only his nostalgia for his native region rings true. The influence, and here and there even imitation, of Puškin and Lermontov is evident, but more in the feeling and content than in versification. As an example, the following poem, written in Batum in December 1924, is quoted:

> Шаганэ ты моя, Шаганэ!
> Потому, что я с севера, что ли,
> Я готов рассказать тебе поле,
> Про волнистую рожь при луне.
> Шаганэ ты моя, Шаганэ.
>
> Потому, что я с севера, что ли,
> Что луна там огромней в сто раз,
> Как бы ни был красив Шираз,
> Он не лучше рязанских раздолий.
> Потому, что я с севера, что ли.
>
> Я готов рассказать тебе поле.
> Эти волосы взял я у ржи,
> Если хочешь, на палец вяжи –
> Я нисколько не чувствую боли.
> Я готов рассказать тебе поле.
>
> Про волнистую рожь при луне
> По кудрям ты моим догадайся.
> Дорогая, шути, улыбайся,
> Не буди только память во мне
> Про волнистую рожь при луне.

Шаганэ ты моя, Шаганэ!
Там, на севере, девушка тоже,
На тебя она страшно похожа,
Может, думает обо мне...
Шаганэ ты моя, Шаганэ.

Oh my Šaganè, Šaganè!
Perhaps because I'm from the North
I want to tell you about the fields,
About the wavy rye in the moonlight.
Oh my Šaganè, Šaganè!

Perhaps because I'm from the North,
Because the moon there is a hundred times larger,
However beautiful is the Shiraz,
It is no better than the fields of Ryazan.
Perhaps because I'm from the North.

I want to tell you about the fields.
This hair I've taken from the rye,
If you want to, wind it round your finger –
I don't feel the least bit of pain.
I want to tell you about the fields.

About the wavy rye in the moonlight
You can guess by looking at my curls.
Darling, please joke and smile,
Only do not awaken my memories
About the wavy rye in the moonlight.

Oh my Šaganè, Šaganè!
In the North there is also a girl,
She looks so very much like you,
Perhaps she is thinking about me...
Oh my Šaganè, Šaganè![27]

5. *ANNA SNEGINA*

More interesting than "Persian Motifs" is the long autobiographical poem
Anna Snegina, also written in Batum in January 1925. In partly narrative,
partly lyrical verse the poet tells us what had happened to him at the time
of the revolution. When he revisited his village after his trip abroad, he
remembered how he had come there in 1917, how he again met the daughter of the local landowner with whom he had been in love when he was
sixteen years old, and he speaks of the changes the revolution had brought.
These memories are described with great vivacity and realism. They are
rich in sincere emotion and expressed in simple and melodic lines.

The poem begins with Esenin's return to Konstantinovo – here called

[27]   *Ibid.*, III, pp. 11–12.

Radovo – after the February revolution. The coachman who drives him from the station to the village tells him the latest news, especially of a battle between the peasants of Radovo and those of a poor neighboring village, Kriuši. In the fight one man from Radovo was killed and, as a result, ten peasants from Kriuši have been sent to Siberia. The poet arrives at the house of his grandparents, where he is warmly welcomed. The old mill with its overgrown garden is full of memories of his youth:

> Когда-то у той вон калитки
> Мне было шестнадцать лет,
> И девушка в белой накидке
> Сказала мне ласково: "Нет!"
> Далекие, милые были –
> Тот образ во мне не угас...
> Мы все в эти годы любили,
> Но мало любили нас.

> Once at that little gate,
> I was then sixteen years old,
> A girl in a white coat
> Told me gently: "No!"
> Faraway and dear events –
> Their image is still alive in me...
> We were all in love in those years,
> But we were rarely loved.

He explains why he has run away from the front. He had understood how terrible it was to kill others.

> Война мне всю душу изъела.
> За чей-то чужой интерес
> Стрелял я в мне близкое тело
> И грудью на брата лез.
> Я понял, что я – игрушка,
> В тылу же купцы да знать,
> И, твердо простившись с пушками,
> Решил лишь в стихах воевать.

> The war had eaten my whole soul.
> In somebody else's interest
> I shot those that were close to me
> And I threw myself on my brother.
> I saw that I was only a toy,
> In the rear were the merchants and rich,
> And leaving the guns forever,
> I decided to fight only in verses.

He had thrown away his rifle and, as "the first deserter in the country", he now has returned to the village.

His grandfather has not changed. He is gay and contented with life as before, but his grandmother complains how afraid she is of the revolution.

She has heard rumors in the village and expects terrible things to happen. Already all prisoners have been freed and even those from Kriuši have returned home, among them their leader, Pron. When he learns this, the poet immediately goes out to visit these peasants he had known before. He finds them gathered at Pron's house and talks with them. This conversation, as we find it in the poem, does not ring very true. Evidently Esenin reports what he now, in 1925, would like to have said in 1917. The peasants at first greet him as a stranger who has never known the hardships of their life, but soon they begin to ask him what he has heard in the city. Surely he must know members of the new government and he should be able to tell them when the land of the landowners will finally be divided among them. The poet doesn't know any more than they do, but when they ask: "Tell us, who is that man Lenin?" he answers, "…He is you." These words are often quoted by Soviet critics in favor of Esenin.

The poet has caught cold during his walk and when he lies in bed with a high fever, his anxious grandfather calls Anna Snegina, the daughter of the landowner, who comes to take care of the patient. When he regains consciousness he recognizes the girl he had loved as a boy. She is married now to an officer who is at the front, but talks about the poet's old love for her and stays with him till dawn. In gentle and delicate lines Esenin describes the rebirth of their love. He had recited his poems from "Moscow the Tavern City" to her—which in reality, of course, were written much later – and Anna is very upset about his bohemian way of life. She suggests that he drank because of an unhappy love affair, and when he assures her that he loves no woman, she says:

> – Тогда еще более странно
> Губить себя с этих лет:
> Пред вами такая дорога…
>
> Сгущалась, туманилась даль…
> Не знаю, зачем я трогал
> Перчатки ее и шаль.
> . . . .
> Луна хохотала, как клоун.
> И в сердце хоть прежнего нет,
> По-странному был я полон
> Наплывом шестнадцати лет.
> Расстались мы с ней на рассвете
> С загадкой движений и глаз…
>
> Есть что-то прекрасное в лете,
> А с летом прекрасное в нас.

> Then it is even more strange
> To ruin yourself at your age:
> There is such a future before you…

> The horizon became clouded and obscure
> I don't know why I touched
> Her gloves and her shawl.
> . . . .
> The moon laughed like a clown.
> And though I did not feel what I had felt before,
> My heart was strangely filled
> With the fervor of my   sixteen years.
> We left each other at dawn
> With the mystery of movements and eyes...
>
> There is something beautiful in summer,
> And in summer something beautiful in us.

The poet meets Anna again when, at the request of the peasants, he goes with Pron to her house to demand her land for the farmers. Pron is drunk and speaks rudely to Anna who has just received word that her husband has been killed. The poet would like to comfort her, but she insults him, angry that he could come at this moment as a spokesman of the peasants. "Go away", she shouts. "What a miserable low coward you are! He is dead and you are here..." Easily offended, the poet leaves with Pron to go to the tavern. He tries to forget her, but when after the Octoberrevolution the Sneginks are forced to give their land to the peasants and have to leave their estate, the miller invites Anna and her mother to stay at his house. Love between Anna and the poet flares up again, but this time they are not happy, knowing that it cannot last. Anna says:

> Конечно,
> До этой осени
> Я знала б счастливую быль...
> Потом бы меня вы бросили,
> Как выпитую бутыль...
>
> Of course,
> Till the autumn
> I would know happiness...
> But then you would discard me
> Like an empty bottle...

After a few days the Sneginks leave the village and the poet soon returns to the city.

The last part of the poem describes his return several years later, probably in 1924. His grandparents are again overjoyed to see him and they tell him what has happened since 1917. The civil war has passed through the village, Pron has been killed in a battle. Then the miller gives the poet a letter which had arrived for him several months before. The letter is from Anna and comes from London. In it she tell him how sad she is and how she longs for Russia. Often she goes to the harbor, just to see a ship with the Soviet flag. The letter hardly moves him. He has already forgotten Anna. Only at night, when he walks through the garden, old memories are awakened. The poem ends with nearly the same lines about the girl at the gate quoted at the beginning. Only the last line is changed:

> Мы все в эти годы любили,
> Но, значит,
> Любили и нас.

> We all loved in those years,
> But, that means,
> We also were loved.[28]

Anna Snegina was published in 1925. Esenin had thought that it would be well received and was greatly disappointed when the critics paid hardly any attention to it. The romantic love affair with the daughter of a land-owner could not interest the Soviet critics or the young readers, who had hoped that Esenin would continue to write in a more revolutionary spirit.

[28]   *Ibid.*, pp. 182–208.

VIII

THE LAST YEAR: 1925

1. ILLNESS AND DESPAIR

In the spring of 1925 Esenin returned from the Caucasus to Moscow, and at first it seemed as if he really would settle down to do some serious work. He lived in the apartment of a good friend, Galja Benislavskaja, who supported him in his good intentions and had an excellent influence on him. His sisters had come to Moscow and lived near him, so that he was surrounded by people whom he loved and who respected his talent. He had brought many new poems, written while he was in the Caucasus, and he was full of hope that the critics would praise his attempts to write for the new Soviet readers. As we have seen, however, the critics were far from enthusiastic and preferred his old lyrics to the new songs about the revolution. Esenin was all the more sensitive about their objections because in his heart he felt that they were right and that he was unable to write about the new aspects of Russia nor for the new generation. His short period of optimism was soon followed by new and more serious attacks of nervousness and despair and, as usual, he sought forgetfulness in drink.

At the end of March he went once more to Baku, hoping to find some rest and perhaps new inspiration, but this time the Caucasus could not help him. He continued to drink and felt more melancholy and desperate after each drunken excess. One evening he went walking in the mountains without a coat and with open shirt and, as a result, caught a serious cold. It seems probable – and he has said so himself – that he wanted to catch cold, and perhaps die.

When he returned to Moscow in May, he looked ill and had completely lost his voice. It was rumored that he suffered from tuberculosis of the larynx and, although this was not true, Esenin did nothing to contradict the rumor. The theme of death, the certainty that his life will soon end, returns more and more often to his work. These moments of despair still alternated with others when he was full of hope and good intentions, when he tried to stop drinking and start a new life.

At Galja Benislavskaja's apartment Esenin had met a granddaughter of
L'ev Tolstoj, Sof'ja Andreevna Tolstaja. They became engaged and were
married in June. For a last time he hoped to be able to arrange his personal life, to find a home and, perhaps, happiness with a woman he loved.
Did he really believe that this time his marriage would solve his problems?
It does not seem probable, especially in view of the following conversation
reported by Viktor Èrlix, who spoke with Esenin shortly before the latter's
marriage. According to Èrlix. Esenin said then:

"Well, here it is, I am getting married! But why should I get married? What is there
left for me in life? Fame? My God! I am not a child! Poetry? Do you think that...
But no! That is also going away from me."

"But your personal life? Happiness?"

"Happiness – that is nonsense! That does not exist. And my personal life... But I
have given it exactly for what I don't have now! Where is my life? Where are my
children?"

"Listen Sergej! Talking about your marriage, they say that you have tuberculosis of
the larynx?"

He gestures with his hand.

"That is not true, I have simply ruined my voice by drinking. In the Caucasus I ran
in the snow with open shirt. I wanted to catch cold, but I didn't succeed." And after
a moment of silence: "But as for dying, I'll die anyhow. And very soon!"[1]

Esenin's wife and friends saw clearly how serious his condition was. They
did everything they could to help him, but he refused to listen to their
advice. He was unable to give up drinking and always found enough so-
called "friends", obscure bohemian writers, who were only too proud to
be seen in his company, who were always ready to drink with him and
make him forget all the good intentions he may have had.

Disgusted with himself and the life he was leading, Esenin several times
went to Konstantinovo, hoping to find some rest there. He could not
stand the quiet life in the village for long and always returned a few days
later, more unhappy and desperate. Once he went there with a large
crowd of his bohemian friends to celebrate the marriage of one of them.
It became a scandalous drunken party such as Konstantinovo had never
before witnessed. The villagers were particularly shocked by the fact that
among the visitors there were women who behaved just as badly as did
the men. When Esenin was back in Moscow, he was furious at himself
because the village had now seen him at his worst. Even there he could
not be respected any more and nothing seemed left of his dream that
Konstantivono would become famous because he had been born there.

V. Èrlix, *Pravo na pesn'*, p. 76.

Neither the good care of Sof'ja Andreevna nor the solicitude of his friends could help Esenin. Nervous and irritable he continued to write, but this did not alleviate his troubles. He felt that his talent was on the decline and that there was nothing left for him to say. His condition seemed to improve slightly when shortly after their marriage the Esenins spent some time in Baku. His poems had been translated into Georgian and he had many friends there who encouraged him to continue his work, but already in September he had to return to Moscow. The State Publishing House was going to publish an edition of Esenin's collected works and he had to be there to make a definite selection of the works he wanted to be included. His wife assisted him and it was mostly thanks to her that the three volumes were prepared. Esenin spent most of the rather large sums of money he received for his works on drink. The atmosphere of Moscow, where the critics did not appreciate his latest work and did not even mention his *Anna Snegina*, for which he had expected high praise, increased his nervous disorders. In October he began to suffer from hallucinations and from a serious persecution complex. He became afraid of being alone and clung to his wife and friends, at the same time resenting any pity or attempt to restrain his freedom. At that time he once told Èrlix:

Listen … I am finished … I am very ill … I suffer mostly from being a coward. I tell you that, my boy … but formerly I would not have told this to a man twice my age. I am very unhappy. I have nothing in my life. Everything has betrayed me. Do you understand? Everything. But that is not what I wanted to say … Listen … Don't ever pity me! Don't pity me! If I ever notice it … I'll kill you! Do you understand?[2]

Those who were near him knew that he planned to commit suicide. Once he had tried to jump out of a window; several times they had had to use force to prevent him from killing himself. Esenin knew that he was very ill, but he refused all advice and medical care. He told his friends that he would take care of his health after he had finished the editing of his works. In November he once said to his friend Ustinov:

"Please write an obituary about me."

"An obituary?"

"Yes, I am going to hide. Some friends will organize my funeral. Articles about me will appear in the newspapers and magazines. Then I shall appear again. I'll hide for two or three weeks to give the magazines time to write articles about me. Then we'll see who is a friend or an enemy.[3]

Evidently Esenin at this time considered everybody who did not praise him an enemy.

[2] *Ibid.*, pp. 80, 81.
[3] I. Gruzinov, "Esenin", *Sbornik S. A. Esenin* (Moscow, 1926), p. 146.

His condition became so serious that his wife and friends were afraid to let him go out alone. Somebody always tried to accompany him wherever he went. But once, toward the end of November, when he had escaped their supervision, he arrived in a state of great excitement at the apartment of his sisters. He told them that he had insulted somebody who had threatened to bring the affair to court and now he was terribly afraid of what would happen to him. His sisters advised him to enter a hospital; once there he would not have to go to court. A few days later Esenin followed their advice. The life in the hospital without alcohol, the treatments he received, seemed to improve his health, but his nervousness did not disappear. He worried about money, about losing time. He wanted to work and write again. The thoughts about suicide did not leave him. He told Mariengof, who, after a long separation, came to visit him, that the doctors were afraid that he would kill himself, that his door was always left open and that all sharp and dangerous objects had been taken away from him.

Esenin stayed only about a month in the hospital. The doctors advised him to remain longer, if he wanted to recover completely, but he refused to listen to them. He felt stronger again and capable of work. Not wanting any supervision or curtailment of his liberty, he decided not to return to his wife and to move to Leningrad, where he had some good friends. He seemed in rather good spirits and was full of plans. He wanted to do journalistic work, to edit a magazine, and life still seemed to hold some promise for him. But unluckily he could not leave immediately, for he had to wait for some money that was due him. This little setback was enough to make him forget his good intentions and he again started to drink.

2. LAST POEMS

In the last year of his life Esenin wrote many lyrics, more than he had written in any other single year. It was as if he had to prove to himself that his talent was as great as ever and that there were still many things he wanted to express. The sad fact was that there was not much left for him to say and he could only repeat himself, often with less strength than before.

Early in the year he still wrote a few poems in which he tried to show that he understood the new Russia and wanted to be part of it. Thus, in January he wrote "Captain of the Earth"[4] commemorating the anniver-

[4]   *Sobr. Soč.*, III, pp. 36–39.

sary of Lenin's death. It is one of the weakest poems he ever wrote. It was printed in a magazine in Baku, but never published elsewhere and he did not include it in the definitive edition of his works.

The autobiographical poem "My Road"[5] adds nothing to what he said before. Again he tried to justify himself, to explain why he had not at first understood what was happening in his country and how his trip abroad had shown him the advantages of the Soviet system.

When his poems in praise of the revolution did not have the success for which he had hoped, he wrote again about his despair, about the terrible feeling of being too old and superfluous. It was always much easier for him to express these emotions and the tragic verses have a tone of greater sincerity and truth. In "Snowstorm" he says why people ought to hang him:

> За то, что песней
> Хриплой и недужной
> Мешал я спать
> Стране родной.

> Because with a hoarse
> And sick song
> I have prevented my country
> From falling asleep.

He says how he hates the roosters who keep you awake at night:

> Но я забыл,
> Что сам я петухом
> Орал во-всю
> Перед рассветом края...

> But I forgot
> That I myself, like a rooster,
> Have shouted loudly
> Before the dawn of my country...

He then sees himself in his open grave. As was the custom, copper coins have been laid on his closed eyelids. The gravedigger will take these coins to buy himself a drink and will say:

> – Вот чудак!
> Он в жизни
> Буйствовал немало...
> Но одолеть не мог никак
> Пяти страниц
> Из "Капитала".

---

[5]   *Ibid.*, pp. 42–48.

What a fool!
He made a lot of noise
In his life...
But he could not even master
Five pages
From the *Capital*.[6]

As often happened, after the deepest despair came a period when he tried
to accept life, when he could settle down again to work and was convinced
that he would develop his talent further. In "Spring",[7] written shortly
after "Snowstorm", he says that he is now reconciled with life. He has
studied Marx again and discovered that Marx has said that poets have
their own law. That cheers him up and, for a little while at least, makes
him feel happy.

A problem which still bothered Esenin as much as ever was the question
to what group of the population he belonged. In his sober moments he
refused to admit that he was a member of the city Bohemia. He had always maintained and been proud of the fact that he considered himself a
farmer. But when he visited his village he could not ignore the fact that
he was not, and never had been, a farmer, however much he might love
the fields and animals. This longing to belong to the village is excellently
expressed in the following poem, one of the gayest and most charming
he wrote in 1925:

Я иду долиной. На затылке кепи.
В лайковой перчатке смуглая рука.
Далеко сияют розовые степи,
Широко синеет тихая река.

Я – беспечный парень. Ничего не надо.
Только б слушать песни – сердцем подпевать,
Только бы струилась легкая прохлада,
Только б не сгибалась молодая стать.

Выйду за дорогу, выйду под откосы, –
Сколько там нарядных мужиков и баб!
Что-то шепчут грабли, что-то свищут косы.
"Эй, поэт, послушай, слаб ты иль не слаб?

На земле милее. Полно плавать в небо.
Как ты любишь долы, так бы труд любил.
Ты ли деревенским, ты ль крестьянским не был?
Размахнись косою, покажи свой пыл."

Ах, перо не грабли, ах, коса не ручка –
Но косой выводят строчки хоть куда.
Под весенним солнцем, под весенней тучкой
Их читают люди всякие года.

[6]   *Sobr. Soč.*, II, pp. 234–237.
[7]   *Ibid.*, pp. 238–240.

К черту я снимаю свой костюм английский.
Что же, дайте косу, я вам покажу –
Я ли вам не свойский, я ли вам не близкий,
Паматью деревни я ль не дорожу?

Нипочем мне ямы, нипочем мне кочки.
Хорошо косою в утренний туман
Выводить по долам травяные строчки,
Чтобы их читали лошадь и баран.

В этих строчках – песня, в этих строчках – слово.
Потому и рад я в думах ни о ком,
Что читать их может каждая корова,
Отдавая плату теплым молоком.

I walk through the valley, my cap pushed back.
My brown hands are in kid gloves.
Far away the rosy steppe is glittering,
Wide and blue is the quiet river.

I'm a careless fellow. Nothing do I need.
I want only to listen to the songs – accompanying them with my heart,
Only that the light breeze should blow,
Only that my young body stay straight.

I go off the road, I go down the slope –
How many festive peasants and women are there!
The rakes are whispering something, the scythes are whistling something.
"Hey, poet, listen, are you weak or aren't you?

On the earth it's better. Stop roaming in the sky.
As you love the dales, thus you should love work.
Aren't you from the village, weren't you a peasant?
Swing then the scythe, show your fervor."

Alas, the pen is not a rake, the scythe is no penholder –
But with the scythe tremendous lines are written.
Under the sun of spring, under the clouds of spring
People read them every year.

Damn it, I take off my English suit.
Come on, give me a scythe, I'll show you –
Am I not one of you, am I not close to you,
Don't I cherish the memory of the village?

I don't care about the gullies, I don't care about hillocks.
It is good to write with a scythe
Grassy lines in the valley's morning fog,
So that horse and sheep may read them.

In those lines there is a song, in those lines is the word.
Therefore I am glad, not thinking about anyone,
That every cow can read them,
Paying for it with her warm milk.[8]

[8] *Sobr. Soč.*, III, pp. 77, 78.

Except for the last stanza, which sounds somewhat forced, this poem is spontaneous and sincere. Even its rhythm is different from that of the other lyrics of this time. The lines of twelve and eleven syllables, with a caesura after the sixth, reflect the joy of work and the pleasant atmosphere of a beautiful spring day.

This mood of happiness was, however, an exception. More and more the visits to his village inspire thoughts about approaching death and feelings of remorse and sadness because he has not fulfilled the promises of his youth. Although he is not yet thirty years old, Esenin is convinced that his life is over, that he has written all he could write. Everything he hears and sees around him tells him that his death is near; the nightingale sings a requiem for him, the flax in the field is crying, his father's house now attracts him as a place where he can die. Although nothing new is expressed in these poems, Esenin was still able to write beautiful melodious verse. If one did not know his previous work, the following stanzas from a poem written in October, two months before his death, would be sufficient to count him among the best poets of his time:

Снова вернулся я в край родимый.
Кто меня помнит? Кто позабыл?
Грустно стою я, как странник гонимый –
Старый хозяин своей избы.

Молча я комкаю новую шапку,
Не по душе мне соболий мех.
Вспомнил я дедушку, вспомнил я бабку,
Вспомнил кладбищенский рыхлый снег.

Все успокоились, все там будем,
Как в этой жизни радей не радей, –
Вот почему так тянусь я к людям,
Вот почему так люблю людей.

Вот отчего я чуть-чуть не заплакал
И, улыбаясь, душой погас, –
Эту избу на крыльце с собакой
Словно я вижу в последний раз.

Again I have returned to my native region.
Who remembers me? Who has forgotten?
Sadly I stand, like a persecuted pilgrim –
The old master of my hut.

Silently I rumple my new cap,
The sable fur is not to my taste.
I remembered grandfather, I remembered grandmother.
I remembered the crumbly snow of the graveyard.

All have grown quiet, we'll all be there,
However much you try in life –
That's why I want so much to be with people,
That is why I love people so much.

That is why I nearly cried,
And, smiling, my soul was dying –
This hut and the dog on the porch,
It is as if I see them for the last time.[9]

The theme of love, which had inspired his "Persian Motifs", returns frequently in his later lyrics, but now it is a tormenting, unhappy love, directed toward a woman he either does not love enough, or less than another one who does not love him. Sometimes the influence of the early poems of Aleksandr Blok becomes again very evident, as in the following lines:

Свет такой таинственный,
Словно для единственной –
Той, в которой тот же свет
И которой в мире нет.

The light is so mysterious
As if it were for the only one,
For her in whom the same light is
And who does not exist in this world.[10]

Generally the women about whom he writes are more concrete and the love he mentions is without vagueness or mysticism. Most of these love lyrics were written between July (when he married Sof'ja Andreevna) and October 1925. At his wedding in July he sang one of them.[11] Although it has the rhythm of a gay folksong, the content is somber and mentions old age and death. Now even when he loved he was unsure of himself, afraid to be laughed at. In his moments of anger and revolt he no longer had strength to be rude and to insult his beloved as he had done before. Thus he wrote sadly in September that his youth was gone and added bitterly:

Пусть она услышит, пусть она поплачет.
Ей чужая юность ничего не значит.
Ну, а если значит – проживет не мучась.
Где ты, моя радость? Где ты, моя участь?

Let her hear it, let her cry.
The youth of another means nothing to her.
And if it means something, she'll live without suffering.
Where are you, my joy? Where are you, my fate?[12]

[9]   *Ibid.*, pp. 103, 104.
[10] *Ibid.*, p. 71.
[11] *Ibid.*, pp. 53, 54.
[12] *Ibid.*, p. 92.

The content of the poems becomes more and more monotonous and re-petitive, but the form remains perfect and the lyrics often have a musical quality which resembles the singing tone of gypsy music. Esenin himself mentions the gypsy violin in the following melodious poem:

Плачет метель, как цыганская скрипка,
Милая девушка, злая улыбка,
Я ль не робею от синего взгляда?
Много мне нужно и много не надо.

Так мы далеки и так не схожи, —
Ты молодая, а я все прожил.
Юношам счастье, а мне лишь память
Снежною ночью в лихую замять.

Я не заласкан – буря мне скрипка.
Сердце метелит твоя улыбка.

The snowstorm is weeping like a gypsy violin,
Dear girl, evil smile,
Am I not shy before the blue glance?
I need a lot and there is much I don't need.

We are so far and so dissimilar –
You are young, but my life has gone by.
Happiness is for the young, but for me only memory
Through the winter night into a violent snowstorm.

I am not spoilt – the storm is my violin.
Your smile is like a snowstorm in my heart.[13]

Or the following six lines, written during the same night in October:

Вечером синим, вечером лунным
Был я когда-то красивым и юным.
Неудержимо, неповторимо
Все пролетело... далече... мимо...
Сердце остыло, и выцвели очи...
Синее счастье! Лунные ночи!

In the blue night, in the moonlit night
I was once handsome and young.
Irretrievably, irrevocably
Everything has fled... further... past...
The heart has grown cold, the eyes lost color...
Blue happiness! Moonlit nights![14]

"Stupid heart, don't beat" is the recurring line in a poem written in August.[15] More and more often the poet pities himself. He has lost faith in his talent. Too often has he failed in what he hoped to accomplish. His efforts to stop drinking and regain his health have been in vain. Nobody

[13] *Ibid.*, p. 110.
[14] *Ibid.*, p. 108.
[15] *Ibid.*, pp. 32, 33.

seems to need him or his poetry. When he had left his wife, he sought consolation with other women, but neither drink nor women could drown
his feeling of self-contempt:

> Что случилось? Что со мною сталось?
> Каждый день я у других колен.
> Каждый день к себе теряю жалость,
> Не смиряясь с горечью измен.
>
> Я всегда хотел, чтоб сердце меньше
> Билось в чувствах нежных и простых,
> Что ж ищу в очах я этих женщин –
> Легкодумных, лживых и пустых?
>
> What has happened? What has become of me?
> Every day I am at other knees.
> Every day I lose pity toward myself,
> Not accepting the bitterness of betrayals.
>
> I always had wished that my heart
> Should beat less in tender and simple feelings,
> What then do I seek in the eyes of these women –
> Superficial, false and empty?[16]

Esenin must have realized that he could not continue writing this same
kind of sad and desperate complaint. When, at the end of December, he
decided to go to Leningrad, he once again hoped to find new inspiration
and, perhaps, new courage.

3. THE END

When he arrived in Leningrad on December 24, Esenin took a room in the
Hotel Angleterre, where his friends, the Ustinovs, were staying. He seemed quiet and full of plans. He told his friend, Èrlix, that he wanted to edit
a magazine, just as Nekrasov had done at his age. It is difficult to know
whether he was sincere when he said this and whether he really planned
to settle down in Leningrad, as he told his friends there, or whether he
only wanted to stay a few weeks and then return to Moscow. For that
was what he had told his friends in Moscow.

 The day after his arrival Esenin said that he wanted to visit his old
friend, Kljuev, whom he had not seen for a long time. In spite of their
now completely different outlook on life, he still loved him and recognized
how much Kljuev had taught him. Both Ustinov and Èrlix, who accompanied Esenin when he went to see Kljuev, have described this visit in
their memorial articles about Esenin. They arrived very early in the

[16] *Ibid.*, p. 134.

morning when Kljuev was still asleep. In the livingroom Esenin looked
with narrowed eyes at the many ikons and wanted to light his cigarette
from the little lamp in front of the ikons, but Kljuev protested so vehe-
mently that he had to give in. When Kljuev left the room to get dressed,
Esenin went up to the ikons, blew out the little lamp and said to Èrlix:
"Don't believe him. It is nothing but affectation. I bet you that he will
not even notice that the lamp is out." Esenin, indeed, won his bet and
felt very pleased about the trick he had played. Kljuev went with them to
the hotel where Esenin recited his latest poems, anxious to hear the
opinion of his former master, who finally said: "Good poems, Seryëža,
very good poems! I you collected them in one little book, it would
become the favorite book of all delicate young girls!" Esenin, of course,
felt deeply hurt by this crushing remark and it destroyed the last traces of
friendship between the two poets.[17]

Esenin seemed anxious to start working. "Only these days we aren't
working", he said, "because of the holidays, but afterwards we'll start."[18]
He spoke about renting an apartment with his friends and about editing
the magazine. When he was alone with Èrlix he confessed how bewildered
he felt, how difficult it was to understand the time in which he lived. "If
I could have been a White officer, I would have understood everything.
There wouldn't really be anything to understand. Villainy is a simple
thing. But now! I don't understand what is happening in this world!"
He also complained that his left hand troubled him. The doctors had told
him that in a few years he would not be able to use it. This may well have
been the result of a suicide attempt in Moscow when he had tried to cut
his veins. Esenin hated all signs of illness or old age and seemed very upset about his hand.

December twenty-sixth passed quietly. At night Esenin was alone in
his room and wanted to write. When he could not find any ink, he cut his
arm and wrote with blood:

> До свиданья, друг мой, до свиданья.
> Милый мой, ты у меня в груди.
> Предназначенное расставанье
> Обещает встречу впереди.
>
> До свиданья, друг мой, без руки и слова,
> Не грусти и не печаль бровей, –
> В этой жизни умирать не ново,
> Но и жить, конечно, не новей.

[17] V. Èrlix, *Pravo na pesn'*, p. 93. G. Ustinov, "Moi vospominanija o Esenine",
Sbornik S. A. Esenin (Moscow, 1926), p. 167.
[18] V. Èrlix, *Pravo na pesn'*, pp. 93, 99.

Goodbye, my friend, goodbye,
My dear, you are in my heart.
The predestined separation
Promises a meeting in the future.

Goodbye, my friend, without handshake or word,
Do not be sad and do not frown –
In this life it is not new to die,
But to live also, of course, is not any newer.[19]

This was his last poem and it seemed as if his decision to kill himself
were definite, but when he joined his friends the next morning they did not
notice anything. He only seemed somewhat more nervous than usual and
even became very angry because the boy who had to prepare his bath had
forgotten to turn on the water when he had heated the stove and could
have caused an explosion. Esenin was convinced that this had been done
on purpose to kill him and he remained upset, though his friends tried to
convince him that nobody was conspiring against him. A little later he
told Ustinov's wife, whom he called Aunt Liza: "By the way, Aunt Liza!
What a shame! There isn't any ink in my room. You understand? I wanted to write and there was no ink. I looked everywhere, but I could not
find any. Look what I have done". He showed her the cut in his arm.
Then he took a piece of paper from his pocket and gave it to Èrlix, asking
him not to read it yet. Èrlix put it away and remembered it only after
Esenin's death. Then he found that it was the farewell poem that Esenin
had written twenty-four hours before his suicide.

During the rest of the day nothing unusual happened. They dined together, but there was very little to drink, since, because of the holidays,
the stores were closed and no liquor could be bought. After dinner a few
friends joined Esenin in his room, but they left early. When toward nine
o'clock Ustinov also left, he promised to come back later. "Come back,
come back in any case, as soon as possible!" begged Esenin. "And tell
them to let me into your room toward morning!" Several times before
Esenin had come to Ustinov's room during the night when he was afraid
to be alone.

Ustinov could not keep his promise and did not come back, but Èrlix,
who had forgotten his briefcase, returned a little later. He found Esenin
seated at the table, quietly reading his old poems. A large carton with
manuscripts stood before him on the table. He had taken off his jacket
and thrown a fur coat over his shoulders. Èrlix said goodbye a second
time and Esenin did not retain him. Toward ten o'clock he went down-

[19]   *Sobr. Soč.*, III, p. 138.

stairs to tell the doorman not to admit anybody to his room. For a long time he remained seated in the lobby, evidently afraid to return to his room. Finally he went back upstairs, but he seems still to have hesitated a long time before committing suicide. Perhaps he waited in the hope that Èrlix would read his latest poem and come to save him. Toward morning he tried to cut the artery at his wrist, but when he did not succeed, he took a rope which had been tied around one of his suitcases and hung himself from a pipe of the central heating system.

When Ustinov's wife knocked on the door the next morning, there was no answer. The director of the hotel was called and the door was forced open. Then they found Esenin's body. Ustinov was struck by the fact that Esenin had not even bothered to make a loop in the rope. He had only wound it twice around his neck.[20] Could this mean that he had not really intended to die? It is, of course, possible that Esenin would not have killed himself that night if Èrlix had read his poem and had returned to argue with him. He had, however, nursed the thought of suicide for a long time and one of the many attempts he made was bound to succeed.

After the necessary formalities, Esenin's body was brought to the Nečaev hospital for an autopsy. It was ascertained that death was caused by suffocation. The brains showed no abnormalities. The time of death was fixed at five o'clock in the morning. The body was then brought to the House of the Leningrad Writers on the Fontanka where his friends and others could pay their last respects. A sculptor made a death mask.

Esenin's widow and his brother-in-law Nasedkin arrived on the twenty-ninth. They had arranged the transport of the body to Moscow where the funeral would take place. In the evening the body was brought to the October station where many people had gathered. There were speeches, verses in honor of Esenin were recited and then the train with the coffin left.

In the afternoon of December 30 the train slowly entered the station in Moscow where thousands of friends and admirers of the poet were waiting. The car which contained Esenin's body was decorated with branches of evergreen. While funeral music was played, the coffin was lowered from the train and càrried by the writers and artists – Pil'njak, Babel', Orešin, Meyerhold, Vsevolod Ivanov and others – brought to the "House of the Press" on Nikitskij Boulevard.

[20] A description of Esenin's last days can be found in V. Èrlix, *Pravo na pesn'*, pp. 93–103; G. Ustinov, "Moi vospominanija o Esenine", *Sbornik S. A. Esenin* (Moscow, 1926), p. 167; E. Ustinova, "Četyre dnja S. A. Esenina", *Sbornik S. A. Esenin* (Moscow, 1926), p. 232.

Esenin's friends formed a guard of honor around the coffin. During the day and throughout the night, except for one hour when only the family and closest friends were admitted, an endless stream of people circulated through the building to pay their last respects to the poet. The funeral was held on the thirty first of December. At nine o'clock in the morning a little girl, daughter of Esenin and Zinaida Rajx, recited a poem by Puškin. Then the coffin was closed. The procession of several thousand people which followed the coffin halted before the "Herzen House", where the chairman of the Union of Writers spoke a few words. When they passed the Kamernyj Theater, the theater orchestra played a funeral march. Finally, Esenin was buried at the Vangankovskij cemetery. At the request of the family no speeches were made and only some poems were recited, some of Esenin's own and some written by others in his memory.

BIBLIOGRAPHY

1. BOOKS IN RUSSIAN AND UKRAINIAN

Авербах, Леопольд, "Памяти Есенина", *Известия* (Москва), 31/XII, 1925.

Авраамов, Арсений, *Воплощение. Есенин–Мариенгоф* (Москва, изд. "Имажинисты", 1921).

Адамович, Георгий, "Литературные беседы (о Сергее Есенине)", *Звено* (Париж), № 1, 1926.

Адонц, Гайк, "О поэзии Есенина", *Жизнь Искусства* (Ленинград), №№ 34, 35, 1925.

Азадовский, Марк, *Беседы собирателя* (Иркутск, изд. 2-е Иркутской секции научных работников, 1925).

Ал. "Есенин", *Диктатура Труда* (Сталино), 8/I, 1926.

Александров, И., "Под народный суд!", *Рабочая Москва* (Москва), 20/XII, 1923.

Алексеев, *Деревня в русской поэзии*. С вступ. заметками. (Берлин, изд. Е. А. Гутнова, 1922).

Алтайский, К., "Рецензия на сборник *С. А. Есенин* изд. ГИЗ", *Коммуна* (Калуга), 3/IX, 1926.

——, "Рецензия на *Собрание Стихотворений* Есенина, т.т. I, II и III", *Коммуна* (Калуга), 6/III, 1926.

——, "Умер Сергей Есенин", *Вятская Правда*, 1/I, 1926.

Ан., А., "Есенина выделить!", *Рабочая Москва*, 20/XII, 1923.

Анибал, Борис, "Около Есенина", *Новый Мир* (Москва), № 6, 1926.

——, "Рецензия на книгу Есенина 'Пугачев'", *Вестник Литературы* (Петроград), № 2–3, 1922.

Аничков, Е., *Новая русская поэзия* (Берлин, изд. И. П. Ладыжникова, 1923).

Анненков, Юрий., "Вокруг Есенина", *Опыты* (Нью Йорк), кн. III, стр. 160–179, 1954.

Апушкин, Я., "Есенин – 'Пугачев'", *Экран* (Москва), 21–28/II, № 22, 1922.

Аренский, Роман, (Гиппиус, Зинаида) "Земля и камень", *Голос жизни*, № 17, 1915.

Асеев, Н., "Избяной обоз (о пастушеском течении в поэзии наших дней)", *Печать и Революция* (Москва), № 8, 1922.

——, "Плач по Есенину", Альманах *Удар* (Москва), 1926.

——, "Три встречи с Есениным", Сб. *С. А. Есенин* (Москва, изд. ГИЗ, 1926).

Б. "Сергей Есенин", *Советская Степь* (Кзыл-Орда), 3/I, 1926.

Н. Б., "Рецензия на книгу Есенина *Стихи*", *Новый Мир* (Москва), № 3, 1925.

Бабенчиков, М., "Есенин", Сб. *С. А. Есенин* (Москва, изд. ГИЗ, 1926).

Бакинский, В., "Поэзия Сергея Есенина", *Звезда*, № 5–6, 1940.

Башмачников, "Сергей Есенин", *Призыв* (Владимир), 9/I, 1926.

Безыменский, А., "Прошу слова, как комсомолец!", *Комсомольская Правда* (Москва), 19/VI, 1926.

Беккер, М., "Рецензия на книгу А. Ревякина *Чей поэт Сергей Есенин*", *На литера-турном посту* (Москва), № 4, 1926.

Белоусов, В., "Сергей Есенин за границей. (Новые материалы к биографии)", *Октябрь*, кн. 5, стр. 182–191, 1958.

Белоусов, Иван, "Цветок неповторимый", Сб. *Памяти Есенина* (Москва, изд. Всероссийского союза поэтов, 1926).

Беляев, И., *Подлинный Есенин. Социально-психологический этюд* (Воронеж, Группа писателей Чернозем, 1927).

Бенни, Як., "Вокруг Сергея Есенина", *Печать и Революция* (Москва), № 6, 1926.

Бергман, Г., "Есенин – знамя упадочных настроений", *Комсомольская Правда* (Москва), 15/VI, 1926.

Березарк, И., "Лирические темы Сергея Есенина", Сб. *Сергею Есенину* (Ростов н/Д., изд. Трудовой Дон, 1926).

Бескин, Эм., "'Кофта' Маяковского и 'скандалы' Есенина", *Театральная Москва*, 7–11/VI, № 43, 1922.

Благой, Д., "Материалы к характеристики Сергея Есенина (из архива поэта Ширяевца)", *Красная Новь* (Москва), № 2, 1926.

Блок, Ал., *Дневник. 1917–1921* (Ленинград, Писатели в Ленинграде, 1928).

Блюм, В., "Есенин – 'Пугачов'", *Театральная Москва*, № 23, 1922.

Бобрышев, И., "Кто в чем виноват?", *Комсомольская Правда* (Москва), 10/VI, 1926.

Бойчевский, В., "Ново-крестьянская поэзия", Сб. *Современная художественная проза и поэзия* (Москва, изд. Новая Москва, 1926).

Борисов, С., "Вечер Есенина", *Известия* (Москва), 23/VIII, 1923.

——, "К биографии Сергея Есенина", *Красная Нива* (Москва), № 2, 1926.

Брайнина, Б., "Есенин в 'Москве кабацкой'", Сб. *Есенин* (Москва, изд. Работник Просвещения, 1926).

Браун, Як., "Без пафоса – без формы", *Новая Россия* (Москва), № 1, 1926.

——, "Деревни последние песни", *Московский Понедельник*, 7/VIII, № 8, 1922.

Бродский, Н. Л. и Сидоров, Н. П. (состав.), *От символизма до "Октября". Литературные манифесты* (Москва, изд. Новая Москва, 1924).

Брюсов, Валерий, "Вчера, сегодня и завтра русской поэзии", *Печать и Революция* (Москва), № 7, 1922.

——, *Основы стиховедения*, 2-е изд. (Москва, ГИЗ, 1924).

——, "Рецензия на книгу Есенина 'Голубень'", *Художественное Слово* (Москва), № 1, 1920.

——, "Смысл современной поэзии", *Художественное Слово* (Москва), № 2, 1921.

Брыкин, Н., "Конец поэта", *Новая Вечерняя Газета* (Ленинград), 29/XII, 1925.

Буданцев, Сергей, "На родине Есенина", *Известия* (Москва), 13/IV, 1926.

С. Б. (Буданцев, С.), "Рецензия на сборник 'Конница бурь'", *Художественное слово* (Москва), № 2, 1921.

Бурсов, Б., "С. Есенин", *Литературный Современник*, № 5–6, 1940.

Бухарин, Н., *Злые заметки, о писательском этике* (Ленинград, Прибой, 1927).

З. Б. (Бухарова, Зоя), "Рецензия на книгу Есенина 'Радуница'", *Нива*, лит. прилож., № 5, 1916.

Быстрый, Мих, "Урок богеме", *Жизнь Искусства* (Ленинград), № 2, 1926.

В., "Встреча Есенина (о вечере в Политехническом музее, 21/VIII, 1923 г.)", *Вечерние Известия* (Москва), 27/VIII, 1923.

В., "Московский вечер в Берлине. (Отчет о вечере Есенина и Кусикова с докладом А. Толстого и А. Ветлугина, 1/VI, 1922 г.)", *Накануне* (Берлин), № 53, 1922.

М. В., "Сергей Есенин", *Рабочий Край* (Иваново-Вознесенск), 3/I, 1926.

Вак, "Крестьянские поэты", *Гудки* (Москва), № 12, 1919.

Васильев, С., "Живая поэзия. К 60-летию со дня рождения С. Есенина", *Огонек* (Москва), № 40, 1955.

Василевский, И, (Не-Буква), "Писатели о себе", *Накануне*, лит. прилож. (Берлин), № 11, 1922.

Вельтман, С., *Восток в художественной литературе* (ГИД, 1928).

Венгров, Н., "Рецензия на книгу Есенина 'Радуница'". *Современный Мир* (Петроград), № 2, 1916.

Венский, К., "Памяти Есенина". *Власть Труда* (Владикавказ), 31/XII, 1925.

Вержбицкий, Николай, *Встречи с Есениным* (Тбилиси, изд. Заря Востока, 1961).

——, "Встречи с Сергеем Есениным", *Звезда*, № 2, 1958.

А. В. (Ветлугин, А.), "Нам хочется вам нежно сказать... (О вечере Есенина и Кусикова 1/I, 1922 г. в Берлине)", *Накануне* (Берлин), 4/VI, № 57, 1922.

Ветлугин, А., "Нежная болезнь", *Накануне*, лит. прилож. (Берлин), № 6, 1922.

А. В. (Ветлугин, А.), "У С. А. Есенина (беседа)", *Накануне*, лит. прилож. (Берлин), № 47, 1922.

Вешнев, В., *Книга характериск. Капризный князь* (Москва, Госиздат, 1928).

——, "Литература памяти С. Есенина", *Учительская газета*, 24/VI, 26/VI, 1926.

Винников, Виктор, "Путь Есенина к смерти", *Коммунист* (Астрахань), 3/I, 1926.

Виноградская, Софья, *Как жил Сергей Есенин* (Москва, Огонек, 1926).

Владиславлев, И. В., *Русские писатели* (Библиография о Есенине), (Ленинград, 4-е изд., ГИЗ, 1924).

Волин, Борис, "Прав ли суд? К делу четырех поэтов", *Рабочая Москва*, № 284, 1923.

Вольпин, Валентин, *Памятка о Сергее Есенине* (Москва, изд. Сегодня, 1926).

——, "О Сергее Есенине", Сб. *С. А. Есенин* (Москва, изд. ГИЗ, 1926).

——, "Пьеса 'Есенин'. (О пьесе Р. Ивнева и О. Леонидова)", *Красная Газета* (Ленинград), веч. вып., 26/III, 1926.

Воронский, А., "Литературные заметки. (С. Есенини и Л. Леонов)", *Прожектор* (Москва), № 5, 1925.

——, *Литературные записи* (Статьи: "Об отошедшем", "Памяти Есенина") (Москва, изд. Круг, 1926).

——, "Литературные отклики", *Красная Новь* (Москва), № 2, 1922.

——, *Литературные типы* (Москва, изд. Круг, 1925).

——, "Мистер Бритлинг пьет чашу до дня", *Красная Новь* (Москва), № 5, 1926.

——, "Об отошедшем", *Красная Новь* (Москва), № 1, 1926.

——, "Памяти Есенина (из воспоминаний)", *Красная Новь* (Москва), № 2, 1926.

——, "Полемические заметки", *Красная Новь* (Москва), № 5, 1924.

——, "С. Есенин", *Красная Новь* (Москва), № 1, 1924.

——, "Сергей Есенин" в *Собрании стихотворений* Есенина, т. I и т. II (Москва, изд. ГИЗ, 1926).

В-ский, "Рецензия на сборник 'С. А. Есенин', изд. ГИЗ", *Вечерняя Москва*, 17/VIII, 1926.

Вяткин, Г., "Сергей Есенин", *Советская Сибирь* (Ново-Николаевск), 30/XII, 1925.

Р. Г., "Рецензия на I-й том 'Собрания стихотворений' Есенина", *Призыв* (Владимир), 16/IV, 1926.

Гайсарьян, С., "Сергей Есенин". В кн.: Есенин, С. *Стихотворения и поэмы* (Ленинград, 1960).

——, "Сергей Есенин", *Литературная Газета*, 8/X, 1955.

Галицкий, Я., "Сергей Есенин без имажинизма (Есенин раньше и теперь)", *Нижегородская Коммуна*, 15/XII, 1925.

Гейне, Яков, "Сергей Есенин", *Красное Запорожье*, 28/I, 1926.

Герасимов, Иван, "В тупике (на смерть Сергея Есенина)", *Вятская Правда*, 3/I, 1926.

Герман, Эммануил, "Сережа", *Вечерняя Москва*, 31/XII, 1925.

Гиляровский, В. А., "О самоубийстве (ответ на анкету)", *Вечерняя Москва*, 7/I, 1926.

Гиппиус, З., "Судьба Есениных", *Последние Новости* (Париж), 28/I, 1926.

Глубоковский, Борис, "Сергей Есенин", *Новые Соловки*, 7/II, 1926.

Голубков, В. В., Горностаев, Н. П., Лукьяновский, Б. Е., Сахаров, В. И. (состав.), *Марксистская хрестоматия по литературе*, 2-е изд. (Москва, Новая Москва, 1926) (Статьи о Есенине А. Воровского и В. Л. Львова-Рогачевского).

—— (состав.), *Писатели современники* (Москва, изд. ГИЗ, 1925).

Горбов, Д., *У нас за рубежом* (изд. Круг, 1928).

Горн, К., "Рецензия на I-й том 'Собрания Стихотворений' Есенина", *Пролетарский Путь* (Ульяновск), 13/IV, 1926.

Горный, Сергей, "С. Есенин", *Руль* (Берлин), № 1544, 1926.

Городецкий, С., "Октябрь в художественной литературе", *Известия* (Москва), 7/XI, 1926.

——, "О Сергее Есенине. Воспоминания", *Новый Мир* (Москва), № 2, 1926.

——, "Памяти С. Есенина", Сб. *Есенин* (Москва, изд. Работник Просвещения, 1926).

С. Г. (Сергей Городецкий), "Рецензия на книгу Есенина 'Пугачов' ", *Труд* (Москва), № 75, 1922.

Городецкий, С., "Сергей Есенин", *Искусство Трудящихся* (Москва), № 1, 1926.

——, "Текущий момент в поэзии", *Советское Искусство* (Москва), № 2, 1926.

Городской, Я., "Сергей Есенин", *Красный Николаев*, 3/I, 1926.

Горшкова, Л., "Опыт социологического анализа творчества Есенина", Сб. *Есенин* (Москва, изд. Работник Просвещения, 1926).

Горький, М., *О писателях. Сергей Есенин* (Москва, изд. Федерация, 1929).

Грандов, М., "О Сергее Есенине", *Бедность* (Москва), 31/XII, 1925.

Грацианская, Нина, "О нечаянной радости (воспоминания о Есенине)", Сб. *Сергею Есенину* (Ростов н/Д., изд. Трудовой Дон, 1926).

Григоренко, О., "Сергій Есенін" (на украинском языке), *Пролетарская Правда* (Киев), 30/XII, 1925.

Григорьев, С., *Пророки и предтечи последнего завета. Имажинисты* (Москва, изд. Саав,1921).

Гриф, "Поэт озерной тоски", *Власть Труда* (Иркутск), 1/I, 1926.

Груздев, Илья, "Рецензия на книгу Есенина 'Москва кабацкая' ", *Русский Современник* (Ленинград), № 3, 1924.

——, "Русская поэзия в 1918–1923 г.г. (К эволюции поэтических школ)", *Книга и Революция* (Петроград), № 3 (27), 1923.

Грузинов, Иван, "Есенин". Сб. *С. А. Есенин* (Москва, изд. ГИЗ, 1926).

——, *Имажинизма основное* (Москва, изд. Имажинисты, 1921).

——, "Как зарабатывают на Есенине (о книгах А. Крученых)", *Красная Газета* (Ленинград), веч. вып., 10/III, 1926.

——, "О смерти Есенина", Сб. *Памяти Есенина* (Москва, изд. Всероссийского союза поэтов, 1926).

——, "Пушкин и мы", *Гостиница для путешествующих в прекрасном* (Москва), № 1 (3), 1924.

——, *С. Есенин разговаривает о литературе и искусстве* (*Воспоминания*) (Москва, изд. Всероссийский союз поэтов, 1927).

Гуль, Р., *Жизнь на Фукса* (Москва, изд. Госиздат, 1927).

——, "Рецензия на книгу Есенина 'Избранное' ", *Новая Русская Книга* (Берлин), № 2, 1923.

Гусман, Борис, *Поэты. Пять характеристик* (Москва, изд. Огонек, 1925).

——, *Сто поэтов. Литературные портреты* (Тверь, изд. Октябрь, 1923).

Г-ъ, В., "Рецензия на книгу Есенина 'Преображение'", *Пролетарская Культура* (Москва), № 6, 1919.

Д., "Беспутный гений. Рецензия на сборник 'С. А. Есенин', изд. ГИЗ", *Рабочий Клич* (Рязань), 1926.

Д., "Неудачная пьеса 'Есенин'. (О пьесе Р. Ивнева и О. Леонидова)", *Вечерняя Москва*, 20/III, 1926.

Дальний, И., "Сергей Есенин", *Борьба* (Сталинград), 10/I, 1926.

Дальний, Степан, "Воспоминания о Есенине", *Известия* (Саратов), 3/I, 1926.

——, "Гибель крестьянского поэта", *Советская Деревня* (Саратов), 6/I, 1926.

Данилов, Мих, "Певец голубени", *Бакинский Рабочий*, 31/XII, 1925.

Деев-Хомяковский, Г., "Правда о Есенине", *На литературном посту* (Москва), № 4, 1926.

"Дело четырех поэтов ('Случай в пивной' перед товарищеским судом работников печати)", *Вечерняя Москва*, 11/XII, 1923.

Дивильковский, А., "На трудном подъеме", *Новый Мир* (Москва), кн. 7, 1926.

Длигач, Лев., "Есенiн". (На украинском языке), *Пролетарская Правда* (Киев), 3/I, 1926.

Д'ор, О. Л., "Сергей Есенин в Америке. Личные воспоминания", *Правда* (Москва), 28/III, 1923.

Друзин, В., "Путь Есенина", *Красная Газета*, веч. вып. (Ленинград), 15/V, 1925.

——, "Сергей Есенин", *Звезда* (Ленинград), № 2, 1926.

——, *Сергей Есенин* (Ленинград, изд. Прибой, 1927).

——, "Сергей Есенин. К годовщине со дня смерти", *Труд* (Ленинград), 9/I, 1927.

Дымшиц, А., "Сергей Есенин". В книге: *Есенин, С. Стихотворения и поэмы* (Ленинград, 1956).

Дынник, Валентина, "Есенин", *Прожектор* (Москва), № 2, 1926.

——, "Из литературы о Есенине", *Красная Новь* (Москва), № 6, 1926.

——, *Лирический роман Есенина*. Отд. оттиск из сборника *Памяти Есенина* (Москва, изд. Всероссийского Союза Поэтов, 1926).

Евгеньев, А., "Перлы и адаманты имажинизма", *Вестник Литературы*, №№ 10 (34), 11 (35), 1921.

Евгеньев-Максимов, В., *Очерк истории новейшей русской литературы* (Ленинград, изд. 2-е ГИЗ, 1926).

Евдокимов, Иван, "Сергей Александрович Есенин", Сб. *С. А. Есенин* (Москва, изд. ГИЗ, 1926).

Ежов, И. С., *Революционная русская поэзия XX века* (Москва, изд. Новая Москва, 1925).

Ермилов, Вл., "Почему мы не любим Федоров Жицей?", *На литературном посту* (Москва), № 4, 1926.

——, *Против мещанства и упадочничества* (Москва, изд. Госиздат, 1927).

Есенин. Жизнь – личность – творчество. Сборник лит.-худ. секции Центр. дома работников просвещения, под редакцией Е. Ф. Никитиной (Москва, изд. Работник Просвещения, 1926).

Есенина, Александра, "Это все мне родное и близкое. О С. Есенине" (Воспоминания). Лит. редакция А. А. Коваленкова, *Молодая Гвардия*, №№ 7, 8, 1960.

Есенина, Екатерина, "В Константинове", *Альманах Литературная Рязань*, II, 1957.

Жаворонков, А., "Два письма С. Есенина", *Новый Мир* (Москва), № 5, 1957.

——, "Образ вождя в поэзии С. Есенина", *Нева*, № 4, 1958.

——, "С. Есенин, 'Анна Снегина'", *Вопросы Литературы*, № 7, 1957.

Жиц, Федор, "Почему мы любим Есенина (этюд)", *Красная Новь* (Москва), № 5, 1926.

——, "Рецензия на книгу Есенина 'Стихи' (1920–1924 г.г.)", *Красная Новь* (Москва), № 3, 1925.

Забежинский, Григорий, "О творчестве и личности Сергея Есенина", *Мосты* (Мюнхен), № 4, 1960.

Залшупин, С., *Портреты и офорты современных русских писателей* (Берлин, изд. Гамаюн, 1923).

Захаров-Мэнский, Н., "Книги стихов 1919 года", *Вестник Театра* (Москва), № 58, 1920.

——, "Московские поэты. (Корреспонденция из Москвы)", *Жизнь Искусства* (Петроград), 19/VI, 1920.

Зелинский, К., "О Есенине", *Октябрь*, № 10, 1955.

——, "О Есенине. К 65-летию со дня рождения", *Смена*, № 19, 1960.

——, "По поводу одного судебного дела. (О литературном наследии С. Есенина)", *Литература и Жизнь*, 5/VIII, 1960.

——, "Поэзия Сергея Есенина". В книге: Есенин, С. *Сочинения* (Москва, 1956).

Земсков, В., "А. Блок и С. Есенин. (Публикация писем, хранящихся в Центр. гос. архиве литературы и искусства СССР)", *Огонек* (Москва), № 48, 1955.

——, "Горький и Есенин. (К истории взаимоотношений)", *Урал*, № 6, 1961.

——, "Как создавался 'Пугачов' Сергея Есенина", *Урал*, № 5, 1960.

——, "Монография о Есенине", *Вопросы Литературы*, № 4, 1961.

——, "Сергей Есенин в Ташкенте. (К биографии писателя)", *Звезда Востока*, № 3, 1960.

Земсков, В. и Правдина, И., "В творческой лаборатории Есенина", *Русская Литература*, № 1, 1960.

Зинин, Денис, "Худощавый и низкорослый...", *Тверская Правда*, 1926.

Зорев, А., "Трагедия богемы", *Вечерняя Москва*, 29/XII, 1925.

И. Л., "О Есенине", *Беднота* (Москва), 21/IV, 1926.

Иванов, Ф., *Красный Парнас, литературно-критические очерки* (Берлин, изд. Русск. Унив. Т-во, 1922).

——, "Мужицкая Русь. (Н. Клюев, С. Есенин)", *Голос Росии*, 20/VII, 1921.

Иванов-Разумник, Р. В., "Две России". Сб. *Скифы*, т. II (Петроград, изд. Скифы, 1918).

——, "Поэты и революция. (Есенин, Клюев, Орешин)", Сб. *Красный Звон* (Петроград, изд. Революционная Мысль, 1918).

——, Поэты и революция", Сб. *Скифы*, т. II (Петроград, 1918).

——, *Россия и Инония* (Берлин, изд. Скифы, 1920).

——, "Россия и Инония", *Нам Путь* (Москва), № 5, 1918.

——, "Россия и Инония", Сб. *Россия и Инония* (Берлин, изд. Скифы, 1923).

——, *Русская литература от 70-х г.г. до наших дней* (Берлин, изд. Скифы, 1922).

——, "Три богатыря. (Есенин, Клюев, В. Гиппиус)", *Летопись Дома Литераторов* (Петроград), № 3 (7), 1921.

Ивнев, Рюрик, "Акростих Есенина", *Вечерняя Москва*, 12/IV, 1926.

——, "О Есенине". Сб. *С. А. Есенин* (Москва, изд. ГИЗ, 1926).

——, "Открытое письмо Сергею Есенину и Анатолию Мариенгофу от 5 декабря 1920 года". Сб. *Имажинисты* (Москва, изд. Имажинисты, 1921).

——, *Четыре выстрела (в Есенина, Кусикова, Мариенгофа, Шершеневича)* (Москва, изд. Имажинисты, 1921).

"Из литературного наследия Сергея Есенина: I. Стихотворения. II. Письма" (Публикация, коммент. Е. Динерштейна), *Вопросы Литературы*, № 3, 1960.

Ильина, А. (Сеферянц), "Русь – Рас...сея – Россия – СССР", Сб. *Есенин* (Москва, изд. Работник Просвещения, 1926).

"Имажинисты и А. В. Луначарский", *Вестник Литературы* (Петроград), № 11, 1921.

Инбер, Вера, "Сергей Есенин", *Новый Зритель* (Москва), № 2, 1926.

Ингулов, С., "В молитвенном экстазе (о книге Есенина 'Березовый ситец')", *Коммуна* (Калуга), 11/VIII, 1925.

Иноков, А. (псевдоним Инн. Оксенова), "Певучий зов (Поэт – крестьянин С. Есенин)", *Жизнь Железнодорожника* (Петербург), № 30, 1918.

Иофанов, Д., "Сергей Есенин (К 30-летию со дня смерти)", *Советская Украина*, кн. 12, 1955.

Ирецкий, В., "Плавильня слов", *Вестник Литературы* (Петроград), № 9 (21), 1920.

К., "Рецензия на сборник 'С. А. Есенин', изд. ГИЗ", *Заря Востока* (Тифлис), 5/IX, 1926.

К. Б., "Сергей Есенин", *Рабочий Клич* (Рязань), 31/XII, 1925.

К. С., "Сергей Есенин", *Степная Правда* (Семипалатинск), 1/I, 1926.

Каверин, В., "О Сергее Есенине (заметка)", *Красная Газета*, веч. вып. (Ленинград), № 316 (1004), 1925.

Камский, Мих., "Сергей Есенин", *Труд* (Баку), 30/XII, 1925.

Кеук, "Рецензия на сб. 'Плавильня слов'", *Книга и Революция* (Петроград), № 3–4, 1920.

Кий, "Рецензия на книги Есенина 'Радуница' и 'Преображение'", *Книга и Революция* (Петроград), № 7, 1921.

Кириллов, Алексей, "Рецензия на 'Собрание стихотворений' Есенина, т. I", *Ленинградская Правда*, 18/IV, 1926.

Кириллов, В., "Встречи с Есениным", Сб. *С. А. Есенин* (Москва, изд. ГИЗ, 1926).

Киршон, В., "Сергей Есенин", *Молодая Гвардия* (Москва), № 1, 1926.

——, *Сергей Есенин* (Ленинград, изд. Прибой, 1926).

Киселев, Алексей, "Мессианство в русской поэзии", *Путь*, 25/III и 1/IV, №№ 32, 33, 1921.

Кисин, Б., "Сергей Есенин", *Рабочий Клич* (Рязань), 3/I, 1926.

Кисин, Веньямин, "Октябрь в отражениях современной литературы", Сб. *Из недр земли* (Рязань, изд. ГИЗ, 1922).

Клейнборт, Л., "Печатные органы интеллигенции из народа", *Северные Записки*, № 6, 1915.

——, "Поэты-пролетарии о войне", *Современный Мир* (Петроград), № 3, 1916.

Клычков, Сергей, "Лысая гора", *Красная Новь* (Москва), № 5, 1923.

Клюев, Николай, *Плач о Есенине* (Нью Иорк, изд. Мост, 1954).

Князев, В., *Ржаные апостолы* (Клюев и клюевщина) (Ленинград, изд. Прибой, 1924).

Коган, П. С., "Есенин", *Вечерняя Москва*, 31/XII, 1925.

——, *Литература этих лет. 1917–1923 г.г.*, 2-е изд. (Иваново-Вознесенск, изд. Основа, 1924).

——, "Памяти Есенина", *Печать и Революция* (Москва), № 2, 1926.

——, "Сергей Есенин", *Зрелица* (Свердловск), № 4, 1926.

——, "Сергей Есенин", *Красная Панорама* (Ленинград), № 2 (96), 1926.

——, "С. Есенин (Литературные силуэты)", *Красная Новь* (Москва), № 3, 1922.

Константинов, Л., "Поэтический обзор за май в Москве", *Знамя* (Москва), № 3–4 (5–6), 1920.

Королев, Вл., "Рецензия на книгу Есенина 'Песнь о великом походе'", *Коммуна* (Калуга), 13/V, 1925.

——, "Русское стихотворчество XX века. Нео-крестьянская поэзия", *Корабль* (Калуга), № 5–6, 1922.

Коряллов, Михаил, "'Есенинщина' и советская молодежь", *Возрождение* (Париж), тетрадь 15, 1951.

Кофанов, Пав., "Еще двое... (Некролог С. Есенина и Анат. Арского)", *Молот* (Ростов н/Д.), 1/I, 1926.

168

BIBLIOGRAPHY

Кошечкин, С., "К вопросу о мастерстве Сергея Есенина", В: *Проблемы социалистического реализма* (Москва, 1959).
Красильников, В., "Вокруг Есенина", *Книгоноша* (Москва), № 22, 1926.
——, "Молодые поэты", *На Литературном Посту* (Москва), № 7–8, 1926.
——, "Рецензия на книги Есенина 'Березовый ситец', 'Русь Советская', 'О России и революции', и 'Персидские мотивы'", *Книгоноша* (Москва), № 26, 1925.
Кр. В. (Красильников, В.), "Рецензия на *Собрание стихотворений* Есенина, т. VI", *Наша Газета* (Москва), 6/I, 1926.
Красильников, В., "Сергей Есенин", *Книгоноша* (Москва), № 1 (122), 1926.
——, "Сергей Есенин", *Печать и Революция* (Москва), № 7, 1925.
Красильников, Павел, "Есенин", *Оренбургский Рабочий*, № 2 (17), 1926.
Крути, И., "Сергей Есенин", *Известия* (Одесса), 30/XII, 1925.
Крученых, А., *Гибель Есенина* (Продукция № 134б) (Москва, изд. автора, 1926).
——, *Есенин и "Москва кабацкая"* (I. Есенин и "Москва кабацкая"; II. Любовь хулигана; III. Две автобиографии Есенина) (Продукция № 135) (Москва, изд. автора, 1926).
——, *Лики Есенина от херувима до хулигана, Есенин в жизни и портретах* (Продукция № 137) (Москва, 1926).
——, *На борьбу с хулиганством в литературе* (Продукция № 140) (Москва, изд. автора, 1926).
——, *Новый Есенин. О первом томе "Собрания Стихотворений"* (Продукция № 138) (Москва, изд. автора, 1926).
——, "Псевдо-крестьянская поэзия. Есенин и его евангелисты", Сб. *На путях искусства* (Москва, изд. Пролеткульта, 1926).
——, *Хулиган Есенин* (Продукция № 141) (Москва, изд. автора, 1926).
——, *Черная шайка Есенина* (Продукция № 136) (Москва, изд. автора, 1926).
Кузнецов, В., "А. М. Горький о С. Есенине", в: *Русская советская литература. Сборник статьей* (Горький, 1958).
Кузько, П., "Поэты из народа (о Клюеве и Есенине)", *Кубанская Мысль*, сентябрь, 1915.
Кулемкин, Александр, "Рецензия на книгу А. Крученых 'Драма Есенина'", *Молодая Гвардия* (Москва), № 2, 1926.
Кулинин, Андрей, "Как работал Есенин", *Советская Украина*, кн. 7, 1957.
——, *Сергей Есенин. Критико-биографический очерк* (Киев, изд. Киевского Университета, 1959).
Кусиков, Александр, "Битюг (Клюев и Есенин)", *Накануне* (Берлин), лит. прилож., № 34, 1922.
——, "Мапа и пама имажинизма". *Вещь* (Берлин), № 1–2, 1922.
——, "'Только раз ведь живем мы, только раз' … Памяти Есенина", *Парижский Вестник*, № 207, 1926.
Л. А., "Сергей Есенин", *Литературная Газета* (Казань), № 2, 1922.
Лавренов, Борис, "Казненный дегенератами", *Красная Газета* (Ленинград), веч. вып., 30/XII, 1925.
Лапшин, Ник, "Стихи Есенина (О I-м томе 'Собрания стихотворений' Есенина)", *Советский Юг* (Ростов н/Д.), 9/IV, 1926.
Левидов, Мих., "'Народная поэзия'", *Журнал Журналов* (Петроград), № 30, 1915.
——, "Смерть учит", *Вечерняя Москва*, № 3, 1926.
Левин, Венянин, "Есенин в Америке", *Новое Русское Слово* (Нью Иорк), 9–13/VIII, 1953.
Левый, "Рецензия на журнал 'Знамя' (М), №№ 7, 8, 9, 10", *Трудовая Мысль* (Тверь), № 1, 1921.
Лежнев, А., *Вопросы литературы и критики* (Москва, изд. Круг, 1926).

——, "Литературный обзор. (О книгах Есенина 'Москва кабацкая' и 'Стихи')", *Печать и Революция*, № 1, 1925.

——, "Памяти Сергея Есенина", *Бакинский Рабочий*, 1/I, 1926.

——, "'Пугачов' Есенина", *Вестник Искусств*, № 22, 1922.

——, "Рецензия на I-й и II-й томы 'Собрания стихотворений' Есенина", *Правда* (Москва), 19/V. (1926).

——, "Рецензия на трагедию Есенина 'Пугачов'", *Казанский Библиофил*, № 3, 1922.

——, "Сергей Есенин", *Правда* (Москва), 30/XII, 1925.

Лежнев, И., "Гошапка (О Есенине, глава 'Две растраты')", *Новая Россия* (Москва), № 1, 1926.

Лейтес, А., "Сергій Есенін (на украинском языке)", *Культура и Побут* (Харьков), 3/I, 1926.

Лелевич, Г., "О болезнях и опасностях". Сб. *Против упадочничества* (Москва, изд. Правда и Беднота, 1926).

——, "О сергее Есенине", *Октябрь* (Москва), № 3, 1924.

——, "По журнальным окопам", *Молодая Гвардия* (Москва), № 7, 1924.

——, *Сергей Есенин. Его творческий путь* (Гомель, изд. Гомельский Рабочий, 1926).

Леонидов, Олег, "Живой Есенин", *Красная Газета* (Ленинград), веч. вып., 26/I, 1926.

——, "Цветок неповторимый. (О сб. 'Памяти Есенина')", *Красная Газета* (Ленинград), веч. вып., 27/V, 1926.

Леонов, Леонид, "Умер поэт", *Тридцать Дней* (Москва), № 2, 1926.

Лесоклинский, Г., "Поэт Сергей Есенин", *Сибирский Гудок* (Ново-Николаевск), 9/I, 1926.

Лесс, А., "На родине Сергея Есенина (По воспоминаниям сестры поэта А. А. Есениной)", *Нева*, № 7, 1955.

Либединский, Юрий, "Воспоминания о Сергее Есенине", *На литературном Посту* (Москва), № 1, 1926.

Либерман, Гр., "Певец земли родины", *Театр и Кино* (Баку), № 11, 1926.

Лигарский, Н. (псевдоним Клестова, Н.), "Заметки о поэзии и поэтах". *Творчество* (Москва), №№ 1–3, 4–5, 1919.

Линковский, В., "О Сергее Есенине. (Рецензия на книгу Есенина 'Страна Советская')", *Заря Востока* (Тифлис), 20/II, 1925.

Л-кин, А. (Липецкий, А.), "Крестьянский поэт Сергей Есенин", *Взаимопомощ* (Москва), № 2, 1926.

Л-ов, Г., "Сергей Есенин", *Советская Мысль* (Великий Устюг), 1/I, 1926.

"Литературное наследие С. Есенина. (Материалы комиссии ССП СССР", *Литературная Газета*, 8/XII, 1956.

Литовский, О., "Памяти Сергея Есенина", *Наша Газета* (Москва), № 1, 1926.

Логвиненко, А., "У героини стихов Есенина (Шагане Нерсесовна Тальян)", *Московский Комсомолец*, 3/XII, 1958.

Лукьянов, Мих., "'Последний поэт деревни', о Сергее Есенине", *Коммуна* (Калуга), 31/XII, 1925.

Лукьянов, С., "Земля и солнце (О вечере Есенина и Кусикова 1/VI, 1922 г. в Берлине)", *Накануне* (Берлин), 4/VI, № 15, 1922.

Луначарский, А. В., *Доклад. Упадочное настроение среди молодежи и прения* (Изд. Коммунистическая Академия, Москва, 1927).

——, "Об имажинистах", *Печать и Революция* (Москва), № 1, 1921.

Луцкий, Ф., "К поэтике С. Есенина". Сб. *Есенин* (Москва, изд. Работник Просвещения, 1926).

Львов-Рогачевский, В. Л., *Имажинизм и его образоносцы* (На части книг местом издания обозначен г. Ревель), изд. Орднас. (Название образовалось из перевернутого слова Сандро – сокращенное имя Александра Кусикова), 1921.

——, *Книга для чтения по истории новейшей русской литературы* (Ленинград, изд. Прибой, 1924).

——, *Новейшая русская литература*, 5-е перераб. (Москва, изд. Мир, 1926).

——, "Новое слово", *Новый Мир* (Москва), № 158, 1921.

——, "Ново-крестьянская поэзия", *Путь* (Москва), № 5, 1919.

——, *Очерки по истории новейшей русской литературы. 1881–1919 г.г.* (Москва, изд. ВЦСПС, 1920).

——, *Очерки пролетарской литературы* (Москва-Ленинград, изд. Моск. Акц. Издат. О-ва, 1927).

——, *Поэзия новой России. Поэты полей и городских окраин* (Москва, изд. Книго-издательство Писателей, 1919).

Лягин, Сем., "Суриковский литературно-музыкальный кружок", *Друг Народа* (Москва), № 1, 1918.

Ляховец, Д., "Есенин", *Тверская Правда*, 20/I, 1926.

——, "Мое интервью (вместо фельетона)", *Вечерние Известия* (Москва), 12/V, 1924.

Мансфред, А., "Гибель Сергея Есенина", *Известия* (Саратов), 1/I, 1926.

Мар, С., "Сгоревший поэт", *Новая Вечерняя Газета* (Ленинград), 29/XII, 1925.

Мариенгоф, Антолий, *Буян-остров* (Москва, изд. Имажинисты, 1920).

——, *Воспоминания о Есенине* (На обложке: О Сергее Есенине. Воспоминания) (= *Библиотека Огонька* № 148) (Москва, изд. Огонек, 1926).

——, "Письмо С. Есенину", *Гостиница для путешествующих в прекрасном* (Москва), № 2, 1923.

А. М. (Анатолий Мариенгоф), "Рецензия на книгу Есенина 'Пугачов'", *Гостиница для путешествующих в прекрасном* (Москва), № 1, 1922.

Мариенгоф, А., *Роман без вранья* (Берлин, изд. Петрополис, 1929).

Марченко, А., "Золотая словесная груда..." (О некоторых особенностях образной системы Есенина-лирика), *Вопросы Литературы*, № 1, 1959.

Масчан, С., "Из архива С. Есенина" (Публикация материалов из архива, принадлежавшего С. А. Толстой-Есениной), *Новый Мир* (Москва), № 12, 1959.

Медведев, П., "Крестьянские предреволюционные писатели", *Литературная Учеба*, № 5, 1935.

Мечтатель, В., "Светлый остров". Сб. *Печаль полей* (Чита, изд. Центр. Дальне-Восточн. К-та Обществ. организ. по оказ. пом. голод. России, 1922).

Миклашевская, А., "Встречи с Сергеем Есениным. (Отрывки из воспоминаний 1923–1924 г.г.)", *Учительская Газета*, 4/X, 1960.

Мкртчан, Л. М., "С. Есенин и город", *Науч. Труды* (Ереванский университет), том 70 (= *Серия филол. наук*, вып. 7, часть I) (1960).

Москвич, "Стружки. Установка на грубость", *Вечерняя Москва*, 5/V, 1926.

Мурашев, М., "А. Блок и С. Есенин". Сб. *Есенин* (Москва, изд. Работник Просвещения, 1926).

——, "Сергей Есенин в Петрограде". Сб. *С. А. Есенин* (Москва, изд. ГИЗ, 1926).

Н., "Опять Наседкин", *На литературном посту* (Москва), № 4, 1926.

Н., "Рецензия на книгу Есенина 'Голубень'", *Сирена* (Воронеж), № 1, 1918.

Н., "Рецензия на книгу Есенина 'Москва кабацкая'", *Сибирские Огни* (Ново-Николаевск), № 4, 1924.

М. Н., "Сергей Есенин. (К выходу II-го тома 'Собрания стихотворений'", *Рабочий Путь* (Омск), 6/I, 1926.

Наседкин, В., *Последний год Есенина* (Москва, Никитинские субботники, 1927).

——, "Село Есенино", *Красная Нива* (Москва), № 26, 1926.

Наумов, Е. И., *Сергей Есенин. Жизнь и творчество* (Ленинград, изд. Учпедгиз, 1960).

Никитин, Николай, "Встречи", *Красная Новь* (Москва), № 3, 1926.

——, "О Сергее Есенине (заметка)", *Красная Газети* (Ленинград), веч. вып., № 316 (1004), 1925.

Никитина, Е., "Поэты и направления. (Пути новейшей поэзии)", Сб. *Свиток*, № 3 (Москва, изд. Земля и Фабрика, 1924).

——, "Сергей Есенин". Сб. *Есенин* (Москва, изд. Работник Просвещения, 1926).

Никонов, В., "Поэт большого сердца", *Стержень* (Ульяновск), № 1, ноябрь, 1925.

Никулин, Л., "Незабываемые встречи. (Из воспоминаний)", *Дон*, № 4, 1957.

Оболенский, С., "Неизвестное стихотворение Есенина", *Нева*, № 11, 1959.

Обрадович, С., "Образное мышление", *Кузница* (Москва), № 2, 1920.

Оксенов, Инн., "В защиту литературы", *Красная Газета* (Ленинград), веч. вып., 12/VI, 1925.

——, "Из воспоминаний о Сергее Есенине", Сб. *Памяти Есенина* (Москва, изд. Всероссийского Союза Поэтов, 1926).

——, "Литературный год", *Новый Журнал для всех* (Петроград), № 1, 1916.

——, "Памяти С. Есенина", *Красная Газета* (Ленинград), 28/XII, 1926.

——, "Рецензия на книгу Есенина 'Москва кабацкая'", *Звезда* (Ленинград), № 4, 1924.

——, "Русская художественная литература за 1924 г.", *Ленинградская Правда*, 1/I, 1925.

——, "Слово пророка (о поэме 'Инония')", *Знамя Борьбы* (Ленинград), 26/V, 1918.

Олендер, С., "Сергей Есенин", *Молодой Ленинец* (Москва), 30/XII, 1925.

Олидорт, Б., "Рецензия на книгу 'Радуница'", *Приазовский Край* (Ростов н/Д.), № 211, 1916.

Ольшевец, М., "О жизни и смерти Сергея Есенина", *Известия* (Одесса), 6/I, 1926.

"О нездоровых настроениях и художественной литературе (сводка писем читателей)", *Комсомольская Правда* (Москва), 13/VI, 1926.

Орешин, П., "Воспоминания. Мое знакомство с С. Есениным", *Красная Нива*, 26/XII, 1926.

——, "Рецензия на 2-й том 'Собрания стихотворений' Есенина", *Красная Новь* (Москва), № 6, 1926.

——, "Рецензия на 'Собрание стихотворений' Есенина, т. I", *Красная Новь* (Москва), № 5, 1926.

Осетров, Е., "На родине Есенина", *Литература и Жизнь*, 5/VI, 8/VI, 1960.

Осинский, Н., "Побеги травы. (Заметки читателя Ш.)", *Правда* (Москва), 4/VII, 1922.

"Отражения революции 1917 года в русской литературе", *Вестник Жизни* (Москва), № 2, 1918.

Павлов, Михаил, "Рецензия на книгу Есенина 'Пугачов'", *Книга и Революция* (Петроград), № 7 (19), 1922.

Павлов, С., "Стихотворения Есенина", *Литературное Обозрение*, № 11, 1940.

Памяти Есенина. Сборник. Статьи, воспоминания и стихи (Москва, изд. Всероссийского Союза Поэтов, 1926).

"Памяти Сергея Есенина", *Целина* (Ленинград), № 2, 1926.

Памятка о Сергее Есенине (Москва, изд. Сегодня, 1926).

Панов, М., "Как поняли приговор суда", *Рабочая Москва*, 20/XII, 1923.

Перелесков, Аким, "Плевицкая в шароварах", *Жернов* (Москва), № 5, 1926.

"Первое выступление Сергея Есенина. (О вечере в Политехническом музее 21/VIII, 1923 г.)", *Трудовая Копейка* (Москва), 25/III, 1923.

Перцов, В., "Маяковский и Есенин", *Вопросы Литературы*, № 3, 1961.

——, "Новое в современной русской поэзии", *Новый Путь* (Рига), 3/VII, № 123, 1921.

——, *Писатели и новая действительность.* стр. 358–364 (Москва, 1959).

Петров, Б., "В семье не без урода", *Рабочая Москва*, 20/XII, 1923.

Петровский, П., "Ответ тов. Правдухину", *Звезда*, кн. 3, 1927.

Пильняк, Борис, "О Сергее Есенине", *Журналист* (Москва), № 1, 1926.

"Письмо в редакцию Р. Ивнева, А. Мариенгофа, М. Ройзмана, В. Шершеневича, Н. Эрдмана (по поводу роспуска группы имажинистов)", *Новый Зритель* (Москва), № 35, 1924.

Плат, П., "Невозвратимое", *Приволжская Правда* (Кинешма), 10/I, 1926.

Плетнев, Р., "Сергей Есенин", *Уральская Новь* (Свердловск), № 1, 1926.

Покровский, Вл., *Три речи против С. Есенина* (Ленинград, 1927).

Покровский, Г., *Есенин. Есенинщина. Религия* (Москва, изд. Атеист, 1930).

Полетаев, Н., "Есенин за восемь лет". Сб. *С. А. Есенин* (Москва, изд. ГИЗ, 1926).

Полонская, Елизавета, "О Сергее Есенине (заметка)", *Красная Газета* (Ленинград), веч. вып. № 316 (1004), 1925.

Полонский, Вяч., *О современной литературе. Сергей Есенин* (изд. Госиздат, 1928).

——, *Очерки литературного движения революционной эпохи* (изд. Госиздат, 1929).

——, "Памяти Есенина", *Новый Мир* (Москва), № 1, 1926.

П. Иль, (Полтавский И.), "Памяти А. Соболя. 'Прохожий человек' (А. Соболь и С. Есенин)", *Красная Газета* (Ленинград), веч. вып., 11/VI, 1926.

Полянин, Андрей, "Рецензия на книгу Есенина 'Радуница'", *Северные Записки* (Петроград), № 6, 1916.

Похомов, Вас., "Памяти Сергея Есенина", *Коммуна* (Самара), 1/I, 1926.

"Поэт Есенин", *Смычка* (Павлово), 10/I, 1926.

Правдухин, В., "От Иванушки-Дурачка до Карла Маркса. О Сергее Есенине", *Звезда* (Ленинград), кн. 3, 1927.

——, "Сергей Есенин. Доклад, прочитанный 28/I, 1926 г. в Ленинграде на вечере работников печати памяти С. Есенина", *Сибирские Записки* (Новосибирск), № 1–2, 1926.

Прокушев, Юрий, "Поэзия Есенина за рубежом", *Литература и Жизнь*, 5/X 1960.

——, "Сергей Есенин. Литературные заметки и публикация новых материалов", *Литературная Рязань, Альманах* (Рязань), № 1, 1955.

——, *Сергей Есенин. Литературные заметки о детстве и юности поэта* (= *Б-ка Огонек*, № 46) (Москва, Правда, 1960).

——, *Сергей Есенин* (Москва, изд. Знание, 1958).

——, Юность Есенина (Москва, изд Московский Рабочий, 1963).

——, "Юношеские годы Сергея Есенина", изд. *Огонек* (Москва), № 2, 1957.

"Против есенинщины. На борьбу с упадочными настроениями части молодежи. (Выступление А. В. Луначарского в Доме Комсомола Рогожско-Симоновского района)", *Вечерняя Москва*, 18/X, 1926.

Против упадочничества, против "есенинщины". (Сборник статей) (Москва, изд. Правда и Беднота, 1926).

Пяст, В., "Погибший поэт", *Красная Газета* (Ленинград), веч. вып., 29/XII, 1925.

М. Р., "Сергей Есенин", *Комсомольская Правда* (Москва), 1/I, 1926.

Радек, Карл, "Бездомные люди (Есенин и Соболь)", *Правда* (Москва), 16/VI, 1926.

——, "Не термометр виноват", *Комсомольская Правда* (Москва), 27/VI, 1926.

——, "Не термометр виноват". Сб. *Против упадочничества*, (Москва, изд. Правда и Беднота, 1926).

Рашковская, Августа, "Мотивы пролетарской поэзии", *Вестник Знания* (Ленинград), № 13, 1925.

——, "Сергей Есенин (1895–1925)", *Вестник Знания* (Ленинград), № 1, 1926.

Ревякин, А., "Есенин и есенинщина", *На литературном посту* (Москва), № 1, 1926.

——, *Чей поэт Сергей Есенин. (Беглые заметки)* (Москва, изд. автора, 1926).

"Рецензия на 1-й том 'Собрания стихотворений' Есенина", *Рабочий Путь* (Смоленск), 21/IV, 1926.

"Рецензия на книгу Есенина 'Собрание стихов и поэм', т. I", *Накануне* (Берлин), лит. прилож. № 27, 1922.

"Рецензия на сборник 'С. А. Есенина', изд. ГИЗ", *Коммунист* (Астрахань), 3/IX, 1926.

Родов, Семен, *В литературных боях. Статьи, заметки, документы* (Москва, изд. Жизнь и Знание, 1926).

Рождественский, Всеволод, "Есенин", *Красная Газета* (Ленинград), веч. вып., 30/XII, 1925.

——, "Есенин". Сб. *Памяти Есенина* (Москва, изд. Всероссийского Союза Поэтов, 1926).

——, "Письмо из Ленинграда. (Воспоминания о последних днях жизни Есенина)", Сб. *Сергею Есенину* (Ростов н/Д., изд. Трудовой Дон, 1926).

Розанов, Ив., "Есенин и его спутники", Сб. *Есенин* (Москва, изд. Работник Просвещения, 1926).

——, *Есенин о себе и других* (Москва, изд. Никитинские Субботники, 1926).

——, "Жизнь и творчество Сергея Есенина", *Народный Учитель* (Москва), № 1, 1926.

——, "Мое знакомство с Есениным". Сб. *Памяти Есенина* (Москва, изд. Всероссийского Союза Поэтов, 1926).

——, "Реквизиция бога (о Клюеве, Есенине и Орешине)", *Понедельник* (Москва), 8/VII, 1918.

——, *Русские лирики* (Москва, изд. Никитинские Субботники, 1929).

Розенфельд, Б., "Есенин и имажинизм". Сб. *Есенин* (Москва, изд. Работник Просвещения, 1926).

Ройзман, Матвей, "То, о чем помню". Сб. *Памяти Есенина* (Москва, изд. Всероссийского Союза Поэтов, 1926).

Ромм, Александр, "О Есенине". Альманах *Чет и Нечет* (Москва, изд. авторов, 1925).

Ряховский, В., "О Сергее Есенине, великих людях и константиновской учительнице", *Рабочий Клич* (Рязань), 26/II, 1926.

В. С., "Рецензия на сборник 'С. А. Есенин' изд. ГИЗ", *Северная Правда* (Кострома), 17/VIII, 1926.

Садофьев, Илья, "Сергей Есенин", *Ленинградская Правда*, 29/XII, 1925.

Сазонов, Н., "Поэтов на суд рабкоров", *Рабочая Москва*, 20/XII, 1923.

Сакулин, П., "Народный Златоцвет", *Вестник Европы* (Петроград), № 5, 1916.

Сало, Жан, "Русская поэзия", *Вещь* (Берлин), № 1–2, 1922.

Са-на, "Имажинисты", *Руль* (Берлин), 11/IX, 1921.

И. С. (Саффьев, Илья), "Сергей Есенин", *Жизнь Искусства* (Ленинград), № 1, 1926.

Саянов, В., "Памяти Есенина", *Нева* (Ленинград), № 7, 1955.

С-в., "Сергей Есенин", *Красная Газета* (Ленинград), веч. вып. 4/I, 1926.

Святополк-Мирский, "Есенин", *Воля России*, кн. V (Прага, 1926).

Семашко, Н. А., "О самоубийсве. (Ответ на анкету)", *Вечерняя Москва*, 7/I, 1926.

——, "О цветах жизни". Сб. *Против Упадочничества* (Москва, изд. Правда и Беднота, 1926).

——, "Угрожает ли нам эпидемия самоубийства?", *Известия* (Москва), 22/I, 1926.

Семенов, Сергей, "О Сергее Есенине (заметка)", *Красная Газета* (Ленинград), веч. вып., № 316 (1004), 1925.

Сергеев, В. (Брянцев, А.), "Их четверо. Что было в пивной", *Известия АОМС* (Москва), 5/XII, 1923.

Сергей Александрович Есенин, воспоминания. Под ред. И. В. Евдокимова (Москва, изд. ГИЗ, 1926).

"Сергей Александрович Есенин", Сб. *С. А. Есенин* (Москва, изд. ГИЗ, 1926).

Сергею Есенину. Сб. статей, воспоминаний и стихотворений под общ. ред. Павла Кофанова (Ростов н/Д., изд. Трудовой Дон, 1926).

Сердцев, Николай, "Певец деревни", *Терек* (Пятигорск), 13/I, 1926.

Сиповский, В., *Поэзия народа. Пролетарская и крестьянская лирика наших дней* (Петроград, изд. Сеятель, Е. В. Высоцкого, 1923).

Слоним, Марк, "Литература наших дней", *Новости Литературы* (Берлин), № 1, 1922.

——, *Портреты советских писателей* (Париж, изд. Парабола, 1933).

Слонимский, Мих, "О Сергее Есенине (заметка)", *Красная Газета* (Ленинград), веч. вып., № 316 (1004), 1925.

Сменин, Михаил, "Рецензия на 'Собрание стихотворений' Есенина, т.т. I, II и III", *Уральский Рабочий* (Свердловск), 18/VIII, 1926.

Ю. С. (Соболев, Юрий), "Рецензия на № 1 журнала 'Новый Мир' за 1926 г. (о поэме Есенина 'Чорный человек')", *Вечерняя Москва*, № 24 (632), 1926.

Сокол, Евгений, "Одна ночь (из воспоминаний о С. Есенине)". Сб. *Памяти Есенина* (Москва, изд. Всероссийского Союза Поэтов, 1926).

Соколов, Б., "Литературные очерки. (Имажинисты)", *Воля России*, 14/I, 1921.

Соколов, Ипполит, *Имажинистика* (Москва, изд. Орднас, 1921).

Сокольников, М., "Сергей Есенин", *Город и Деревня* (Москва, № 1, 1926).

Соломонин, В., "Испугавшийся жизни", *Тихоокеанская Звезда* (Хабаровск), 4/II, 1926.

Сосновский, Л., "Испорченный праздник", *Рабочая Газета* (Москва), 22/XI, 1923.

——, "Развенчайте хулиганство", *Комсомольская Правда* (Москва), 19/IX, 1926.

Спасский, Сергей, "Поэзия в современности", *Зарево Заводов* (Самара), № 1, 1919.

Ст., "Сергей Есенин", *Трудовая Правда* (Пенза), 7/I, 1926.

Старцев, Иван, "Мои встречи с Есениным". Сб. *С. А. Есенин* (Москва, изд. ГИЗ, 1926).

Стор, Николай, "Сергей Есенин", *Заря Востока* (Тифлис), 30/XII, 1925.

Стрелец, "Поэт", *Новая Россия* (Москва), № 1, 1926.

Стуков, Виктор, "О Сергее Есенине", *Красный Алтай* (Барнаул), 31/I, 1926.

Табидзе, Тициан, "С. Есенин в Грузии", *Заря Востока* (Тифлис), 6/I, 1927.

Тарабукин, Николай, "Рецензия на книгу Есенина 'Избранное'", *Горн* (Москва), № 8, 1923.

Титов, Е., "Рецензия на 'Собрание стихотворений' Есенина, т. 2-й", *Тихоокеанская Звезда* (Хабаровск), 27/VI, 1926.

Тихонов, Н., "Из встреч с Есениным", *Красная Газета* (Ленинград), веч. вып. № 316 (1004), 1925.

——, "Из встреч с Есениным". Сб. *Памяти Есенина* (Москва, изд. Всероссийского Союза Поэтов, 1926).

Толстой, Ал., "О Есенине", *Тридцать Дней* (Москва), № 2, 1926.

——, "О Сергее Есенине (заметка)", *Красная Газета* (Ленинград), веч. вып., № 316 (1004), 1925.

——, "Памяти Есенина", *Новая Вечерняя Газета* (Ленинград), 30/XII, 1925.

——, "Рецензия на книги Есенина 'Трерядница' и 'Исповедь хулигана'", *Новая Русская Книга* (Берлин), № 1, 1922.

Топоров, А., *Крестьяне о писателях* (Москва, изд. Госиздат, 1930).

Торов, М., "Поэты из народа", *Вестник Жизни* (Москва), № 1, 1918.

Треплев, К., "Сергей Есенин", *Кочегарка* (Артемовск), 3/I, 1926.

"Триэмия", "Рецензия на книгу Есенина 'Трерядница'", *Книга и Революция* (Петроград), № 1, 1920.

Троцкий, Л., "Вне-октябрская литература. Литературные попутчики революции. С. Есенин", *Правда* (Москва), № 224, 1922.

——, *Литература и революция. Сборник статей* (Москва, 2-е дополн. изд. ГИЗ, 1924).

——, "Памяти Сергея Есенина", *Известия* (Москва), 19/I, 1926.

——, "Памяти Сергея Есенина". Сб. *Сергею Есенину* (Ростов н/Д., изд. Трудовой Дон, 1926).

——, "Памяти Сергея Есенина", *Правда* (Москва), 19/I, 1926.

Трусов, Андрей, "Урок", *Рабочий Путь* (Омск), 28/II, 1926.

Трушкин, В., "Лирика Сергея Есенина". Есенин, С., *Лирика* (Иркутск, 1958).

Тугенхольд, Я., "Старый стиль и новая деревня", *Вечерняя Москва*, № 12, 1926.

Турабов, С., "Есенин в Азербайджане (к биографии поэта)", *Литературный Азербайджан*, № 10, 1959.

Тынянов, Ю., "Промежуток", *Русский Современник* (Ленинград), № 4, 1924.

"Умер Есенин", *Волховский Труженик*, 6/I, 1926.

Урицкая, П., "Произведения Есенина". Сб. *Есенин* (Москва, изд. Работник Просвещения, 1926).

Устинов, Георгий, "Годы восхода и заката". Сб. *Памяти Есенина* (Москва, изд. Всероссийского Союза Поэтов, 1926).

——, *Литература наших дней* (Москва, изд. Девятого января, 1923).

——, "Мои воспоминания о Есенине". Сб. *С. А. Есенин* (Москва, изд. ГИЗ, 1926).

——, "Не с того конца", *Известия* (Москва), 6/IX, 1922.

——, "Очерки новейшей русской литературы. I. Искусство и политика", *Известия* (Москва), 23/IX, 1922.

——, "Сергей Есенин и его смерть", *Красная Газета* (Ленинград), веч. вып., 29/XII, 1925.

Устинов, Е., "Четыре дня С. А. Есенина". Сб. *С. А. Есенин* (Москва, изд. ГИЗ, 1926).

Ушаков, Д., "К смерти Сергея Есенина. (Письмо из Ленинграда)", *Северная Правда* (Кострома), 6/I, 1926.

Б. Ф., "Рецензия на I-й том 'Собрания стихотворений' Есенина" (на украинск. яз.), *Пролетарская Правда* (Киев), 3/VI, 1926.

Ф. Р., "Рецензия на книгу 'Преображение'", *Гори* (Москва), № 2–3, 1919.

Файнштейн, Лев, "Сергей Есенин в Баку". Сб. *С. А. Есенин* (Москва, изд. ГИЗ, 1926).

Фельдман, Цецилия, "Мало ли есть вкусных ядов" (Письмо в редакцию "Комсомольской Правды"), Сб. *Против упадочничества* (Москва, изд. Правда и Беднота, 1926).

Финк, Виктор, "О казненных дегенератами", *Красная Газета* (Ленинград), веч. вып. № 316 (1004), 1925.

Фомин, Семен, "Из воспоминаний". Сб. *Памяти Есенина* (Москва, изд. Всероссийского Союза Поэтов, 1926).

——, "Ширяевец и Есенин. (К годовщине смерти Ширяевца)", *Красная Нива* (Москва), 22–30/V, 1926.

Фриче, В., "Литературное одичание (о группе имажинистов)", *Вечерние Известия* (Москва), 13/II, 1919.

——, "Литературные очерки. Пора отмежеваться!", *Вечерние Известия* (Москва), 24/II, 1920.

Хераскова, Е., "Приемы композиции в стихотворениях Есенина". Сб. *Есенин* (Москва, изд. Работник Просвещения, 1926).

Хлипкий, Филипп, "Сергей Есенин", *Советская Правда* (Челябинск), 6/I, 1926.

Ховряков, Николай, *Сергей Александрович Есенин* (*1895–1925*). *Памятка читателю* (Караганда, 1958).

Ходасевич, Владислав, "Есенин", *Современные Записки* (Париж), кн. XXVII, 1926.

Хомчук, Н., "Есенин и Клюев (По неопублик. материалам)", *Русская Литература*, № 2, 1958.

Храповицкий, Л., "Краса (о вечере группы 'Краса' в Петрограде", *Рудин* (Петроград), № 1, 1915.

Цейтлин, А., "На родине Сергея Есенина", *Красная Газета* (Ленинград), веч. вып., № 45, 1926.

——, "На родине Сергея Есенина", *Красная Нива* (Москва), № 8, 1926.

Цинговатов, А., "Есенин на переломе", *Комсомолия* (Москва), № 7, 1925.

——, "Сергей Есенин", *Под знаменем Лининизма* (Пенза), № 3 (80), 1926.

——, "Сергей Есенин", *Учительская Газета* (Москва), 31/XII, 1925.

Чагин, П., Предисловие к книге Есенина *Русь Советская* (Баку, изд. Бакинский Рабочий, 1925).

Чаров, А., "Вхутемасовцы развлекаются", *Комсомольская Правда* (Москва), 7/VI, 1926.

Чириков, Евг., "Инония", *Общее Дело* (Париж), 28/II, 1921.

Читатель, "Чужой и близкий. (Заметки читателя о связи Есенина с деревней)", *Орловская Правда*, 6/I, 1926.

Чихачев, Петр, "Московские встречи (Воспоминания о В. Я. Брюсове и С. Есенине)", *Дон*, № 3, 1958.

Чока, "Сергей Есенин", *Звезда* (Екатеринослав), 3/I, 1926.

Ч-ский, В., Первые шаги", *Звезда*, кн. 4, 1926.

Чужак, Н., *Правда о Пугачове, опыт литер.-историч. анализа* ("*Пугачов*" Есенина) (Москва, изд. Всесоюзн. О-ва Полит. каторжан и ссыльно-поселенцев, 1926).

Ш. Нина, "Памяти Сергея Есенина", *Курская Правда*, 31/XII, 1925.

Шамурин, Е. И., "Рецензия на книгу Есенина 'Пугачов'", *Культура и Жизнь* (Москва), № 2–3, 1921.

Шапирштейн-Лерс, Я., *Общественный смысл русского литературного футуризма* (*Нео-народническая литература XX века*), с предисл. А. В. Луначарского (Москва, изд. А. Г. Миронова, 1922).

Шафир, Я., "Сменовеховская табакерка (о журнале 'Новая Россия', 1926, №№ 1, 2)", *Книгоноша* (Москва), № 13, 1926.

Швейдель, М., "Литература о Есенине, библиография". Сб. *Есенин* (Москва, изд. Работник Просвещения, 1926).

Шемшелевич, Леонид, "Разговор о Есенине", *Дон*, № 9, 1957.

Шепеленко, Д., "Рецензия на книгу Есенина 'Стихи'", *Пролетарий Связи* (Москва), № 4, 1925.

Шершеневич, Вадим, *2×2=5 Листы имажиниста* (Москва, изд. Имажинисты, 1920).

——, *Жмет кому руку* (на титульн. листе: *Кому я жму руку*) (Москва, изд. Имажинисты, 1921).

——, "Не слова, а факты. (О пребывании Есенина за границей)", *Театральная Москва*, 7–11/VI, 1922.

——, "О друге". Сб. *Есенин* (Москва, изд. Работник Просвещения, 1926).

——, "Открытое письмо Александру Кусикову", *Накануне*, лит. прилож. (Берлин), № 34 (551), 1924.

——, "Памяти Сергея Есенина", *Советское Искусство* (Москва), № 1, 1926.

——, "Поэт Сергей Есенин", *Заря Запада* (Витебск), 15/I, 1926.

——, "Поэты о театре", *Театральная Москва*, № 34, 1922.

——, "Рецензия на книгу Есенина 'Ключи Марии'", *Знамя* (Москва), № 2 (4), 1920.

——, "Театр не для поэтов", *Театральная Москва*, № 34, 1922.

Шипов, Андрей, "О Есенине", *Народный Учитель* (Москва), № 2, 1925.

Шулепников, С., "Имажинисты", *Приволжская Правда* (Кинешма), 20/VI, 1925.

А. Щ., "Заметки читателя о С. Есенине", *Нижегородская Коммуна*, 5/I, 1926.

Щеглов, М., "Есенин в наши дни", *Новый Мир* (Москва), № 3, 1956.

Эвентов, Исаак, *Сергей Есенин* (Ленинград, 1957).

Эренбург, Илья, *Портреты русских поэтов* (Берлин, изд. Агронавты, 1922).

——, *Портреты современных поэтов* (Москва, изд. Первина, 1923).

——, "Рецензия на книги Есенина 'Трерядница' и 'Исповедь хулигана'", *Новая Русская Книга* (Берлин), № 1, 1922.

И. Э. (Эренбург, Илья), "Рецензия на книгу Есенина 'Пугачов'", *Новая Русская Книга* (Берлин), № 2, 1922.

Эрлих, Вольф, *Право на песнь* (Ленинград, изд. Писатели в Ленинграде, 1930).

——, "Четыре дня". Сб. *Памяти Есенина* (Москва, изд. Всероссийского Союза Поэтов, 1926).

Юзовский, Ю., "Сергей Есенин", *Лава* (Ростов н/Д.), № 1, 1926.

——, "Сергей Есенин". Сб. *Сергею Есенину* (Ростов н/Д., изд. Трудовой Дон, 1926).

——, "Сергей Есенин", *Советский Юг* (Ростов н/Д.), 1/I, 1926.

Ю-н., "Рецензия на книгу Есенина 'Радуница'", *Новое Время* (Петроград), № 14539, 1916.

Якубовский, Г., "К итогам литературного года", *На литературном посту* (Москва), № 3, 1926.

——, "Лирика и современность", *Октябрь* (Москва), № 5, 1926.

——, "Поэт великого раскола. О лирике Сергея Есенина", *Октябрь* (Москва), № 1, 1926.

Ярмолинский, А., "Есенин в Нью Иорке", *Новый Журнал* (Нью Иорк), кн. 51, 1957.

2. OTHER LANGUAGES

Berg-Papendick, Wanda, "Sergej Jessenin, der letzte Sänger des russischen Dorfes. Zum 10. Todestage des Dichters", *Ost-Europa* (Königsberg, Pr.), 11 (1935), p. 182–190.

Bhushan, V. N., "Two Soviet Poets", *Twentieth century*, vol. 3 (Allabahad, 1937), p. 406–419.

Černikovská, Jiřina, *Sergej Jesenin* (Praha, Orbis, 1957).

Duncan, Irina and Macdougall, Allan Ross, *Isadora Duncan's Russian Days and her last Years in France* (London, Victor Gollancz Ltd., 1929).

Ehrenburg, I., "Sergej Jesenin", *Die literarische Welt* (Berlin), No. 3, 15/I, 1926.

Laffitte, Sophie, *Serge Essénine. Une étude* (Paris, Editions P. Seghers, 1959).

Lindenberg, Wladimir, ... *Die Unvollendeten*; *Lebensläufe früh verstorbener Dichter* (Hamburg, H. Dulk, [c. 1948]).

Manning, A. Clarence, "The Tragedy of Esenin", *The Slavonic Review* (London), vol. VII, No. 21 (1929).

Pascal, Pierre, "Esénine, poète de la campagne russe", *Oxford Slavonic Papers*, 2 (Oxford, 1951).

Pavlova, Nelia, "Essénine et Isadora Duncan", *Revue Mondiale* (Paris), 1/I, 1930.

Пешић, М. М., *Сергије Јесењин. О Јесењину. Јесенин о себи. Преводи из Јесенина* (Белград, Штампарски завод Орао, 1931).

——, *Сергеј Јесенин; живот и дело* (Београд, 1957).

Poggioli, Renato, *The Poets of Russia* (Cambridge, Mass., Harvard University Press, 1960), pp. 269–276.

Pozner, V., *Littérature russe* (Paris, éd. Kra, 1929).

Préface dans l'édition française de "Requiem" de Serge Ésénine (Paris, éd. Nouvelle Revue Française, 1930).

Тарановский, К. Т., *Из јесењинове лирике. Избор песама. У преводу и са студијом о Јесењину* (Београд, Скерлић, 1931).

SLAVISTIC PRINTINGS AND REPRINTINGS

Edited by Cornelis H. van Schooneveld

Some Titles on Literature:

12. DMITRIJ ČIŽEVSKIJ: History of Russian Literature from the Eleventh Century to the End of the Baroque. 1960. 451 pp., 34 plates. Cloth. Glds. 38.—

13. J. VAN DER ENG: Dostoevskij romancier. Rapports entre sa vision du monde et ses procédés littéraires. 1957. 115 pp. Cloth. Glds. 10.—

14. LAWRENCE L. STAHLBERGER: The Symbolic System of Majakovskij. 1964. 151 pp. Cloth. Glds. 20.—

15. ROBERT L. JACKSON: Dostoevky's Underground Man in Russian Literature. 1958. 223 pp. Cloth. Glds. 20.—

17. MILADA SOUČKOVA: The Czech Romantics. 1958. 168 pp. Cloth. Glds. 15.—

19. GEORGETTE DONCHIN: The Influence of French Symbolism on Russian Poetry. 1958. 242 pp., 7 ills. Cloth. Glds. 24.—

20. Dutch Contributions to the Fourth International Congress of Slavicists, Moscow, September 1958. 1958. 249 pp. Cloth. Glds. 24.—

21. American Contributions to the Fourth International Congress of Slavicists, Moscow, September 1958. 1958. 427 pp. Cloth. Glds. 40.—

23. PETER K. CHRISTOFF: An Introduction to Nineteenth-Century Russian Slavophilism. Volume I: A. S. Xomjakov. 1961. 301 pp., 2 plates. Cloth. Glds. 33.—

27. Studies in Russian and Polish Literature. In Honor of Wacław Lednicki. Edited by Z. Folejewski, † M. Karpovich, F. J. Whitfield, A. Kaspin. 1962. 250 pp., portrait. Cloth. Glds. 36.—

28. WACŁAW LEDNICKI: Henryk Sienkiewicz. A Retrospective Synthesis. 1960. 81 pp., 7 plates. Glds. 15.—

29. A. M. VAN DER ENG-LIEDMEIER: Soviet Literary Characters. An Investigation into the Portrayal of Soviet Men in Russian Prose, 1917-1953. 1959. 176 pp. Cloth. Glds. 16.—

31. Taras Ševčenko, 1814-1861. A Symposium. Edited by Volodymyr Mijakovs'kyj and George Y. Shevelov. 1962. 302 pp. Cloth. Glds. 32.—

35. CHARLES E. PASSAGE: The Russian Hoffmannists. 1963. 261 pp. Cloth. Glds. 30.—

36. VSEVOLOD SETCHKAREV: Studies in the Life and Works of Innokentij Annenskij. 1963. 270 pp. Cloth. Glds. 32.—

40. MILADA SOUČKOVA: The Parnassian Jaroslav Vrchlický. 1964. 151 pp., plate. Cloth. Glds. 20.—

42. CHARLES A. MOSER: Antinihilism in the Russian Novel of the 1860's. 1964. 215 pp. Cloth. Glds. 22.—

43. RENÉ WELLEK: Essays on Czech Literature. Introduced by Peter Demetz. 1963. 214 pp., portrait. Cloth. Glds. 23.—

45. Dutch Contributions to the Fifth International Congress of Slavicists, Sofia, 1963. 1963. 162 pp. Cloth. Glds. 36.—

52. WACŁAW LEDNICKI: Tolstoy between War and Peace. 1965. 169 pp., 4 facsimiles. Cloth. Glds. 25.—

56. N. S. TRUBETZKOY: Dostoevskij als Künstler. 1964. 178 pp. Cloth. Glds. 28.—

MOUTON & CO · PUBLISHERS · THE HAGUE